MORTON M. HUNT

The World
of the
Formerly Married

Allen Lane The Penguin Press
London 1968

MADE AND PRINTED IN GREAT BRITAIN BY
LATIMER TREND AND CO. LTD, WHITSTABLE
MADE IN ENGLAND

To Robert Lescher,
Guide, Mentor, Friend

This is a description of the special world of the separated and divorced in America, an eye-witness report on the mores, problems, and experiences of people who inhabit a half-secret subculture outside the realm of conventional marriage and family life. It is neither an analysis of the causes of divorce nor a guide to divorce law, but a picture of how separated and divorced people live.

I have limited myself almost entirely to the middle class. At the bottom and at the top of American life, the meanings of marriage, divorce, and the post-divorce life are so unlike those at the central core that had I included them all, I would have been writing not one book but three.

Like a cultural anthropologist, I have lived among the natives, sharing their way of life, looking and listening intently, and striving to record not only the form of their daily experiences but the inner meanings these have for them. Like the anthropologist, I have sought to report and interpret, rather than to exhort or give advice. This is not a "how-to" book, and it contains no prescriptions for how or whether to go about separating or getting divorced, speeding the adjustment to that status, or behaving while in it.

Not that I am uninterested in being helpful. On the contrary, I earnestly hope that this book *will* prove helpful, as such a book would have proven to me in my own time. But prescriptions are most apt to be healing when one knows the individual patient; failing that, they may be valueless or even noxious. I offer the reader, therefore, vicarious experience from which he can derive his own wisdom. Each potentially or actually divorced person can sample here the kinds of behavior to be found within the subculture, and observe the various modes of adaptation or maladaptation to the divorced life. If he is only considering it, he can judge for himself whether to risk it or try instead to repair a disappointing marriage. If he has already decided against the latter alternative, he can select for himself the behavior patterns here portrayed which are cut to his measure, and avoid those which are not.

Finally, even the durably and happily married may find the book of value: if they have been mystified, disturbed, or shocked by those friends who have left marriage and taken up another way of life, they may here learn enough to understand and be tolerant of them, and so keep their friendship. For it is easy to disapprove when we do not understand, but almost impossible when we do. Plutarch tells of an ancient Roman who divorced his wife; when friends reproved him, pointing out that she was chaste, rich, and beautiful, he pulled off his shoe and held it up to them, saying, "Yes and this shoe looks fine and new, does it not? Yet not one of you can tell where it chafes me." I trust that my readers will learn from this book how the shoe feels.

The material presented here comes from interviews, a national questionnaire survey, personal observation, and the published psychological and sociological literature of divorce. Those who are interested in further details will find them in the Notes on Sources at the end of the book.

All direct quotations and case histories are taken from the interviews or questionnaires, unless otherwise indicated in the text or the Notes on Sources. To protect the persons involved, I have altered various unessential details; all names used in case histories are, of course, fictitious.

ACKNOWLEDGMENTS

So many people have been of help to me that I cannot list them all, and I must ask the indulgence of those who are omitted.

First and foremost, I thank all those people who told me about their lives in person or in writing. I am grateful to Parents Without Partners, and especially to Mimi Seligman of its national headquarters, for helping distribute some of my questionnaires across the country, and to all the marriage counsellors and sociologists connected with the 1965 Groves Conference on Marriage and the Family who did the same thing. The Family Service Association of America answered many of my queries, the U.S. Bureau of the Census and the U.S. Public Health Service were prodigal with data, and the Minnesota Family Study Center of the University of Minnesota provided many bibliographical suggestions.

Among the individuals who helped me in one way or another during the research phase were Dr. Robert Bell of Temple University, Dr. John F. Cuber of Ohio State University, Dr. Reuben Hill of the University of Minnesota, Jeanne Knakal, formerly of the Family Service Agency of Marin County, California, Dr. Donald McKinley of Teachers College, Columbia University, Dr. Emily Mudd of the Marriage Council of Philadelphia, Dr. Ira L. Reiss of the University of Iowa, and Dr. William Reynolds of Queens College; also, Janet Frank Egleson, Rose Migas, William Bernstein, and Al Bossinger. Three friends—Dr. Louis R. Ormont, Bernice Kohn, and Merle Shain—read the manuscript and gave me many useful suggestions. Dorothea Chotzinoff diligently and carefully rechecked a number of facts. Mr. Frank Furstenberg of the Bureau of Applied Social Research, Columbia University,

ix

coded my questionnaire and helped me develop the tabulations and cross-tabulations I needed; his excellent assistant, who did much of the scoring and calculating, was Mrs. Harriet Rossetto. Violet Serwin was, as always, my superb amanuensis.

CONTENTS

THE WORLD OF THE FORMERLY MARRIED

CHAPTER ONE

The Unknown Society

1 · *Separate Species, Separate World*

At the Bella Vista Motel, the man in Room 27 is having a bad night of it: his light has been on and off half a dozen times since midnight. Room 27 is comfortable enough: the motel is hardly four years old, everything is still new and attractive, the bed is firm, the air conditioner is working properly. But the buttons in the mattress annoy him, the air conditioner seems noisy, the lights of passing cars make patterns through the Venetian blinds. He gets up and turns off the cold air, but in ten minutes is sweltering; he turns it on again and soon is chilled. He pulls up the blanket, sighs, and begins to drift off, only to wake with a start, thinking, *Is it really true? Can this be happening to me?* Sweat breaks out all over him; he goes to the bathroom for water and a tranquillizer, sees himself in the mirror and winces: the fleshy face looking back at him, usually strong and ruddy, is ashen, dough-soft, and red-eyed. *What am I to do now?* he wonders. He will be forty years old in two weeks: *Too early to give up, too late to start again.* He scowls at himself and utters a curse, disgusted at his own rather ridiculous self-pity.

Rather ridiculous, because he is facing neither imprisonment, ruin, nor major surgery. What happened to him this evening happens to three thousand Americans every day of the year: he and his wife have just broken up and are headed for divorce. He had expected it, had even wanted it for months; tonight's quarrel was merely one more, his wife's waspish comments merely a shade worse than usual, but suddenly as in some cliché-ridden TV show, he was flinging clothing into a valise and storming out.

All in all, a commonplace, inglorious, third-rate sort of tragedy, with faintly comic overtones (he had to storm back in, a moment later, to get his briefcase). Instead of feeling tragic, perhaps he should feel free, exultant, and delighted. But he does not: instead, he has that eery feeling one has during many a nightmare ("What am I doing here?"), and he cannot stop an old spiritual from going round in his head: *Sometimes I feel like a motherless child.* . . . It exasperates him to feel this way; he would be horribly embarrassed to have anyone know that he, Eugene Wilson, engineer, home-builder, and member of the town planning commission, could feel lost, alone, and vaguely frightened. He kicks back the covers again, angry at himself. *Sometimes I feel like*—stop it, goddamn it! . . . And eventually, in mid-measure, he drifts off to sleep.

The man in Room 27, and men and women like him, have a surprise ahead. They are not really alone; instead of being cast out into solitude and the unpeopled night, they will shortly find that they are part of a large, half-hidden society in which they will rapidly become comfortable and at ease—an underground subculture of which they knew nothing in advance, a veritable World of the Formerly Married, with its own rules of conduct, its own mechanisms for bringing people together, its own patterns of adjustment to the separated or divorced life, its own opportunities for friendship, social life, and love. As they discover this world, they will cease feeling like outcasts or motherless children, and think of themselves instead as new citizens of an unfamiliar country, new members of a cohesive and reassuring association.

For separated and divorced people in the United States are,

like the Mormons or the Amish, like lower-class Negroes or the Chosen Ones of the *Social Register,* like the natives of a remote village in Maine or the members of Broadway's inner circle, a subinstitution or subculture. They are part of the overall American culture and interact with its members on its own terms; but elsewhere they have a private and special set of norms that guide them in their interactions with each other, and from which they derive their own customs, moral values, rules of fair play, and devices for coping with the problems special to their condition. Many of their daily experiences, and many of the feelings they have about each other, their married friends, and themselves, are distinctly different from those of the inhabitants of the larger world around them.

In all these respects, the separated and the divorced are basically alike and should be considered together. An emotionally genuine separation constitutes the death of a marriage, and divorce is merely its burial; moreover, most separated people rapidly become part of the society of formerly married men and women, and even in advance of divorce behave in most ways as if they were legally disengaged from their mates. But there exists no term that lumps together both the separated and the divorced, of both sexes; I shall refer to them, therefore, as "the Formerly Married," or as "FMs." *

The customs, feelings, and behavior of people in the subculture have gone largely unnoticed, in part because the subculture itself is so new, and in part because FMs are secretive about much that is special to their way of life. But nearly every newly separated person soon senses that some kind of consensual alliance exists among FMs. Feeling at first like an ignorant novice, he strives to learn the unwritten rules that he gathers must exist, soon begins to perceive the subtle bonds

---

* When I do, on occasion, refer to divorce separately, I mean it to include annulment. Despite its technical meaning, annulment is used today very largely as a device for dissolving marriage in states with difficult divorce laws. It plays only a small part in the overall picture; in 1962, annulments accounted for three per cent of all legal dissolutions of marriage in the United States.

of common understanding and fellowship among the separated and divorced, and starts to recognize their special and often unspoken means of communicating with each other.

The married man may a hundred times have walked into a roomful of strangers at a party, and been unaware of which women were married and which were divorced; yet having himself become an FM, he experiences something different the very next time he enters such a room. Signals are being transmitted, inaudible to the uninitiated: there is a subliminal broadcast of attitudes and responses, of unspoken inquiries and promises. Is it that the eyes of FMs meet and hold a half-second longer than the eyes of others? Or is there something special about the smile—a difference too slight to be measured, too subtle to be caught by a camera? Or some unconsciously special tone of voice, choice of words, tilt of head?

One hardly knows, but it is incontestable that FMs often do communicate with each other unperceived under the very noses of their married friends and acquaintances. The novice, highly sensitized by his own feelings, learns this secret language as rapidly and instinctively as a child—often, indeed, without knowing that he is doing so. After a short time—only weeks, perhaps—he finds that he, too, has begun communicating his position in words, gestures, even his stance; he discovers that he, too, has become instantly recognizable to other FMs as one of them.

In the same way, many purely trivial experiences of the novice FM teach him or her that this is a different way of life, with its own values, rules, and purposes. A woman married fifteen years and brand-new to the FM world is astonished and offended to be invited out for a cocktail but not for dinner; she flies for comfort to a long-time divorcee and professes to be insulted, but is patted on the hand and told that this is par for the course and that it is mutually protective, since two FMs may quickly discover that they don't particularly like each other—in which case, why waste an evening? Likewise, a male veteran tells a male novice, "You know, of course, that you should *never* commit yourself to a whole evening with a date you haven't known before. Tell her ahead of time that you're going to have to work in the evening or visit your children or something, so you can get away after an hour—unless you like her, in which case you go to a phone booth and fake a call cancelling your plans so you can take her to dinner. Both of you know what's going on, but both of you pretend, because it's better for you that way." FMs, especially those beyond their twenties, are in a hurry to establish a new relationship or give it up and look further; they are at once fiercely eager to try—and fearful of being caught in a relationship less than ideal.

The novice finds that there is an unpublished body of rules of behavior covering many of the situations which, beforehand, seemed to him to have no guidelines whatever. What manner shall separated or divorced people use toward each other in front of their children? To how many close friends should one offer explanations of what happened, and how detailed or intimate should they be? How should a woman behave, in front of her own children, when a date comes to call? After how long may an FM man make a pass at an FM woman? And since she is surely no virgin, on what grounds can she refuse (if she wants to refuse) without looking silly or offending his pride? There are no categorical answers to any of these questions, of course; the answers embrace a range of possibilities, but fall into recognizable patterns, with one of them, in each case, expressing the prevailing subcultural norm.

All of which comes as a surprise to most new FMs; as married people they knew relatively little of what it is like within the FM world, for almost nobody within it tells the truth about it to the outsider. The FM man or woman learns not to harp on his or her recurrent bouts of despair or loneliness; it bores and finally estranges the married friend. Equally, however, one learns not to reveal much of the surging feeling of renewal, the delight in freedom, the joy and pride of rediscovered sexuality; such confessions are disturbing to the married, and bring disapproval and even the loss of friendship. One learns not to dwell too often upon problems with the children, the ex-spouse, or the former in-laws; friends listen and sympathize, but behind their kindly replies there often lurks an unuttered rebuke: "You needn't have had these troubles. . . . *You* chose to make them for yourself, *we* chose to remain in marriage."

Yet although so much about the way of life of FMs has perceptible patterns, there is also much that remains formless and ambiguous. The society of formerly married people is still too new to be fully developed; besides, its members come from all bands of the broad spectrum of American life, bringing with them widely divergent attitudes about sex, love, child-rearing, and the value of family life. What should the brand-new FM say to an old acquaintance who, all unknowing, asks about his wife? There is no standard answer, or even set of answers; one must be guided by his own personal discomfort, inner feelings, and sense of propriety. He may choose to be serious and stiff-of-upper-lip: "We've just been divorced. . . . It's for the best. . . . Things didn't work out." Or non-committal and brutally direct: "She just got back from Reno four weeks ago." Or surprised, to soften the reply: "Oh—you hadn't heard about us? . . . You don't know? . . ." Or brightly and falsely jocular: "Who?—Oh, you must mean my ex-wife!— She's fine, I think." It is a minor problem, perhaps, but symptomatic of what sociologists call "the ambiguity of the social role of divorced persons in American society."

And such ambiguity can be deeply disturbing when it includes hundreds of situations for which there is no prepared and rehearsed way of behaving. How shall the two who once loved each other divide the physical things they jointly cared about? Money, though it be fought over, is almost easy in comparison to favorite books, records, the bit of Meissen found in a junk shop, the two-generation-old sterling—and who, in heaven's name, gets the photo album, the movies of the children as babies, the wedding pictures?

More importantly, there is no well-established pattern as to what people should tell their children regarding the break-up; it is difficult to explain it in any way that makes sense without also making them fear that all love (including the parental) is perishable. And how shall ex-husband and ex-wife resolve any differences they may have about the children's schooling, religious education, and other matters? For they can no longer compromise through tenderness and love, nor through a *quid pro quo* involving other shared concerns. Where, for that matter, should they meet to discuss such things? Her home, where the children may overhear? His place, where she will feel the invisible presence of other women? In a bar, a parked car, a lawyer's office—each objectionable for one reason or another? Each location sets a different mood; the two people must choose carefully—but according to what criteria?

Coloring everything is the largest ambiguity of all—the overall appraisal of divorce as an act of choice; that is, an act which can and must be morally evaluated. Is it, in simplest terms, a good or bad, beneficial or hurtful, moral or immoral, thing to do? Must the FM regard his or her own divorce as a sign of failure, the final stage of incurable disease? Or dare he think of it as an affirmation of life and hope, the needful cut of the surgeon's knife that restores health and makes happiness possible?

To this ultimate question there is no clearcut answer in the minds of married people and most new FMs. The novice is usually quite ambivalent about it; as for his married friends, they are not even sure what is the right way to react to his announcement of the separation or divorce. A generation ago they had no doubts; the proper behavior, in most circles, was a sorrowing look, a murmured regret, a warm handclasp, as if hearing of the death of the friend's father or mother; among the upper-level sophisticates, however, the chic thing was to be brittle and gay about it. Today, neither seems appropriate, but one has no real idea what is, and therefore is apt to proffer a marbled slice of comment, part light and part dark: "I hear you've got your 'freedom' at last. . . . What do I say? . . . Congratulations!—I guess."

But despite the ambiguities that remain, the World of the Formerly Married is rapidly developing answers—not only to the practical problems of the separated and divorced, but to the ultimate question itself. For even if married people and the newly separated are unsure of its moral value, the prevailing feeling of the Formerly Married is that divorce is painful but necessary, temporarily destructive but finally creative, and not only an act of courage, but an affirmation of one's belief in the value and the possibility of happy marriage.

II · *What Is a Typical FM?*

Who are the members of the hidden society of the Formerly Married, and what are typical FMs like? Are there an archetypal man and woman, formerly married, as universally relevant to that condition as, say, Cressida is to all faithless mistresses, Don Juan to all heartless seducers, Pierrot to pale and wan fond lovers, Kate to shrews? No; not if one is honest about it. The typical FM man or woman, like the typical American, German, or Italian, is a statistical abstraction. FMs, as a category, tend to share certain kinds of experience and certain mores and values, but they arrive at this consensus by many different routes, and use the common culture in very different fashions.

Let us look in momentarily upon a handful of FMs to see what this means:

—Manhattan, the fashionable East Side, late one morning in January. Bright sun, street noises; behind the darkened window of an apartment, however, all is still dim and quiet. Then the alarm rings, the woman stirs and wakes: ah, yes, time to get up—lunch with Doris at the Modern Museum, an auction at Parke-Bernet, cocktails with the New Man, dinner with the children (a bore, but the right thing to do). How were they this morning?—all right, no doubt; the maid always gets them off to school on time so Mother can sleep; she *needs* her sleep after getting in at four A.M. from an evening of the discothèques. What a life!—better than the one she knew at college or as a single working girl; and sweeter, too, for having been wrung, after a long battle, from that impossible dolt of a husband. Thank god, at least he's well-off—the only good thing about him; alimony keeps everything going, though a bit on the thin edge now and then. A self-indulgent, selfish life?—yes, but why not?—one lives only once, and she's not hurting anyone by it, is she? At thirty-eight, she has years of a boring marriage to make up for. *Carpe diem;* Old Time is still a-flying, and all that. What a joy *not* to be saddled with one man, and still to be attractive enough (but some days only after much effort) to be propositioned by nearly every man she goes out with. And she knows the secret now: ask nothing of them—no emotion, no commitment—be gay, playful, seductive, give in when you wish, but *ask nothing*—and you will be popular, and busy, and happy; perhaps it can't last indefinitely, but the end is not in sight and meanwhile her ex-husband has to pay for it all, and it serves him right.

—Suburb of Hartford; sleet is driving down, and winter night has fallen, although it is only six P.M. A car pulls into a driveway, and out steps a weary-looking slender woman of thirty-two, home from a full day in the insurance office, carrying a heavy briefcase full of business papers. She enters, and is leaped upon by two exuberant little boys; the teen-aged baby-sitter, meanwhile, puts on her coat and leaves. Now to start dinner (while keeping up a running conversation with both boys), then serve, clean up, help the boys with homework, get them bathed and bedded; then rinse out some things, wash her hair, pick up a dozen toys, make sandwiches for their school lunches; then an hour or so with her business papers; then a phone call from a male friend who wants her to come with him for a weekend at an inn near Danbury (she'd love to, though she's too tired to feel the Urge, but how could she leave the boys for a whole weekend?); and, setting the clock for seven A.M., into bed after midnight, when suddenly and unexpectedly, after turning out the light, she succumbs to a fit of tears and convulsive sobbing.

—The cocktail lounge of the Mayflower Hotel in Washington. A trim, tanned man of thirty-four, handsome though prematurely bald, is explaining with a disarming grin and twinkling eye to the Young Thing with him why he is a dedicated run-around, twice-divorced and separated now from his third wife. "I think it's something about my endocrine system," he says (and she cannot tell if he is teasing her or means it), "because after a year or so, no matter how jolly the lady I'm living with or married to, I find myself unable to resist the temptation of some new girl—you, this time, but just because we're a terrific thing already, don't figure it's forever. I'm hopeless—but charming. Besides, you seemed to *like* my endocrine system. . . ." She blushes and looks nervously about, thinking back upon the afternoon. But she feels in her heart that he is teasing her only to hide his deeper feelings, so she smiles at him and studies him with shining eyes.

—A run-down lower-middle-class neighborhood in Cleveland; a somewhat shabby home converted into a rooming house. On the third floor (musty smell of rotting carpet; feeble bulb overhead leaking yellow light), behind a closed door, a paunchy grey-haired man (but only forty-one), pallid and waxy-looking, lies on the bed in wrinkled clothes and stares at the TV set. For over two years, since the break-up of his marriage, he has gone directly from the drafting room at five-thirty P.M. to a short-order joint for the $1.75 blue-plate special (the counterman sings out the order to the kitchen as he comes in, without even asking him); from there he either goes to a movie, walks the streets for hours and stares in shop windows, sits in some bar, drinking very slowly and never talking to anyone, or comes home to watch TV. He is not looking for company; he has turned down invitations from old friends until they have stopped asking him, and has even carefully managed not to open his door at the same time as the man across the hall for these two years. He luxuriates in his suffering and wears the hairshirt of loneliness against his quivering skin to atone for some unnamed failure to have loved well enough. Once a month or so he picks up a prostitute at one of the nearby bars when he is drunk, but he can never quite remember in the morning whether it was any good or not.

—A cocktail lounge in a hotel in St. Louis. A small woman in her forties, chubby but pretty, is sitting alone and toying with a Brandy Alexander. The house detective passes through, spots her, and shakes his head; he cannot figure it out. This is the fifth day; each day he has seen this woman—who looks to him like a suburban housewife (he is right), well-bred, demure, and rather prissy—hanging around near the bar, accepting drinks, and leaving for dinner with different men. She is surely not a hooker, but what is she? He could not guess the truth: she is a desperate, panicky divorcee on a one-week binge of seduction after a year of chastity and a lifetime of propriety; this week is the first and only she will ever spend in this fashion. Having been cast off by her husband for another woman, after twenty-some years of marriage, she has wept, fasted, shrieked out loud at night until the room rang, haunted the doctor's office, and at last flung herself into this desperate effort to prove something that can never be permanently proved. Each day she allows herself to be picked up ("But it's so easy!" she says to herself, shocked), taken to dinner, escorted to a room and stripped and possessed (she pretends passion, but feels anesthetized); then, feeling victorious but befouled, she goes to her own room, drinks herself to sleep, awakens full of horror and shame—and by late afternoon, the passion for revenge returning, starts out all over again.

—A pleasantly furnished small apartment overlooking the lake, in downtown Chicago; a man of fifty, strong-featured and well-built, is unpacking his bags, having just arrived back from one of his many sales trips. He thumbs through a date book—nothing on for tonight—then through an address book, and makes three calls until he finds one of his female friends who is free and will come over, later on, to talk to him, make dinner for him, and sleep with him. She knows what he is—a divorced man who has lived this way for ten years, dislikes it but is hopelessly embittered about marriage, and has nothing to offer her but light camaraderie and sex (the moment any woman hints at deeper feelings, or begins to arouse them in him, he suddenly becomes completely busy, or rude, or hyper-critical, until the danger is eliminated). He is pessimistic and self-critical, calls his own behavior promiscuous, selfish, and unreliable; but he also says he thinks this is the way it has to be, since he could succeed neither in marriage nor in any of the three deep relationships he tried right after divorce. When an old friend asked him about loneliness, he said that he was never troubled by it. "I have lots of friends," he explained, "money enough to go out whenever I want, and there are always plenty of women available to give me whatever relief I need. I tell every woman I meet just what I am, but she always hopes for the best—and while she's finding out the truth, at least we're temporarily keeping each other from feeling the emptiness of our lives."

Which of these could we call typical, which the master de-sign, the universal pattern? All and none. And we might have seen many more, all varied. We might have looked in on beatniks, surfers, or ski bums, young, tanned, bored, casual, often promiscuous, rarely involved—many of them the debris and detritus of wrecked marriages. But they are no more repre-sentative of all FMs than are the thickwaisted, greying men and women in discussion groups of Parents Without Partners chapters throughout the country, earnestly exploring under the guidance of psychologists the reasons for marital failure and the problems involved in remarriage.

There are young ones, the new breed, who marry and divorce while still childless, too soon to have had any deep emotional ties to sever; one cannot tell them from never-married people by word or deed (it is always a surprise to learn that they have been married and divorced), and some of them, if they ever talk about it, say that they broke up not because they quarrelled, but because they were bored, or fell out of love, or simply drifted into separate ways without noticing what was happening. In their late twenties, they can hardly recall anything— sometimes not even the looks—of the mates they once slept with. Typical?—yes, of themselves; but infinitely remote from those others, married half a lifetime, who, when the children are grown, are amazed to discover that they can no longer endure the confinement of a frustrating union and start out late—terribly late—to try to remake their lives. Writes a cultured woman professor, passively married for twenty-five years to an uncouth, overpowering man, "In middle age I couldn't keep up the front. It is in middle age that one gives up hope that things will change, and the situation, which before was only distasteful, becomes unbearable. One can't live without hope." But even with late-won hope, such a person will for the rest of his life be bound to him: nearly all her memories, her adult experiences, are engraved upon her brain in the form of *"we* visited," *"we* saw," and *"we* used to have. . . ."

FMs, in short, inhabit a territory of their own, but enter it by many a road and make many different kinds of adjustment to it. Rather than a single archetype, there are numerous archetypes; we will keep an eye on them all, and try to identify the several main groups or patterns into which they fit, the major kinds of experience they have, and the principal ways in which they handle the situations that confront them.

III · *Some Vital—*
and Frequently Surprising—Statistics

If we cannot symbolize the FM population through one or two typical specimens, we can at least get some fairly clear idea of who and what the FMs are by examining a handful of statistics. And despite the depressing sound of that word, we will find some of them interesting, for the bright light shed by exact numbers shows up many a popular misconception.

First, however, there is one common notion that the statistics do *not* disprove—namely, that the chance of divorce is about one in four. In 1962, the latest year for which detailed and accurate analyses are available, there were 413,000 divorces and 1,577,000 marriages in the United States—about a one-to-four ratio. Some statisticians say this does not indicate the risk, since it compares current marriages to divorces of marriages made in earlier years, when the number of marriages per year was appreciably less. But when statistician Paul Jacobson made an exceedingly subtle analysis of the year-by-year fall-out rate of marriages made earlier, and extrapolated his findings to the present day, he found that marriages now being made do, in fact, have about a one-in-four chance of ending in divorce. He points out, however, that this is the risk for all marriages, including remarriages (whose risk is higher than normal); if one considers only *first* marriages, the risk of divorce is about one in five.

And who were the 826,000 or so people who got divorced in 1962? The risk of divorce is one in four, but not for every segment of society. Any given couple's chances will vary greatly from that figure according to such factors as where they live, what the husband does for a living, or the color of their skin. Census data show, for instance, that the divorce rate among farm laborers and farm foremen is over twice as high as that among professional and technical men; that eight per cent of all actors but only one third of one per cent of all clergymen, are currently divorced; and that the divorce rate is nearly four times as great in the West as in the Northeast. San Mateo County, California, may take the prize for the highest rate; a recent state legislative report indicated a ratio of seventy divorces per hundred marriages in that county. (Among other surprises, it is worth pointing out in passing that the American divorce rate, though currently the world's highest, is far from the highest known in history; in recent times, Japan, Algeria, Israel, Russia, and Egypt have all topped it.)

Neither the risk-of-divorce figures nor the annual crop of divorces gives us any true picture of the size of the World of the Formerly Married. In 1962, data from the Census Bureau showed a total of 5,498,000 separated or divorced persons—but even this huge number is probably lower than reality, since some deserted women and deserting men are either ashamed or afraid to tell the truth.

One very widespread misconception is that within this population of formerly married persons there are several times as many left-over and discarded women as men; it is often said, in fact, that a divorced woman can hardly find any suitable divorced men. In actual fact, the ratio—though unfavorable to women—is only about three-to-two, both among the divorced and the separated. The misconception arises from the far greater ease with which men can hunt out female companions. Because it is so much more permissible for men to make the advances, they have far less need to use neutral meeting-grounds such as clubs, parties, resorts, and cruises—and it is therefore at just such places that one often sees five or ten times as many unattached women as men, senses the female desperation in the face of the odds, and gets an exaggerated notion of the sex ratio in the FM world.

Another erroneous notion is that divorce is the chosen pattern of the upper classes, and desertion or domestic-relations court the pattern of the lower ones. All the popular media—television, movies, tabloids, novels, plays—reinforce the impression that it is the chic, the well-off, the college-educated professionals and businessmen, who are most prone to divorce. Yet for at least fifteen years, every analysis by statisticians and sociologists has shown that the divorce rate is higher among those of low socio-economic status than among the middle and upper-middle classes. According to the computations of various researchers, for instance, unskilled or semi-skilled laborers are about three times as likely to get divorced as professional people and proprietors; low-income families are about twice as prone to divorce as those of average or above-average income; and non-whites, whose average socio-economic status is markedly lower than that of whites, have been more divorce-prone than whites in every census year but one since 1890.

A great deal of the writing and comment about divorce in recent years has correctly emphasized the risk of divorce among those who marry too young: teen-age husbands have a divorce rate more than three times, and teen-age wives almost four times, as high as that for the total population; one out of four men and two out of five women getting divorced are under twenty-nine. But figures like these tend to make us forget that people get divorced at all ages, even though the rate declines with age: half of all divorcing men are over 34.5 and half of all divorcing women are over 31. Moreover, the youngest divorced people remarry rapidly and disappear from the ranks, while older ones take their time, or are less desirable and so tend to linger a while. As a result, the World of the Formerly Married is not a world of very young adults; half of all divorced persons, and nearly half of all separated persons, are between their mid-thirties and their mid-fifties, as appears in the following summary of census figures for 1962. (I have combined the figures for men and women; the distribution of each sex is generally similar, though women are not quite so concentrated in the 45-to-54-year bracket as men.)

Age	Separated	Divorced
14 to 24	265,000	155,000
25 to 34	558,000	611,000
35 to 44	621,000	714,000
45 to 54	510,000	813,000
55 to 64	282,000	516,000
65 and up	201,000	252,000
	2,437,000	3,061,000

Another exaggerated belief that the figures belie is that the great bulk of divorces occurs very early in marriage. It is undeniable that more break-ups occur during the first year or two than later, and that divorces resulting from these early break-ups reach a maximum rate three years after marriage; but this is only the peak of the curve, and not the bulk of the cases. In actual fact, the divorce rate diminishes only gradually, year by year, after that peak; nearly forty per cent of all broken marriages last ten or more years before being dissolved, and thirteen per cent last more than twenty years. For the United States as a whole, the median duration of marriage at the time of divorce is 7.3 years. ("Median" means that as many marriages ending in divorce lasted more than 7.3 years as lasted less.)

And while it is true in general that the longer a marriage lasts, the smaller is the risk of divorce, there are certain groups of marriages which show increased risks after many years. People who married in 1933, for instance, had a higher divorce rate between the tenth and fifteenth years of marriage than in either of the previous five-year periods; perhaps economic difficulties in the Depression delayed marital break-up until they could afford to make one household into two. Some students of American divorce think that if a census were taken of recent middle-class divorces—none now exists, since the published government data make no class distinctions—one would find a definite secondary peak of late marital break-up around the fifteenth year—a time when children are beyond the critical nursery and grade school years, and the forces binding man and wife together have begun to diminish. My own modest survey hints at this, showing eighteen per cent of separations as coming in four or less years, twenty-nine per cent between the fifth and ninth years, thirty-one per cent between the tenth and fourteenth years, and twenty-two per cent in or beyond the fifteenth year.* One might guess that this is due to the slower achievement of maximum career potential among such people, or to their greater concern about the psychological impact of divorce on children. But possibly even more pertinent is a finding of the Kansas City Study of Adult

* On the nature of this survey, see Notes on Sources.

Life, made by a team of social scientists from the University of Chicago several years ago: by age forty or so, lower-status people have more or less given up on life, and no longer see the future in terms of expansion and fulfilment but in terms of decline towards death; middle-class people of that age are generally only just reaching the pinnacle of their powers and see themselves as still young, healthy, and vital. It may well be that middle-class persons are willing to take a chance on divorce and remarriage long after lower-class persons have abandoned hope of improving their lives.

According to a treasured folk belief, children hold marriages together; the inevitable deduction would be that most FMs are childless. But statistics show the notion to be inaccurate; in fact, the more acceptable divorce becomes to Americans as a solution to marital difficulties, the less force children exert in keeping marriages intact. People used to feel that they should endure their miseries and stay together for the sake of the children; today they are giving ever greater weight to their own right to happiness, or perhaps coming to think that it is no favor to children to maintain an unhappy marriage for their benefit. The change is taking place rapidly: in 1948 only forty-two per cent of divorcing people had children under eighteen, but by 1955 the figure was up to forty-seven per cent, and by 1962 had leaped to sixty per cent, involving 537,000 children that year. For some reason, the trend is most marked in the Northeast, where sixty-nine per cent of divorcing people now have minor children.

If the belief about children's effect on marriage seems to be rebutted by the statistics, the one about "the family that prays together stays together" seems to be upheld, as advertised; devout churchgoers, whatever their brand of belief, are less likely to join the ranks of the Formerly Married than non-churchgoers or people of weak belief. But this does not prove that the devout have happier or more successful marriages; it proves only that strong religious ties tend to inhibit the urge to divorce. Even this, however, is changing: Catholics are the largest religious denomination in which divorce has been all but forbidden, but the divorce rate among them is steadily increasing.

Another popular impression only superficially validated by statistics is that divorce is a product of the sinful big city: the data indicate that divorce is about fifty per cent more common among urban people than among farm families. But this does not constitute proof that the city corrupts people; it may merely allow them more latitude to carry out wishes that they and their country cousins alike harbor in their souls.

The Formerly Married are not the only inhabitants of their special world; several other kinds of people drift in and out of it, the most numerous being the widowed and the never-married. Widows and widowers outnumber FMs two to one, although fewer of them are evident in the World of the Formerly Married than this might lead one to expect; the reason is that most of them are considerably older than most FMs and four-fifths of them are women for whom it is socially unacceptable—and not often possible, to begin with—to date or have relationships with much younger partners. Moreover, at any age widows and widowers do not interact easily even with FMs of their own age; although both face many of the same problems of loneliness, disruption of habits, and practical difficulties in running their home, the psychological make-up of the widowed and their feeling about what has happened to them are profoundly different from those of the Formerly Married, and each finds in the other much that is suspect, unsympathetic, or even antagonistic.

Never-married people—"single" people, in popular terminology—also interact with FMs, particularly at the younger age levels, where the very briefly married are almost indistinguishable from those who have never tried; indeed, the former are as apt to seek out the society of single people as that of the Formerly Married. At somewhat older age levels, a certain number of chronic bachelors and unmarried women mix with FMs, but mutual suspicion of each other, lack of common experience, and difference in outlook are even more effective as deterrents to choosing each other than in the case of the Formerly Married and the widowed.

Such is the polymorphous World of the Formerly Married —more lower- than middle-class (though we shall henceforth concentrate on the latter), more parental than non-parental, more nearly middle-aged than young; a world not of frivolous, hedonistic, footloose youths but of earnest, conscientious, somewhat harassed but hopeful adult Americans.

IV · *On the Making of FMs*

How did all these varied people come to be citizens of the World of the Formerly Married? I shall not here attempt any major inquiry as to the ultimate causes of divorce. That is another book; this one is about what becomes of the divorced. Yet the behavior of every FM is shaped, in part, by the experiences that caused him to seek, or unwillingly to agree to, the dissolution of the marriage; and though we need not swim the Hellespont of causation, let us put one toe into it.

First of all, we need to remind ourselves that what is said in divorce courts and reported in the tabloids has very little to do with the real reasons for marital break-ups. In every state, the law requires that one spouse sue the other for divorce on one or more of the legal grounds allowed in that state. Whatever the actual causes of conflict or unhappiness in that marriage, the divorce suit must fit the Procrustean bed of the law; the result is that in ninety per cent of divorce suits, the testimony offered in court is a sham battle, planned in advance, agreed upon by both lawyers, and uncontested by the defendant—the aim being to dissolve the marriage on the easiest and least unpleasant legal ground. Adultery, for instance, has become less and less common as a legal ground for divorce over the decades, and now accounts for only two per cent of all divorce suits, although in reality it is a causative factor in many times that percentage of divorces; its decline is due not to any decrease in adultery itself, but to the growing availability of such less objectionable and more easily proved grounds as cruelty or desertion.

If we took the legal complaints literally, we would have to believe adultery to be ninety-three times as common in Virginia as in Oregon, drunkenness twenty-two times as common in Florida as in Michigan, and a great deal of other nonsense. The figures on the legal grounds used for divorce reveal not why people break up their marriages, but in what ways they are forced to do so by the law. Even the three-fifths of all American divorces now granted on grounds of cruelty, indignities, and mental suffering are a legal artifact, not a reflection of true causes; when people are allowed to use an even less unpleasant ground such as "incompatibility," they choose it almost exclusively. In Alaska, which permits the use of that ground, over ninety per cent of divorcing couples prefer it to any other. Unquestionably, if incompatibility were made a legal ground in other states, the "causes" of divorce as recorded in court would suddenly and dramatically change.

At the opposite extreme are those analyses made by social scientists which turn away from individual feelings and experiences, and seek the causes of divorce in large-scale social and psychological phenomena. Sociologists, writes Professor William J. Goode in *After Divorce*, are not interested in the question, "What went wrong in this marriage?" but in such impersonal questions as, "Under what types of institutional arrangements is divorce to be found?" and "What characteristics are associated with marital stability or instability?" At that level of thinking, the principal causes of divorce are abstract social and cultural factors such as increased industrialization, increasing urbanization, the decline of religious opposition to divorce, vertical social mobility, the high demands made on the affectional side of marriage, the independence of women, and the like.

Each of these factors undoubtedly has a significant relationship to the high divorce rate in America, yet none of them can, or is meant to, explain the failure of any given marriage, or the success of any other. Increased industrialization, for instance, is certainly connected with the increased divorce rate, and yet three out of four marriages, even in our highly industrialized society, last a lifetime. Birth control has enabled some couples to remain childless and such people are more likely to divorce than those with children, yet most childless couples remain married. The sociological reasons for divorce therefore describe the kind of environment in which divorce is fairly common; they explain the increased likelihood of divorce in general, and are causes in the scientific and statistical sense, rather than in the sense of actual everyday experience.

An unhappily married person, however, does not feel or experience probabilities or large environmental factors, but rather those specific episodes and conflicts which make his marriage painful or unendurable; whatever the social conditions making divorce likely, he sees the episodes or conflicts themselves as leading to the separation and the divorce, and for him, therefore, they are the causes.

What, then, do FMs name as the causes of their own divorces? A hundred, a thousand different things. There are certain areas in which complaints repeatedly occur, and researchers have often compiled lists of these complaints, arranged by category. Financial troubles (insufficient support, quarrels over money, etc.) usually rank high; the control or domination of one partner by the other often ranks second or third; adultery, drunkenness, personality differences, and irresponsibility or lack of interest in home life come further down the scale in frequency; and toward the bottom are such old staples as cultural differences, immaturity, desertion, influence of relatives, and sexual incompatibility.

But even these compilations are misleading, for different FMs may experience the same cited cause in very dissimilar ways. One woman may name her husband's heavy drinking as a major problem, seeing it only as a bad habit, or self-indulgence, or simple meanness on his part; another woman may name the same thing, but see it as the result of her husband's lack of business success, or his sexual incapacity when sober. One man may say that he and his wife were incompatible, and that they both knew it after only a few months of marriage; another has the same complaint, but says that they became incompatible over a fifteen-year period, as separate interests, promotions, and child-rearing changed them from what they had been. One woman says her husband never gave her enough money because he was stingy and irresponsible by nature; another woman names the same trouble, but feels that her husband was forever punishing her for having a mind of her own, especially when it came to sex.

Perhaps, then, we will come closest to understanding how FMs feel about the causes of divorce if we classify them not by kinds of complaints, or subjects of disagreement, but according to the manner in which they are experienced—that is, according to the simplicity or complexity with which the individual sees them and the degree of insight he shows. For it is what the FM himself sees or believes about his own case that most affects his thinking about himself and his adjustment or maladjustment to his new status.

There are, for instance, quite a few people who see their marital breakdowns in terms of a single, simple cause inherent in the situation, and which inevitably had to wreck the marriage. A woman says that her husband was a wonderful man in every way except that he was a chronic gambler; after six years of crises and disasters due to his gambling, she brokenheartedly left him. A man says that his wife was, in his somewhat old-fashioned term, a "gold-digger"—she never could get enough, never was satisfied, and after a decade of this he left her. Another man says that he realized his wife was highstrung and sensitive, but had no idea she was a borderline schizophrenic; after some years of marriage and motherhood, she was in the mental hospital more often than not, and finally he divorced her for the sake of his children.

In each of these cases, the thoughtful observer might well

feel that the simple cause inherent in the situation was an insufficient explanation: the gambler must have needed his gambling for some deep-rooted reason, as the gold-digger needed her spending—and each was chosen originally by a spouse who responded, in some way, to the very qualities that later became unendurable. The husband of the schizophrenic sees her illness in simple terms, but a woman does not become severely schizophrenic in the same simple way in which she catches a cold; the husband's own personality and demands must have played some part in pushing her over the border. None of these people, however, sees things in more than a simplistic fashion, and for each of them their perception of what happened is a reality that will shape their subsequent actions, perhaps committing them to similar mistakes or perhaps making them more fearful or vengeful than they need be.

A second group of FMs experience marital break-up in terms of a single cause external to the marriage—an accident of fate which upsets the equilibrium of an otherwise good relationship. Consider, for instance, the following statement which comes from a thirty-four-year-old woman in a city in Massachusetts:

> Husband always known to be a good boy. Eight years after we were married, he joined bowling league at work, had too much to drink one night, ended up necking in the parking lot with a married woman. Thereafter acted like a love-sick calf, had no relations with me for eight months, stayed out crazy hours, hung around bars telling his troubles to bartenders and waitresses. I couldn't stand it, begged him to straighten out and give her up, and when he wouldn't, moved him out bag and baggage.

To this wife, the whole thing was a species of misfortune visited upon their marriage from the outside; in none of her comments does she question whether she had played any part in his behavior or ask herself why he should have been so vulnerable to a mere peccadillo. This limited perception may well be the reason she has been slow to adjust to life as an FM, has had very few and almost all abortive relationships, and has not yet remarried after six years.

Another woman thinks her marriage was fine until her husband's parents moved nearby and became a disruptive influence in their lives. A man whose company moved him to a Southern city thinks that what made his wife leave him was the boredom, the drinking, and the fast company she fell into, none of which would have come her way if they had been allowed to remain in Akron. Even success sometimes seems to people like an outside and fateful force, breaking up what would otherwise have endured; the former wife of an actor writes:

> For eight years he was a struggling young nobody, lucky to get walk-ons and supporting roles. All that time I was doing my best to encourage him, and helping earn a living; we were a devoted, very close couple. Then he got his big break, and made it in a lead role, after which came TV and movies. He became arrogant and demanding, uninterested in me, a really different human being. Maybe he felt I wasn't as glamorous as some of the women he could now afford. If he hadn't ever hit it big, we'd still be happily married. It changed him. It ruined the sweet sincere guy I was married to.

Each of these people is probably right in identifying the external cause—except that in each case it is only the proximate cause, the triggering action; it acted upon a situation already loaded and primed for detonation. Had it not happened, something else probably would have; and to the extent that these people fail to see this, they run the risk of repeating their mistakes and misjudgments the next time.

Another group of people experience the causes of their break-up in more complicated and psychological terms. If they complain about drinking, gambling, or adultery, they rightly regard these as the symptoms of psychological disorder.

But some of them only sense this dimly, without having any deeper perception. They say things like this:

> As his drinking got worse and worse I tried my best to help him, but nothing I did or said was any good. I have wondered a thousand times how I failed him, and quit wondering.

> She was a good housekeeper, a good friend, and a good mother, but she couldn't meet my need for emotional warmth or sexual responsiveness. She tried, but she couldn't give whatever I needed.

In each case, the speaker is aware that some sort of neurotic difficulty existed, but has no idea how complex and profound it was. For a woman who chooses a weak or alcoholic man often does so by way of unwitting defense against the threat of male sexuality and strength; such a woman is consciously tormented—and unconsciously comforted—by the failure of her husband to be a satisfactory male. A man who chooses a sexually blocked woman may be selecting her on the basis of unconscious infantile wishes; he wants someone like his mother, but the incest-barrier makes him select a relatively frigid woman with whom sex may be frustrating but will not produce anxiety.

Sexual problems are, in fact, the most familiar complaint of those who sense neurotic difficulty but perceive only its symptoms. According to nearly every serious researcher, sexual problems are not a major cause of divorce, and yet every marriage counsellor and psychiatrist, and many a lawyer, reports that sexual problems do exist in a great many troubled or dissolving marriages. This seeming paradox probably means that only a small number of people have severe, innate sexual disabilities, but that a far greater number become sexually maladjusted by way of expressing the neurotic conflicts between themselves and their mates. Sexual problems are thus not very often a fundamental cause, though many FMs experience them as if they were; such people realize that a kind of emotional illness is involved, but cannot identify it or recognize their own part in the sickness of the relationship.

A young woman who had been married for eight years later married a bachelor of forty-two; the marriage was turbulent from the beginning and lasted only a year. Her view of it is that he was immature, petulant, demanding, bossy, and given to temper tantrums when she paid too much attention to her son. But she thinks that behind all this, the trouble was sexual. "During our short courtship," she says, "what I mistook for respect turned out later to be lack of desire, better known as impotence. I tried to get him to see a doctor, and when he finally did and was referred to a psychiatrist, he refused to go." But why didn't she herself go? Shouldn't she have wondered why she chose an immature man to begin with, or how, after an eight-year marriage, she could have been so unaware of a man's lack of desire as to marry first and burn later? Ought she not have wondered whether a mistake of that order was not partly her fault? But she does not wonder; we can only wish her an accidentally better choice the next time.

Other people have considerably more insight and see not just the symptoms, but the fundamentally inappropriate or neurotic basis of their own choice of partner, or the neurotic reasons for the conflict between them. Many better-educated people today try to grope for insights and think in terms of psychodynamic mechanisms, whether or not they have ever had any psychotherapy. Such groping may not always yield the most profound self-knowledge, but it does result in a subtler evaluation of their experience, and a different and perhaps better adaptation to FM life. Such people make statements like these:

I guess I must have been looking for a father-figure.

When I married her, I thought love doesn't pay any heed to the color line. But now I think a large part of it was that I was defying my parents, and busting loose.

He was a brilliant man, but quite lacking in the cultural back-ground and breeding I had. I thought I would be very good for him, but that was a mistake; that's not a healthy reason for marrying someone.

Even though the forces that impelled these people to love and marry unsuitable mates were unconscious, they did even-tually recognize that there had been something unhealthy about such a choice and grasp some part of the truth. And this awareness modifies their view of themselves, and hence their behavior in the future. A forty-six-year-old television writer, now very happily remarried, sees his own first marriage with considerable insight, although he has never had any profes-sional treatment:

I couldn't have picked worse if I had tried. I met her down South, and she was young and pretty and sexy, and I was a lonely soldier, far from home. Even if she didn't know what I was talk-ing about half the time, doesn't love conquer all? No, it doesn't. But it was marvelously flattering to a homely shrimp like me to have a pretty thing hanging on his arm and listening to every brilliant word he said. We were completely incompatible and I must have been stupid not to realize it. She likes big parties; I don't. She likes night clubs; I don't. She likes loud people; I like polite people. She thinks I'm square; I think she's cheap. Even when I found all this out, I would have stuck with her for the sake of the kids, but I couldn't stand her continual and out-rageously open infidelities. She even carried on in the living-room while I was upstairs in bed, believe it or not.

But I think now that I probably instigated the whole thing. She was always jealous of the fact that I'd had affairs before marriage, though she'd been a virgin; maybe I talked too much about them to her. She was such a terrible scold about it that finally one night I told her to go out and even up the score, if it would make her feel any better about it. It was just as though I'd given her a hunting license—off she went to the city on business the next morning, and by the time she came back that night she'd scored one already. From there on it got worse and worse until finally

I packed up and left her. Only later did I see that in the things I used to tell her, and in the go-ahead I gave her, I was unconsciously encouraging her to give me the justification for leaving.

Another category of divorce causation, as FMs themselves feel it, is inexperience, unripeness, imperfect expectations, or misjudgments. "Immaturity" of self or mate is one of the reasons most frequently offered by the people I interviewed or queried, and usually they meant not a pathological failure to mature but mere inexperience. A young woman who married while still a junior at college offers a typical explanation:

We were both very immature and from very dissimilar backgrounds, but we didn't realize that that would affect us. We thought we were in love, but it took less than a week after marriage for us to discover that neither of us had married the person we thought we were marrying. We had very little to give each other, and to make it worse, the few things we did have were the wrong things. I had no desire to learn to hunt and fish, and he resisted all my efforts to introduce him to poetry and opera, and so it went. It is easier to explain why we divorced than why we married.

Inexperience and immature expectations also explain the divorces of those young people who find marriage disappointing rather than painful, and boring rather than wretched. A young man of twenty-seven says that his marriage broke up because he simply "wasn't ready to settle down," felt restless and trapped at home, and found married love "just too bland." The young divorcee, according to an article written by one and published in *Harper's*, faces the crisis of marriage when, after a few years, she sees life stretching before her, even, routine, and undramatic, and asks herself in horror, "Is this *all* there is going to be *forever?*" Having expected marriage to fulfill all her emotional needs, she is disenchanted when it does not, and feels that she has fallen out of love; it then seems necessary to fight her way out of the marriage and try again.

If she is lucky, she realizes that she had been unrealistic, and eventually adopts a different and more adult expectation of what marriage should mean.

There are surely many other ways in which FMs experience the causes of divorce; I shall conclude this handful with only one more. It is the one in which the individual perception of the causes probably comes closest to what a skilled objective observer would say: it is the experience of divorce as caused by a whole set of interacting forces, no one of which is a sufficient cause, yet each of which is probably an essential ingredient. I suspect that the more intelligent, honest, and insightful a person is, the less he can pinpoint in simple or clearcut terms what went wrong, and the more he sees the break-up in multi-causal terms.

A good example of this comes from a California schoolteacher, now in her mid-forties, who had been married to a physicist, and who offers this remarkably honest and searching series of conjectures:

> It is very difficult to say just what went wrong. Our marriage was thrillingly happy for years. When this state had ended without our even being aware of it, and we were contented rather than happy, my husband fell passionately in love with another woman. One could put it another way and say that as our sex life lost its real thrill and spontaneity, he (and I, perhaps) became vulnerable to new partners. But the best I can do is to set forth the questions I have asked myself time and again; it is quite easy to make a case for any of the following possibilities, but after several years of thinking about it all, I am not in the least sure what the right order of their importance is.
>
> 1. Was it because we had different tastes in sex? He liked artifice; I preferred spontaneity. He wanted flowing hair, sexy nightgowns, arch looks; I felt foolish, trying to be like that, and wanted to be more direct and lusty.
>
> 2. Was it the result of our total personality interaction? He is very dominant and strong; I submerged my own individuality

bit by bit until, after ten years, I was a shadow, a sounding-board, an echo of him. Because it seemed to make him happy, I allowed this to happen—and the result was that I became dull, while he became more vibrant and free. Somewhere in all this, motherhood and my devotion to the children plays a part, but I'm not sure where or how.

3. Was he more vulnerable, in general, to a new love than most other people? He went through many hobbies and many work interests over the years; perhaps he had a shorter attention span than most people.

4. Was it that he found someone more suited to him, totally, than I? Where he and I complemented each other, he and she virtually mirror each other.

5. Did we just "use it up"? We lived a very close life, had more wonderful hours and shared more deeply and fully, talked more and did more together in ten years, than most couples do in a lifetime.

6. Did marriage carry the seeds of its own destruction? Is there something about it that is bound to kill off, in the end, the very things that brought us together into it? Was there a dulling of sexual pleasure as a result of the knowledge that sex was "expected"? Was it too comfortable for too long, making for a monogamy so binding that it became an intolerable burden? Was there no room for a sense of adventure, of personal rediscovery?

7. Was all this inevitable, or did he perhaps purposely destroy our relationship in order to be freed to pursue the new one?

As I say, I have thought too long about all this to know, any longer, what "the" cause of our break-up was. The question may be meaningless; perhaps the only cause is the entire complex of things that yield the result.

And with that final statement even the philosopher, for all his intricate theorizing about the meaning of causality, can wholeheartedly agree.

v · *The Road to FM Land*

Whatever the causes, and however they are experienced, the
marital break-up they bring about is the end of a long and
intricate process of disengagement. When does it begin? At
what point is the future determined? One is hard put to pinpoint it. Eugene Wilson, the man in Room 27 at the Bella Vista
Motel, would have been unable to say, that first night; even
a year later, after gaining perspective and composure, he was
not quite sure. As he wrote to an old friend:

> It's something like asking when death begins. I've heard that
> you aren't really dead for eight minutes after your heart stops,
> until the brain is ruined from lack of oxygen. But you could also
> say that death does begin with the final beat of the heart, because
> the rest is inevitable. In another sense, though, it begins as soon
> as you start losing your youth. And in yet another sense it begins
> when you are born—born mortal and destined to die. Maybe a
> marriage that fails is like that—maybe it was born mortal.

In a more down-to-earth mood, Wilson has tried to pinpoint
for himself the exact time and place when the process began.
At a large and cheerful buffet, four years earlier, he flirted
with a pretty young actress and then glanced at his wife, seeing,
as if for the first time, her already matronly figure and her prim
tight mouth; he felt displeased, and was filled with dismay at
his own disloyalty and all that it might mean. There was a
time even earlier—his own thirty-fifth birthday—when he and
she stayed home (he had a briefcase full of papers to go over),
drank a toast or two late in the evening, and perfunctorily
made love; afterwards, his engineering training coming to the
fore, he found himself mentally computing the number of
meals, evenings, and copulations he had shared with her thus
far, and the number they would share in the second half of
his life. He shuddered to think that he would grow old and die

without ever knowing anything else but this, and was shocked at himself for the thought.

But perhaps these were only passing moods; perhaps the true beginning was the night, about a year before their separation, when they quarrelled bitterly (he cannot even recall about what) and went to bed in silence; there had been many such occasions in the previous two or three years, but this was the worst. Lying next to her in the dark, he found himself thinking for the very first time that perhaps something was really happening to them, that perhaps their marriage was breaking up. He instantly forbade the thought, thrust it away, denied it; it just as instantly came back and would not be refused. He found himself spinning dreadful fantasies of what the children would think, where he would go to live, what his friends would say, what sort of life he and she would each lead; the thoughts were loathsome and melancholy, and he could not understand why they so fascinated him. Perhaps that night was the moment when he first actually set foot upon the long road that leads from marriage to divorce.

And yet an hour later, still wakeful, he heard her sigh, spoke to her, broke the spell with a gentle touch; then came the tears, the clinging, even a brief rush of passion, and for a while, the thought of separation seemed impossible and absurd, a waking nightmare. But the next time, and the next, it seemed less absurd, less startling; eventually it became almost natural.

That took many months. Some people, especially Europeans, think that Americans divorce impulsively and in haste, as they turn in their old cars for the gleaming new models in the window. But this is untrue. Americans take months or years to work their way painfully down that road. Dr. Goode, in a survey of divorced women in Detroit, found the median time from the "first serious consideration" to the final decision to be about four and a half months—and even at that, the first serious consideration may come long after the idea has been hovering ominously in the shadowed background of the mind.

John F. Cuber and Peggy B. Harroff, in *The Significant Americans: A Study of Sexual Behavior Among the Affluent*, report that among upper-middle-class people the decision to divorce typically comes after three or four, or even more, years of awareness that the marriage is unsatisfactory and that an eventual break-up is possible.

During this period the movement toward dissolution is not smooth and continuous, but irregular and halting, being broken by waverings and brief retreats followed by new and bigger advances. So it was with the Wilsons; after each new quarrel they would have a time of making-up and warmth, but each new quarrel was more reckless, each reconciliation less reassuring. They ceased making love regularly, but several times, after weeks of not touching each other in bed, they would come together again fiercely, almost desperately, each assuring the other that it was better than ever; in truth each was growing used to the idea that desire for the other could wither and disappear.

And there were the talks—those long, searching, inconclusive talks, by which they sought to turn back toward safety and yet willy-nilly pushed further toward the unknown. Sometimes he and she were fairminded and utterly "civilized," sometimes they sought to slash each other with words (she with icy sarcasm, he with bellowing rage). But whatever the tone, they always thought they were trying to search, to probe for the truth, and so to clarify, to correct, and to repair. Only in retrospect does he see how absurdly mistaken they were, for there are many truths that should never be told, that only damage the other person, and that can never be taken back.

The less articulate people of the lower class are, in large part, propelled down the road to separation and divorce by physical acts and bad behavior; people of the middle class are propelled by earnest talk, unveiling, and truth-telling. The Wilsons each said (and believed) that their only purpose in all this was to work it out, to clear up the difficulties, and to achieve a sounder basis for marriage, but each was also half-aware that the more they talked, the less chance there was of going home again, and that the talks were leading them inexorably to the frightening, hateful, and yet oddly desired end. Every such searching examination, every exposure of truth, whittled away at love, added to their supply of grievances, and conditioned them to treasonous thoughts until treason to their marriage became patriotism to themselves.

And yet again and again came the brief resurgences of love and warmth, the vows to forget all that had been happening, the sweet illusion that all problems had been resolved. But these moods became briefer and more tepid as time passed. One sociologist has drawn a symbolic graph of the process: a curve descends from left to right, but not smoothly—a jagged mountain range, with peaks of love and valleys of conflict, each peak being lower than the previous one, each valley deeper, until it plunges into the sea of separation. It is, in fact, remarkably like the curve of the progress of cancer—the declining state of health, the upthrusting remission produced by surgery, the new and deeper declines, the new and less important remissions brought about by radiation and drugs, and then finally the last steep descent to the point where the curve breaks off.

Some few couples are fortunate; they merely drift apart. Childless, or with children who are grown and gone, they see less and less of each other, develop other interests, perhaps other loves, and one day admit to each other that they should no longer be married. But for most people it is not so; there are a thousand strands of affection and habit, of duty and loyalty, holding them together even after they have come to desperately desire escape.

No wonder, then, that ordinarily sensible and well-behaved people become enraged over trifles, say vicious things to each other in thick alien voices, slam doors, break dishes, suffer vomiting spells or diarrhea. Anger is the knife with which they slash away at the remaining bonds, and free themselves. Even Eugene Wilson, a product of prep school and an Ivy League

college, tore up their wedding picture one night and threw
the pieces on her lap; even she, a proper Bostonian, flung a cup
of coffee in his face in a downtown restaurant (after pausing
for a second to be sure it was not too hot), ran out into the
street, and leaped into a cab. And yet, most curiously, even
these shameful, foolish deeds, even the strangling rages, were
fascinating and perversely pleasurable. For anger is needful;
it is the exquisite pain that forces the process to a conclusion
and thus brings surcease.*

By this gruesome but compelling process, one finally arrives
at the border and falters a moment, fearing to take the final
step—and then does so. The moment of crossing over takes
many a different form.

A young woman, whose husband torments her not by quarrelling but by stony nonresponsiveness, lies next to him one
night in suffocating silence until three A.M.; then she cannot
tolerate another moment of it, leaps out of bed and turns on
the lights, and in a few minutes is on her way by taxi to a
hotel.

A normal, respectable middle-aged businessman comes
home at midnight, drunk, profane, and abusive, and tells his
wife of the last twenty-one years to clear out in fifteen minutes
or he will get out his .22 rifle and load it; she flees, half-
dressed and almost hysterical, to the nearby home of friends
and pounds on the door until they wake and let her in.

A young man quietly and gently asks his wife during a long
talk one night if she doesn't feel that he ought to move out
for a little while until he can "straighten out his thinking"
about what he wants in life, and she agrees; in the morning,
after a tearful embrace, he leaves her, ostensibly for a week
or two, but both of them suspect he will never move back in.

* It is also probably true, as Dr. Goode suggests, that some of the anger
is due in many cases to deliberate provocation by the partner who first wants
to escape, and who behaves objectionably in order to make the reluctant
spouse willing to give up the marriage. But even the one who first wants to
escape needs to generate a good deal of anger in himself, in order to feel
justified in his disloyalty.

The wife of an actor who is spending half a year in Hollywood, far from her and their home, gets a fat envelope one morning from a lawyer in Ciudad Juarez; she reads the papers with shaking hands, unable to believe the words, but finally realizes that he has gotten a Mexican divorce without telling her in advance or getting her consent to the action. It is fraudulent and not binding, but she will have to go to court to fight it, and in any case, whatever her legal status, she has abruptly become an FM.

As for Eugene Wilson and his wife, they had been speaking of a trial separation for months before they finally parted. He was the one who first suggested it, but she grew panicky (she had never worked or lived on her own) and he had to shelve the idea. He brought it up tentatively, again and again, and the more she pleaded for him to stay, the more he longed to go. But after a while she apparently grew used to the notion, for one night during some unpleasant words, she told him he could pack up any time he wanted to and leave—she had had quite enough, and life without him could certainly be no worse than life with him had been. To his own surprise, he was suddenly unwilling to do so, wanted her to beg him not to, and slouched off to bed without anything more to say. The following night, after the children were asleep, she caustically asked when he was planning to leave, and said she didn't understand what he was waiting for; he answered sharply, she counteranswered, and all at once he found himself on his feet and beginning to take down the valise from the storage closet. Once he had begun, there was no way for him to stop, nor did she seem to want him to. He snapped the valise shut and said goodbye without looking at her, walked out, came back in half a moment for his briefcase (blurting out his purpose the instant he walked in, lest she think he came back to beg her forgiveness), and left again. As of that moment, although their actual divorce lay more than a year and a half away, Wilson and his wife began their lives as formerly married people.

CHAPTER TWO

The Novice

I · *A Case of Mixed Feelings*

Not all brides and grooms are equally happy at weddings, nor all mourners equally sad at funerals; still, at least they all know what society and their own consciences expect of them. But the man or woman whose marriage has just broken up has no clear directives, external or internal, as to his or her appropriate behavior and feelings. The traditional attitude of the world around him or her is that the moment of separation, like any death-bed scene, is tragic and depressing; yet the emerging ethos of the World of the Formerly Married holds it to be also liberating and encouraging, since it is a rebirth or, at the very least, the immolation prerequisite to a Phoenix-like rearising.

What is even more perplexing to the FM is to have feelings quite the opposite of those he or she expected to have—feelings which, in the circumstances, seem to make no sense. One would imagine, for instance, that where two people are desperately unhappy with each other, are both in favor of the separation, and have no children to worry about, their immediate reaction to separation would be pure relief. But sometimes it is quite the opposite. A young businesswoman, cheerful in manner and attractive despite a severely simple, pulled-back hairdo, says she was taken quite aback by her own unpredictable emotions:

Bob and I had known for months that we couldn't make a go of it any longer, and by the time we agreed to separate it was a thing we both felt necessary, and wanted, for both our sakes. But my God!—the day he moved out I felt absolutely broken. I went to work that morning, and all day long I sat at my desk and just *shook*. People would look at me and ask, was I sick or something? When I went home at the end of the day and sat in the living-room alone, knowing there would be no one coming home, I felt scared, and sick at the stomach. Yet for many months the marriage had been awful for both of us, and this was supposed to be a blessed relief.

Or if a man's wife, deeply discontented with their marriage, has badgered and tormented him until he agrees, against his wishes, to leave his home and children, one would expect him to feel only rage and deep depression; he may, however, be astonished to find a very different mood arising within himself, as did this forty-seven-year-old insurance salesman:

The first night was one of the few times in my adult life that I actually wept. But toward midnight I suddenly realized that I could go to bed without the prospect of one of those awful hysterical fights she used to provoke at bedtime. As terrible as I knew I ought to feel, I couldn't get over the queer pleasure I actually felt. It was like being on a plane or boat trip and getting away from it all.

We might work out a set of predictions as to the feelings, upon separation, of the different kinds of FMs—those who wanted to escape and those who did not, those who were married a short time and those who were married many years, those who experienced the causes of marital discord in a simple fashion and those who experienced them in all their subtlety and complexity. But with these and many other variables to consider, and so many imponderables outside of our reckoning, we would probably guess wrong distressingly often; as with the sociological causes of divorce, we might get a set of statistical correlations rather than predictions applicable to individuals. Perhaps future generations of social scientists, equipped with computers, will be able to feed the many human variables into the machine and come out with reliable answers; until then, we may be better off to ask only the end result: How is any newly separated man or woman "taking it"—that is, what is his or her location along the spectrum running from the wholly negative to the wholly positive?

There are a few people who experience only dark and distressing feelings upon separation. Some women burst into tears a dozen times a day, are unable to eat or sleep, wear little make-up and frumpy clothes, cannot properly run their households, and look and act like persons in a state of shock; some men fumble with their work all day long, sit alone at night staring mindlessly at television, and drink themselves into a joyless stupor before going to bed. A woman medical technician who had finally separated, after fourteen years, from her chronically unfaithful husband, put it this way:

> I felt worthless, no good, unwanted, rejected, *fouled*. I was in a state of complete and devastating depression. Driving a car, I would often forget where I was, and where I was going. It was terrifying. I had my first auto accident, and got my first speeding tickets. I also had a severe rash on one wrist that doctors couldn't clear up for months.

A manly and ordinarily strong-minded real-estate agent of thirty-four felt just as depressed:

> I had a remarkable tendency to cry, remembering good past experiences. I was always wondering what she was doing now (and especially if she was having sex with anybody else and liking it). Felt a vast aloneness from the whole world. Stomach had a hole in it (actually). Went mechanically through the motions of my work, there being nothing to work for. Couldn't concentrate enough to read at night. Took pills to go to sleep, but would wake at three or four A.M. and find myself unable to get back to sleep. This went on for many weeks.

All sorts of physical and emotional symptoms plague these people: sleeplessness troubles some (although others find themselves requiring ten and twelve hours of sleep every night); the lack of appetite or, conversely, overeating, are fairly common; some people are unable to interest themselves in anything, and cannot seem to keep their thoughts from returning again and again to the same exasperating reflections; some fly into rages at their children on little provocation, and then are bitterly ashamed; and some become chain-smokers, or use sleeping pills, alcohol, or anti-depressant drugs. Some become sufficiently disturbed or alcoholic to seek psychiatric treatment, but others who should get treatment fail to, with tragic consequences: the suicide rate among divorced women is three times as high, and that among men is four times as high, as those for married women and men respectively.

In contrast to this bleak picture is the experience of those at the opposite end of the spectrum. For varied reasons, a few FMs seem to feel almost nothing but positive emotions after the parting. "We'd been married three years," says a dynamic young career woman, "and it was a mistake from the first week. It was like being in jail. The day he moved out I felt simply great. It was like having made the clean break in a love affair that has gone sour, only ten times stronger. I called up my closest friends and told them the good news, then I went out and spent $175 in Lord & Taylor's, and I went to a party that same night."

A man of forty-one who, for the sake of his children, had remained married long after the relationship had deteriorated, felt almost manic after the separation. "As I walked around town that first evening," he says, " I felt so light-hearted and excited that I had to tell someone—anyone—and finally I called a girl I'd once had an affair with years earlier, and who I knew was now divorced. She was just great about it—she changed her plans and told me to come on over, and we talked until five in the morning. I went home and wasn't sleepy or

even tired. I never went to bed that night. For weeks I practically luxuriated in the feeling of being alive again. I felt
interested again in everyone and everything—including myself."

Instead of developing physical disorders due to the separation, such people usually lose those they may have had. A
woman of thirty-five was freed, within a week of separation,
from constipation of several years' duration; a prominent stage
director stopped biting his nails after doing so for over a decade; a woman of fifty says she "stopped vomiting for the first
time in months"; a man who had difficult and slow urination,
due to tension and anger, found himself making water like a
boy. The recapture of health and of the *joie de vivre* can be
intensely sensuous. A warm and emotional young woman who
had been married for five years to an undemonstrative and
inhibited man recalls how she felt after she finally got him to
move out:

> After achieving this, I experienced only great relief, a marvelous
> unloading feeling, tranquillity in my surroundings and myself
> for the first time in years. I became generous, warm, giggly, and
> peaceful. I slept much better, looked better, felt sensuous and
> proud of my body (for my own sake, not for anyone else's),
> even slept without nightclothes and enjoyed the sheets against
> my skin. Felt a general rebirth and awakening; felt almost in-
> toxicated. This lasted six weeks and then slowly diminished to a
> more normal level of well-being.

And yet neither extreme represents the typical mood of the
newly separated. The majority of them have a bewildering and
changeable mixture of feelings that conflict with and contradict
each other. A childless man of twenty-eight, debonair and
youthfully handsome, says, "It was great to get back into the
swing of things with my single friends. I had a ball. But I
was hyperemotional for a long while, and I used to burst into
tears even at happy movies or sometimes in the middle of
talks with friends. It was damned embarrassing." A housewife

of forty-one, with two children, felt like this after breaking up a lengthy marriage: "I was so relieved!—I felt able to breathe, I went around humming, I talked to myself and laughed out loud. I'd known for a long, long while that I would eventually have to do it, and it was a great hurdle finally overcome. But in the middle of all this I had acute colitis and stomach pains that lasted several months." A forty-nine-year-old artist who left his home and two children says:

> The day I finally walked out on her with just one little suitcase and almost no money, and got on the bus for New York, I felt dazed and unseeing but glad, like somebody who has just come out into blinding light after being lost in a cave. For weeks I hardly even cared about my children, and I had no sex drive at all—I didn't even bother to visit the woman I'd been having an affair with—but from the very first I did feel able to paint once again, and I got to work with energy and fresh ideas for the first time in a long while. Work was all I needed for a couple of months.

The wife of a well-to-do banker, thirty-two at the time of her separation, recalls her mixed feelings as follows:

> When he first left, I felt a rather cautious exhilaration. I kept saying to myself, "I'm free. . . ." But at the same time, and increasingly, I felt a heaviness, an emptiness, that came over me like an actual pain. I remember realizing one day that it was like an invisible sobbing, underneath, inside my chest. Or sometimes after a spell of feeling gay, I would for no reason feel like a balloon with a pinprick, and the air very slowly seeping out. Having gotten rid of a husband who couldn't arouse me sexually, I was suddenly very awakened and screaming with desire, but too frightened and unsure to know what to do about it.

In the same fashion, many novice FMs have a mixture of physical ailments and signs of returning health. One man finds he no longer drinks too much, but is frequently sleepless; a woman no longer suffers from almost chronic cystitis, but smokes heavily and has trembling hands. Some people have spells of tachycardia (irregular heartbeat), others develop skin ailments, still others have migraine headaches, backaches, or loss of hair; yet most people soon find themselves sleeping better, looking and feeling younger, and having a greater capacity for work.

There are various reasons for the illogic and the ambivalence of the feelings of the newly separated. People tend to feel what they know is expected of them, but the novice FM does not know with any certainty what *is* expected. Again, the mutual truth-telling that precedes the actual break damages the ego of the escapee as well as the ego of the abandoned one; both are demeaned and humiliated, and thus the former, even in the moment of escape, may have the joy he feels in his freedom contaminated by despair and depression. Similarly, separation nearly always signifies a kind of rejection—explicitly, to the one who was originally unwilling to have the marriage break up, but implicitly, to the one who first wanted it to. A woman may be sexually unresponsive, and her husband may be the one who wants to leave, but he cannot avoid the thought that perhaps her unresponsiveness was due to a dislike of him or a distaste for his person. Or perhaps a man is cold and critical, and his wife is the one who wants to be free of him; yet she cannot escape the feeling that his coldness and criticism were due to her own shortcomings.

As a result, even those who feel considerable relief are often sufficiently distressed and disorganized to seek professional or semi-professional help in dealing with their turbulent emotions. One-sixth of all the family heads who go to the three-hundred-odd family agencies throughout America are separated or divorced persons in search of counselling. Most of the 166 chapters of Parents Without Partners, a national organization of the separated, divorced, and widowed, schedule discussion groups or group therapy sessions led by psychologists or marriage counsellors, many of which are designed to help FMs recover from the trauma of their experience. A survey made for the congressionally chartered Joint Commission on Mental

Illness and Health found that among separated and divorced people, one-fifth of the men and two-fifths of the women seek help for their emotional problems from psychiatrists, clinics, social agencies, general practitioners, or ministers; another one-eighth of the men and one-fifth of the women did not, but felt they could have used it.

Yet at the same time, even those who are primarily grieved, unhappy, or distraught at the moment of separation frequently have curiously admixed with these feelings a sense of self-preservation, health, and comfort. When someone we love is slowly dying, we shed tears for what is to come; when at last he is dead, we still weep but with a difference. The pain we feel is almost welcome because we know that now the vigil is done, the hurt is going to diminish rather than grow worse; the prospect ahead is no longer of death, but of readjustment and new life. So it is, too, with the death of a marriage.

There may even be a sense of impending growth and achievement, the stirring of something positive, the excitement of challenge. Separation may in many people trigger certain health-producing mechanisms in the psyche, even as infection does in the tissues. Both in this country and elsewhere, a few leading psychologists have begun to think that the greatest spurts of personality growth and reorganization occur during periods of crisis and psychological upheaval. Some psyches are permanently damaged by emotional crises, but most, according to the new view, react as the body does to exercise or effort—with an outpouring of energy and an increase of strength. And this may be why many FMs who should seemingly be crushed by separation are actually galvanized by it. They become earnest, energetic, hyperactive, and—much to their own surprise —somewhat pleased with themselves. Like many a mourner at a funeral, they are disconcertingly aware that in the midst of sorrow they feel keenly aware of their own power to survive, and have a sense of well-being and almost of excitement in their ability to endure and to surmount the obstacles ahead.

All of which explains why novice FMs are so often astonished and perplexed by the mixed and shifting nature of their own feelings, and hardly know how to explain them to others—or even to themselves. They look in the mirror, expecting to see the worst, but are surprised to find little evidence of ruin, and perhaps even some of restoration. They are half-delighted and yet half-disappointed that, like Shakespeare's Richard the Second, they can say,

> No deeper wrinkles yet? Hath sorrow struck
> So many blows across this face of mine,
> And made no deeper wounds?

II · *"Alone, alone, all, all alone"*

Of all the negative feelings of the newly separated, none is more common or more important than loneliness. Only a minority fail to suffer from it, and even those who most keenly desired the end of the marriage often find the initial loneliness excruciating. The man comes home to his rented room or apartment at dusk, and opens the door to his sanctuary. All is still and peaceful in his own little haven; he lights a lamp, puts something on the stove, pours a drink, and sinks down with a magazine in bachelor freedom. But the silence that washes over him is menacing, the air seems sodden and heavy, he struggles to fill his lungs. He turns the page but does not remember what he has just read, has an absurd feeling that something dreadful is about to happen, and can sit still no longer; he leaps up, turns off the stove, and rushes out to a restaurant, a bar, a movie—any place where he can be near other bodies, other faces, other voices.

The woman gets her children fed, bathed, and bedded, and quiet settles upon her house—quiet that pulses in her ears, and is full of foreboding. She watches TV, but there is no one to laugh with or make comments to; she tries to read, but it is curiously comfortless compared to doing so in a room where someone else is reading, too; she plumps up the sofa on which he so often annoyingly sprawled without taking his shoes off, and she is astonished that her eyes fill with tears at the thought. In the bathroom closet at bedtime she comes across some of his old prescriptions, abandoned in his getaway; how long, she wonders, will it be before all traces of his living in this home are erased? In bed, she delays turning the light off; the darkness is full of nameless fears when one is alone. Finally she does turn it off, but stays on her side of the bed, as if he were still there; the night presses upon her, the house makes mysterious noises that cause her heart to skip, and she waits for something to happen. At last, falling asleep, she rolls over, unconsciously reaches out an arm—and wakes with a start because no one is there.

Why the premonition of doom, the oppressiveness of being with one's own self? Were we not all alone before marriage, without feeling like this? Of course, but married love is an experience that changes us so we can never be what we were before. It is not just the side-by-side comradeship of two who are alike, but the fitting together of two who are different, and who complete each other. Whatever loneliness may mean to the child, the bachelor, the unmarried girl, it means something else to the Formerly Married—an amputation, a dismemberment, an incompleteness where once there was something whole.

What pleasure is there for her in preparing a dinner, with no man to admire her for it? What satisfaction is there for him in fixing things that do not work, if there is no woman to praise his skill? The home she was proud of is a burden now, and keeping it lovely is a bore. The small daily triumphs he achieves over the world seem flat and insipid now that there is no one who will taste and relish them with him.

The loneliness of the FM is due in large part to what is technically called "role disturbance." The greater the number of specialized roles a man or woman had in marriage, the greater the disturbance caused by separation; hence it is that the separated parent is even lonelier than the separated nonparent. Obviously, the man misses his children; what is less obvious, but very real, is that he misses the acting out of fatherliness in himself, and the special fellowship of being a co-parent. Even when he visits and plays with his children, and is replenished by their love, he lacks the special satisfaction of being loved in the role of father by his wife. An elbow is scraped, and he fixes it; an argument between the children flares up, and he plays Solomon to them; great questions are asked (*"Why* do people down South hate Negroes?"), and he answers them wisely; but he does all this by himself, and it is not truly satisfying.

The woman has the children with her nearly all the time, but paradoxically is more alone, for there is no one to approve of her when she handles them well, console her when she does not, laugh with her at their pranks or smile with her at their discoveries. She may even try to phone him, once in a while, to share some special moment, but though he is grateful and pleased to hear these things, he no longer radiates that remembered warmth upon her for her motherliness, and when he hangs up she is even more alone than before.

For the parent with custody—and nine-tenths of the time this means the woman—loneliness also has a grimly practical side. She has an endless series of problems that must be solved every day. If she has to move into smaller and cheaper quarters, she must find them, pack, move, and unpack, all by herself. But even if she stays put, what is she to do about the oil burner, the living-room Venetian blind with a broken cord, the banging radiator? What about the insurance, the bank statements, the increased real-estate assessment? If she has to work, when on earth is she to shop and clean and cook, let alone pay attention to her children? If she washes her hair in the shower, will she hear the baby cry? No wonder she sometimes thinks, "If only I didn't have the children"—and then chokes back the thought like a regurgitation in the throat, scalding and vile.

The newly separated have a variety of ways of reacting to loneliness and dealing with it. A fortunate few are able merely to ignore it; they are the self-sufficient souls for whom the intimacy and interaction of marriage may have proven uncomfortable and overly demanding, and who are happier in limited, uncommitted relationships. Such persons find the FM state relatively comfortable, even at the beginning, and may be genuinely pleased to be rid of the partner. They savor their solitude lovingly, as though it were a fine wine. They can buy what they like, move the furniture around to their taste, visit only the friends they prefer, without opposition or the need to compromise. At night after work, or when the children have fallen asleep, such people enjoy the silence and the freedom to do whatever they please. They can eat two peanut-butter sandwiches for dinner, read in the tub for an hour, go to bed at nine P.M. or at three in the morning, shut the bedroom windows tight or fling them wide open—all just as they choose, without asking anyone's permission.

A very different minority, made up of the severely wounded, treasure loneliness as an unguent and dressing against other contact until the healing has begun. A man in his forties makes a fetish of seclusion, regards his loneliness as "a friend and protector," looks through the peepsight of his apartment door before going out in the morning so as to avoid his neighbors, and avoids all human contact outside of work for months until he feels ready to face people again. A young woman uses her vacation time for three weeks of romantic retreat in a remote cabin by a beach; she wants to drain the cup of loneliness to the dregs, and to gain strength by forcing herself to face the worst at once.

For the majority of the newly separated, however, loneliness is a recurring pain for which they frantically seek relief. Many, when they feel themselves sinking, clutch at the telephone as if it were a life preserver; they seize it, and through it grasp at friends or relatives, talking about nothing, something, anything—only to be in touch with someone else. Sometimes, in a desperate moment, they will call in the middle of the night, waking their friends, or will phone someone a thousand miles away and gabble of trivia for half an hour. Others find relief in scribbling long, rambling letters to far-away friends or former lovers; the act of writing the letter, even though there is no immediate response at hand, makes them feel less alone.

Some pamper themselves. Men, as well as women, may spend money on new clothing, lavish care on the body, lie in the sun, buy a jar of caviar and eat it alone at home; these mild analgesics are gifts of self-love, replacing the love formerly received from someone else.

Some use liquor. Instead of their customary drink or two before dinner, they find themselves using three or four, and having more all evening. But alcohol is unreliable: though it often dulls the senses and yields a temporary contentment, it also sometimes unlocks the feelings and releases a maudlin yearning for love; then one unwisely phones dear friends and spills forth confused repetitious plaints, perhaps broken by spells of crying, that embarrass and weary even the most loyal.

Many find that a full regimen of activities is the only way to fend off the bad spells. Women build against loneliness an inflexible routine of shopping and housekeeping, cooking and child care, tennis and dance classes, local politics and volunteer work, dates and community activities. Men do the same with work, sports, evening classes, parties, dates, and professional meetings. Weekends need a particularly well-built bulwark of scheduled events, to keep solitude from seeping in. The novice —especially the supposedly carefree male—learns by dreadful experience not to leave the weekend to chance; it is enough, once, to find himself watching the clock on a rainy Sunday, waiting for the next time to eat, turning on the TV for a while and restlessly turning it off when bored, reading the paper from front to back, and looking forward to Monday morning as a blessed escape from his own vacuity.

Some people who cannot cope with loneliness in any of these ways rush into new full-time relationships almost at once;

in fact, they may often delay separation until they have some new person standing by to fill the gap. One might call them "chain lovers,"—they never stub out one love until the next is lit. Sometimes the new liaison is a genuine love affair; more often it is a mere act of desperation designed to fend off loneliness at whatever cost.

Of all the resources the novice draws on for help, friends and relatives are the most important; many a newly separated person finds their physical presence the only real antidote to loneliness. The end of the afternoon comes, the light fails, and the novice may find himself unable to face the prospect of the evening alone; he phones friends and chats casually until one of them suggests they get together that evening. But sometimes one cannot wait for such a suggestion: an FM, whether man or woman, will sometimes call a very close friend and say, without pretense, "Can I drop in on you for a while after dinner? I can't stand being alone tonight." And as soon as the date is arranged for hours later, the black mood vanishes; loneliness has no malignant power once the FM knows that after a given amount of time he is due to be with someone.

But there are difficulties involved in turning to one's friends or relatives for comfort. First of all, they are unsure how to behave. Should they inquire into what has happened and into the FM's feelings, or pretend to ignore the whole matter, talking normally and cheerfully about other things instead? If they have seen his spouse, should they tell him? Not to do so might seem a sign of some guilt on their part, if he later finds out, but to tell him they have seen her may spoil the mood of the evening.

And how much should the newly separated person tell his friends? To tell them a great deal may fascinate them at first, but burden them with complicity and all but force them to be on his side (although they may prefer to remain friends of both), or to feel dishonest when they see her later and listen

sympathetically to her. Morover, if he speaks freely, he makes
his friends privy to his weaknesses and failures; later he will
resent their knowing, since the exposures make it hard for him
to recapture his dignity. No man is a hero to his valet—or to
his confidantes.

Yet to tell them nothing or very little is to create a gulf
between himself and them. A newly separated man may, for
instance, visit old married friends for the first time since the
break-up; after the first greetings and mumbled regrets about
his situation they wait for him to take the initiative, and meanwhile talk of politics, books, children, and mutual friends,
wondering if he will bring up the subject of what went wrong
and how he feels these days. But perhaps, though he came for
human warmth, he is too proud or too ashamed to let them get
that close; he wants to be touched, but his nerve-endings will
not endure it. When he leaves, they look at each other in dis-
belief: how could he consider them dear friends, and yet not
confide, not explain, not make sense of it at all? And though
they may not say so, they mean in part: Why did he not
reassure us—for unless we understand his case and see that it
is nothing like ours, how can we be sure that it will not happen
to us? But only a minority of novice FMs—perhaps ten to
twenty per cent—explain nothing to any of their friends. The
large majority do offer some explanations to anywhere from a
few to all. Some consider it a painful but necessary duty to let
their friends know what happened, but most of them have a
great need to discharge their grievances and to be reassured
that they are still acceptable.

Indeed, whatever the potential penalties of pouring out
one's heart, many of the newly separated cannot do otherwise.
A young woman, feeling herself nearly suicidal, begs a married
couple to let her come visit with them, and spends the whole
night, until first dawning, talking it all out; they wisely neither
praise nor blame her, but simply listen responsively, and finally
put her to bed exhausted but saved from immediate danger.
A middle-aged man, upon the collapse of his second marriage,

finds himself making the rounds of all his friends and explaining the separation in "incriminating detail" to each, because he "had a great need for their absolution." A woman in her thirties relates her whole story in excruciating detail to four close friends because, as she puts it, "Telling everything to a few real confidantes was the nearest thing to psychotherapy, and definitely helped me get better." She is quite right; such confiding can, indeed, be therapeutic. As mere "ventilation," it gives temporary relief from symptoms, and when it takes the form of rationalizing—the building of explanations that save face and reduce one's feelings of guilt—it has even more lasting value.

But though friends can serve as psychotherapeutic agents, the process makes both the FM and the married friends keenly aware that there are differences between them now—a narrow crevasse across which they can leap, but which may soon widen into an impassable chasm. Telling too much widens it the sooner: one man who got through his darkest hours by spilling out all sorts of intimate details and grievances to a few friends hardly sees them any more because "they've drawn away from me as though I were a leper."

But the FM's complaining is not the only thing that repels friends and relatives; the positive or pleasurable components in his mood tend to scandalize and alarm them. They may smile and approve, to hear of the FM's delight in his freedom and his exuberant rediscovery of well-being, but inwardly they are affronted and shocked that anyone should enjoy himself at such a time. They could more thoroughly forgive him his trespass against marriage if it brought him no joy; his revealing it to them is an act of sedition, and if there is any flaw in their loyalty to their own marriage, they feel the threat and resist it by secretly disapproving of him.

For these and other reasons, the newly separated person loses some of his friends almost at once, some of whom take his spouse's side and some of whom drop both of them. He is gratified by the ones who choose his side or neither, but very deeply hurt by those who defect, particularly if the latter were old dear friends. He is seldom aware of the meaning his marital break-up may have had for them. A very attractive woman may have been close and dear to her female friends, as long as she was half of a married couple; as a separated woman, she suddenly becomes threatening to their marriages, and they drop her. A man who has been unfaithful wonders why one of his oldest friends never has the time to see him any more; he has no idea that the friend too was formerly unfaithful, confessed all to his cwn wife, and cannot now associate with him without arousing new suspicion.

The divided loyalties of some of the FM's friends, and the desertion of his cause by certain others, augment and exacerbate the loneliness and isolation he feels as a novice. In time, a gulf of incomprehension and divergent interests will yawn between himself and most of his married friends, even those who unequivocally showed sympathy toward him; if he could see all this clearly in the beginning, it would add greatly to the distress of the novitiate period. Happily, he cannot see it that clearly; and at a time when he is first learning to combat loneliness, it is just as well that he cannot.

III · *Of Freaks, Failures, and Fair Game*

The novice FM has not only lost part of himself, and some of his friends (or some of the intimacy of his friendships), but also is now partly alienated and estranged from the culture around him. At first, formerly married men and women are often rather paranoic about this alienation; they say things like this:

> Everyone looks at me differently now, trying to figure out what's wrong with me.

> I feel as if I'm a social misfit. As if I don't *belong* any more.

> It was a nightmare at first. My business associates acted funny, like they were trying to figure me out, like I was a peculiar person. I felt like a freak.

In part, this is a distortion by the novice, who fears he might be looked at as a freak and thereupon imagines he sees what he fears. But in part it is real. A man hears that a woman in his firm, whom he has known for several years, has just broken with her husband; when he first sees her that day, he cannot help searching her face for some change, some hint of what is going on inside.

The FM is now a person outside the realm of normal experience, and a renegade from his culture. He has doubted the primacy of the family, lost his faith in the permanance of love, denied the sanctity of the marriage vow; he has become a heretic, an apostate, a deviant. It has long been so; the alienation of the divorced goes back to the time of the early Christians. Prior to the triumph of Christianity, the Romans had considered divorce an acceptable part of the pattern of adult life. If one wished to end his marriage, that was his own private affair, provided he went about it in approved fashion; the state and the various churches had nothing to say about it, and if friends or acquaintances sometimes disapproved of his divorce, they did so only as they might have disapproved of the cut of his beard, or the way he served a dinner: he was guilty of no more than poor judgment or bad taste.

But Christianity gradually brought marriage under ecclesiastical domination. By the twelfth century, ecclesiastical rules and courts had won complete control over this branch of law, supplanting Roman practices; marriage was considered a sacrament, and divorce was no longer a private matter, since it had become impossible on doctrinal grounds. Only the high and mighty could afford to dissolve their marriages through bribery, and then only in the guise of annulment.

By the Renaissance, however, new forces were at work. Princes and kings, parliaments and courts, were hungry for powers the church had long exercised, and when the leaders of the Reformation denied the sacramental character of marriage, both marriage and its dissolution fell under civil control. Divorce became possible again, and just in time: the rising middle class, absorbing the ideals of romantic love into marriage, needed greater freedom to divorce, for where marriage was supposed to embody love, there had to be an escape from marriages in which love had died.

Yet such is the inertia of culture that even three centuries later, in the largely Protestant and highly individualistic United States, the act of divorce was still viewed with deep suspicion and hostility. In a number of states the divorce laws were rather liberal, but divorce itself was rare. When President Timothy Dwight of Yale spoke in 1816 of the "alarming and terrible" divorce rate in Connecticut, he meant that about one out of every hundred marriages had been legally dissolved. Plays and novels dealing with divorce during the nineteenth century almost all portrayed it as an unmitigated evil, and divorcing people as selfish, foolish, or wicked.

Divorce nevertheless became more common as the century progressed, and in consequence the attitude of society toward divorced people had to change: one's friends and acquaintances began to include people who had left marriage, and it was important to develop an acceptable way to feel about them. The liberal attitude emerging after the turn of the century held that divorce was not so much wicked as tragic, and the divorced person less a sinner than a failure, less self-gratifying than suffering and in need of sympathy. Actually, this was only a minor modification of the older moral condemnation: the wicked are suffering, as they should, but the liberal speaks not of their wickedness but of their pain. No wonder married people so rarely perceive, or are so unwilling to see, the relief and rebirth in so many of their divorcing friends. Even the orthodox psychoanalytic view of divorce as the neurotic's way out of a neurotic conflict is, according to Professor Kingsley Davis, a long-time researcher in marriage and divorce, "a sly way of condemning divorce" rather than a scientific evaluation of it.*

* Nevertheless, even divorce is coming to be regarded as more normal than not marrying at all. Especially in large cities, many a girl in her early

Even today, after several decades in which divorce has been a common part of the American scene, the married world remains subtly hostile towards it, and even persons who think themselves liberal on the subject are very often quite ambivalent about it. Dr. Cuber and Mrs. Harroff report, in *The Significant Americans,* that many upper-middle-class people are tolerant of divorce in the abstract but resentful of individuals who practice it, willing to acknowledge its beneficial aspects and yet hostile toward FMs who seem to be enjoying life instead of feeling miserable.

The heritage of the past is felt by almost all of the separated and divorced in subtle and covert forms, but in many smaller communities, and even in large cities in the "Bible Belt," it may be unsubtle and overt. The man feels it when he is quietly dropped as chairman of the meeting, fails to be put up for the presidency of the club, does not get the expected promotion within the company, is not invited to certain social functions to which he always went. The woman may experience it far more cuttingly: in some small towns or suburban neighborhoods other women speak to her only with frosty politeness, her children have mysterious difficulties in getting other children to play or come home with them, and in a few cases she is treated almost as a Scarlet Woman. The experience reported by a high-school teacher in a town in New Jersey is not unique:

> I moved to a new job, and people were friendly until they found I was divorced. Even ministers reacted to the stigma. When male teen-age students came to my house to talk—with my children there—neighbors complained to the principal that I was corrupting their morals. At the same time, I knew of widows in the same town who were receiving all the help and sympathy they needed.

---

thirties or bachelor in his forties would rather have been married and divorced than never married; the status of FM is the less embarrassing of the two. As Samuel Butler said, turning the trick on Tennyson, " 'Tis better to have loved and lost than never to have lost at all."

Even more painful was the treatment given a housewife in the Midwest:

> All but two of my friends dropped me, and even our closest friends, a couple we spent almost every evening with, who lived across the street, have never spoken to either of us since the break. I rceived crank phone calls, my position as speaker on a PTA program was suddenly withdrawn, and all sorts of evil and unjust rumors circulated about me which I learned about from one or two loyal friends, who tried to counteract them with the truth.

Still, the attitude of the great majority of Americans is one of apparent tolerance and sympathy; the inherited disapproval is expressed indirectly. The people who criticize a divorcee's children as unruly and troublesome often imply that they got that way because their mother selfishly chose to break up, rather than to endure, her unhappy marriage; the friends or relatives who want to "fix" the broken marriage if they can, or who urge the new FM to seek marital counselling and try for a reconciliation, seem to assume that the separation was the result not of a rational adult decision, but a neurotic or immature one.

The novice also feels their subtle moral judgment in the form of the assumptions made by many friends and acquaintances about his or her sexual morality. It is distressing to many a newly separated man to learn from some close friend that people are speculating as to which women he had been "playing around with" before the break-up; men who had not been unfaithful feel belittled by this assumption, while many of those who had been unfaithful feel misunderstood, since they sought outside solace because of marital disaffection rather than mere self-indulgence.

It surprises many a novice to find that even while he is in the throes of his novitiate and may have little or no sex drive, acquaintances and friends assume he is carrying on like a barnyard rooster. Men friends, after a drink or two, pluck him aside by the sleeve and ask, with a knowing crinkle around the eyes, "Are you getting much these days?" The wives of friends either act flirtatiously with him, make gay little remarks about the exhausting bachelor life he must be leading, or say, when they call to invite him to a family dinner, that they can never catch him at home; their oh-you-naughty-man tone of voice clearly means that he must have been out tomcatting for all he is worth.

But this is trifling compared to the experiences of many newly separated women. The cliché "gay divorcee" is badly dated, but men seem to believe as strongly as ever that a separated or divorced woman must be hungry, even desperate, for sex on any terms; as for moral scruples, she is supposed suddenly to have lost them all ("I mean, why *not?* After all, what have you got to lose?"). She is "fair game" and ostensibly an "easy lay"—an especially degrading attitude when she sees it in married men who for years have treated her with decency and respect. "It was astounding and very upsetting," says a nurse, "to see how many married men came out of the woods the minute they heard I was separated. Men I'd known and worked with for years would phone me and put it to me in the crudest way, as though I was now in the market for it with anybody, any time." Another woman says she was deeply humiliated to have all but two of the husbands of her closest married friends try to date her or call up on some thin pretext to ask if they could drop by at night. Many women have experiences like these:

> What surprised me most was to find how many married men looked to me as a willing partner, regardless of how little I knew them. But it was even more shocking when it was someone with whom my husband and I had been friends, and whom I regarded as "solid." It really threw me off balance for a while.

> Many men seem to think that, once a woman has been married and is now living alone, sex is the thing she misses most. They seem to think we "need it," we "can't do without it."

I was shocked and very angry at the men who immediately made passes at me—my colleagues, my neighbors, mostly married men; they were crude enough to assume that I'd be glad to take whatever I could get.

An old friend, married and with four children, called up and asked me if I would go to the shore with him for the weekend, as his family was away. I was disgusted and said so, and he said, "Well after all, you're divorced, and we could have a lot of fun."

It is demeaning that so many of these men make no pretense of emotional involvement or romantic feeling, though they would undoubtedly do so with a single girl. As a worldly woman put it in a recent Broadway comedy, "If she's unmarried, a man feels like Prince Charming even if she knows every haystack in town. But . . . a man feels he's *entitled* to a divorcee. It's like the free bread in a restaurant." That can be funny in a Broadway comedy; in real life, unfortunately, it hurts.

In these and many other ways the traditional social condemnation of the divorced person, though softened and modified in recent generations, is still manifested and contributes to the FM's own view of himself or herself as a failure, a defective, a person of selfish or immoral character. He will learn to live and cope with the public attitude toward him, and with his feelings about himself—indeed, he may be about to experience a notable rejuvenation and expansion of personality—but in the initial phase of his life as an FM he is likely to experience a loss of self-esteem and a feeling of embarrassment at his own identity. Every time he meets some old acquaintance who innocently asks after his wife, he stumbles over the words, "We're separated" or "We've broken up"; only after a while does he develop a neutral, flat, self-composed way of saying this. And for some time he may betray his own self-contempt when he sits in a roomful of friends or relatives: his laugh may be too loud, his hands may shake as he lights a cigarette, a muscle in his eyelid may twitch uncontrollably. He is fully and properly dressed, but feels somehow naked and ashamed.

Happily for the great majority of FMs, recovery from their psychological wounds and the regaining of self-esteem is usually a natural and spontaneous process. Unlike the process of recovery from a physical wound, convalescence from a broken marriage involves a series of pleasurable, exhilarating, and enhancing experiences along with some fresh hurts and setbacks. But even if the newly separated person suspects that there are such better things in his future, he has no idea during the darker hours of this period how very near at hand the future is.

IV · *First Steps*

The formerly married person is not who he was; he is another person—but who? The process of convalescence requires a redefinition of his identity, the acquisition of a new sense of who and what he now is. This means the working out of a number of new roles toward people around him. First and foremost, the husband and wife need to establish some new kind of relationship with each other.

Childless persons, of course, have far less need of a stable working relationship than parents. Some of the former bypass the problem by dealing through lawyers and using the divorce negotiations as remote-control warfare; they acknowledge themselves to be implacable enemies who cannot even face each other and communicate directly. Others strive to develop an even, controlled, amicable relationship. They talk to each other on the phone or meet to work out their arrangements, acting rueful, decent, and rather uneasy, like former lovers, regrettably but unavoidably become friends.

Those who fail to work out some clearcut definition of what they now are to each other may remain stuck in a violent oscillation between old love and hate, between fruitless efforts at reconciliation and new furious leave-takings. They may meet

in a restaurant to discuss the details of dividing their possessions, but instead of getting down to the subject, make small
talk about all sorts of other things. He notices, since he knows
her very well, that she has dressed carefully, in order to look
her very best; her hair is soft, shiny, and its fragrance reaches
him when he leans close to light her cigarette—something he'd
gotten out of the habit of doing a year or so ago. Neither one
recognizes that a kind of courting is going on, that each is
curious to see whether old feelings may revive so strongly as
to sweep away all the accumulated emotional debris. But then
upon some point of their business, the bubble bursts: perhaps
he asks if he can move certain pieces of furniture out by the
end of the month, and she says it would be better for him if he
left them a few more weeks; he says she might give more
thought to his problems and she says he might give more to
hers; he grows cool and sarcastic, as he used to do, and she
cuts him off again, as she did so often before ("Ask for the
check, please. Now! I want to get out of here."). They may
alternate between the two moods for many months, unless
some new force nudges them off dead-center; until other people
engage their attention, they may prefer the sweet-and-sour dish
to total fasting.

Couples with children have far greater imperatives for per-
ceiving the new roles they must play with each other, and working out their details. Many a newly separated man, for instance, still pays all his wife's bills, balances her checkbook,
and gives her household money, just as he did when living
with her, but after a while he recognizes that this only perpetuates in part the marital relationship that they meant to end,
and that he needs to cease being the head of the family. At this
point he changes over to giving her a lump-sum payment and
requiring her to run her own affairs. Conversely, she may for
some time continue to act helpless, consulting him about every
decision and looking tearful at the thought of taking things
upon her own shoulders; then gradually she sees that this role

is outworn and unhelpful, and starts taking over and re-defining her identity.

The husband asks himself, "How much should I give her?", but the question means something much more complex than it seems to on the surface; he is really asking himself, "What should I feel about her now?" At first, he may answer, out of guilt, "I want her and the children to have everything they always had," or at the other extreme, "Let her sue me." She too may answer the question with guilt: "I don't care about money, I only want enough to take care of the children," or with hostility: "He's not going to rob me and the children of anything that's rightfully ours." But as he and she begin to lay aside the roles of battling husband and wife, and start re-hearsing their future roles of ex-husband and ex-wife, they find themselves thinking in quite other terms: "How much do she and the children actually need to get along?" "How much does he need to lead a separate life?"

Their final answers to these and similar questions are still a long way off, and will probably be arrived at by a series of negotiations through lawyers; the answers will eventually be formally stated in a written agreement or "legal separation," which becomes part of the divorce decree. But long before those final terms have been worked out, the husband and wife have to strike temporary bargains about money, visitation, and certain items of property. In only two or three per cent of the cases are they so totally unable to make such bargains that one or the other—usually the wife—has to go to court and obtain a judicial decree setting forth temporary terms; all the other couples manage to arrange these things informally between themselves, usually with some difficulty and ill-will, yet at least well enough to avoid the court fight. Getting from this point to the final legal agreement is far more than a business matter; it is difficult and prolonged precisely because it involves the work-ing out of an emotional, as well as a practical, redefinition of the relationship between the man and woman, a process we will look at later on. But even in reaching their informal temporary arrangements, the husband and wife have taken the first real step toward that redefinition.

During this period of change, one or both have to decondition themselves to each other's seductive gestures. Some people impulsively rush back to each other once or twice, only to find that they have made the same mistake they made before; after a while, like mice being trained by electric shocks, they stop pushing the wrong button. One man left his wife of ten years after what seemed to him a long-term dwindling of a formerly satisfactory sex life. After only two weeks of separation, he visited the children one Sunday, and when they had gone to bed his wife fairly flung herself upon him in an unusual outburst of passion. He was both astonished and deeply gratified, and moved back in the next day. Before the week was out, however, everything was back where it had been, and after several ghastly discussions he moved out once more. Some weeks later, he says, she tried again, this time more subtly:

> I came in to visit the kids and Lucy was sitting in front of a log fire wearing a hostess gown. It was getting dark, and snowing out, and the firelight was playing on her face. She looked very sweet and tender, and a little melancholy. A favorite record of mine was on the player, and there was a pitcher of Martinis ready. It all seemed so warm and wonderful that I got a lump in my throat and wanted to sweep her in my arms and say it *had* to all be all right with us. But I remembered the last time, and how she'd finally told me that she'd had only a dozen or so orgasms in eight years of marriage, and almost always faked it, and couldn't imagine wanting me to touch her again. I fought back the feeling that everything could still be all right, and acted pleasant but very businesslike, and in a little while it had gone away. When I left that evening I felt I'd really made it this time.

Along with learning to avoid or to nullify seductive situations, they learn to adopt new and workable ways of speaking to each other. Some of them cultivate and manage to preserve an even, neutral, civil manner, neither too warm nor too chilly.

Discussions of their health and current interests, of the children's school grades, teeth, and camp plans, the cost of food, and events in the lives of mutual friends, are conducted in an artificially polite, emotionally anesthetized style.

Many others attempt the same thing, but lose control time and again. Such a couple may, for instance, start out discussing finances or school problems with each other quietly, but perhaps the man gets annoyed at some stubbornness on his wife's part, raises his voice, and she icily demands that he speak to her quietly or perhaps warns him that he is courting a heart attack. The scene goes from bad to worse and ends with an abrupt click of the phone or a slamming of the front door; then later, there comes another call, a mumbled apology, a renewal of the discussion, and eventually an agreement on the point at issue. Neither the anesthetic nor the explosive style is final or workable for long; but before they can arrive at a wholesomely tranquil and stable way of communicating with each other, they will have to labor long at the job of emotional detachment.

Even one's behavior as a parent has to change, to fit the new conditions of life. The father usually develops a regular pattern of visiting, and the days and hours of his visits start to assume a regular place in his life and that of the child. The activities —at first so contrived and unnatural—come to be relatively familiar and expected; the child can count on Daddy to play certain games with him, let him get away with things he cannot do at home, please him and almost woo him. The mother will begin to devise new rules and a *modus operandi* for life in a fatherless home. She may assign certain duties and privileges to her children out of sheer necessity, compensate for her lack of masculine authority by becoming pals with them, or use temper outbursts or call in a grandfather, uncle, or the missing father, at times when she simply cannot manage them any other way.

She and her ex-spouse also both learn to have thought-out answers ready for the repeated questions about their relationship: "Why don't you and Daddy love each other any more?" "If he's still my Daddy, and you're still my Mommy, why aren't you and he still related?" "Are you going to find me another Daddy besides my real Daddy?" "Even if you and Mommy don't love each other, why can't you live here same as the maid?" Each learns to be prepared for the heart-breaking and naïve efforts of the small child to bring his parents together again. One boy of four told his father, who was visiting him in the living-room, that Mommy wanted him to stay for dinner, then ran to the kitchen and told his mother that Daddy wanted to stay for dinner; it worked on two occasions, before the thoroughly uncomfortable parents compared notes and found out what was happening. A five-year-old girl begged her father, who would drop by in the morning on his way to work, not to leave: "Why do you have to go, Daddy? To make money? Don't go. I have a surprise for you. I have money for you, from my piggy bank. You don't have to go away—Daddy, why are you looking at me so funny?"

And each is also learning to be something new and strange: a single parent. No longer the magic word "We" or the phrase "Mommy and I" when talking to a child about bedtime, or homework, or fair play; instead, time and again, the parent must ask the child, "What did Mommy tell you about it?" or "What did your father say?" The child rapidly senses that what was once a parental team is now two isolated parents who can be played off against each other; his own power to do so makes him uneasy until the single parents learn to live their new roles comfortably, and to consult each other often, without quarrels.

After the first weeks or months, when the shock of dislocation is subsiding and the process of detachment from the spouse has gotten under way, a reorientation toward the outside begins. Even if falling in love again and remarrying seem infinitely remote or even repugnant, the FM starts to reconstruct his self-image, redefining how he thinks he must appear to other unattached people, both of the same and of the opposite sex.

For though many a novice is unready to actually start, or even look for, a new relationship, the paramount hope in his mind after the initial period is over is that some day he will find another and better love, and make another and better marriage. The appearance of this mood, however remote the possibility seems to him, is a sign of returning health—not that remarriage is the only available solution to his life, but rather that such a turning-outward of his attention indicates his abandonment of the ruins of marriage and readiness to seek or to build a new edifice.

But initially he may be too unsure of his own potential to risk even the minimal intimacy of a few hours together with someone of the opposite sex. There is a very marked difference in this regard between various categories of FMs. Those who wanted to escape from the marriage start seeking dates and new relationships relatively soon (indeed some of them had already been doing so before the final separation), but those who have been left against their wishes are often nearly as damaged and grief-stricken as widows and widowers, and make no effort to seek new relationships, or even to date casually, for many months. The very young, for the most part, slide back easily into single, dating society, but older people, having been married many years, have no idea how or where to begin. People whose marriages disintegrated without much rancor are often readier to seek new companions than those whose marriages broke up after prolonged arguing.

Aside from these variations, the central or most common reaction is that the novice, even when finally ready to venture beyond the boundaries of his own shattered family and his married friendships, is fearful of trying himself out on someone of the opposite sex. The man, still battered and bruised of ego, feels apprehensive about meeting some new woman (suppose that at the very first glance she finds him homely or too old?), or talking to her (what on earth will he talk about?) or making some advance towards her (how does one make the first move toward a strange woman, after years of doing so only to a wife?). The woman has the same kinds of feelings, but often even more strongly; she is full of alarm at the thought that a date may take her to places she doesn't want to go, talk to her about things she can't reply to entertainingly, or make a pass which she has to deal with. How on earth is she to handle these situations? Her techniques of doing so go back anywhere from five to thirty years, and would look as silly on her now as a pageboy bob and dirty white saddle-shoes.

And therefore many formerly married people take the first steps towards this aspect of redefinition of the self by seeking out and talking to friends of the same sex who have already been through it, and by venturing gingerly into such neutral territory as the cocktail party or the summer resort, postponing dating for later. Most seasoned veterans are pleased to pass on their knowledge to the newcomer, and their very air of expertise makes the novice aware that there is some kind of consensus, some body of customs and connections, linking the Formerly Married. The man may be told all sorts of useful and eye-opening things: "If she's over thirty and never been married, forget it. There's got to be something wrong." "I can name you half a dozen different cocktail lounges where almost nobody but divorced people go. The girls go there to be picked up—and they're nice girls, too, not hookers." "Stay away from the girls your married friends have in mind for you. They're hopeless." "Whatever you do, be careful. Don't get yourself tied up too soon. A man is in real danger of rushing into the wrong thing right after the break-up."

The woman will be equally interested and surprised by some of what she is told: "What's so bad about a blind date? Take a chance. You have to." "Don't turn anything down. Go to anything you can, with anybody, until you get back into circulation." "They almost all try—even the nice ones—and most of them don't come back if you refuse. But it's par for the course, so don't get upset about it." "You'll get used to the loneliness after a while. Nearly everybody does." "Don't get into the rut of hanging around with your married friends. You have to go where the unattached people are."

Where the unattached people are—that rings a bell. The novice perceives that there are ways to behave, places to go, a grapevine of information—that there is a special world of whose existence he had not really been aware. There is a look on the face of the Old Hand—something knowing, tolerant, a little weary and yet rather cheerful, a trifle sad but surprisingly zestful, youthful and yet very adult, hopeful but worldly-wise. The novice perceives, in this composite mood, something of the distinctive flavor of the subculture he is about to become part of; he finds it reassuring that this special world is made up of people who understand how he feels and have been through experiences comparable to his own. He begins to see that FMs are not just millions of isolated left-overs of marriage, but a loosely integrated, semi-secret society-within-a-society.

Throughout America, in every major community, that inner society exists like subsoil water, infiltrated through the structure of American society proper. (In most large cities it is relatively well-developed and easy to find, although in many small towns it may be almost non-existent.) The novice who feels ready to end his isolation and begins to venture out into FM society usually finds it both alarming and comforting. It is alarming because its structure is freer and more fluid than the world he or she has known, and because it involves a turbulence and ferment of human relationships unlike those he has been accustomed to. Yet it is comforting because it is a confraternity of people who seem to understand each other and communicate with each other in rich, condensed, allusive fashion, like members of a family or the same profession. At a party, a resort, or a cocktail lounge filled with FMs, he can sense both the ferocious competition and the communality among them; they *understand,* and this more than makes up for their readiness to prey upon each other.

The newly separated man goes to his first big party: there are a few married couples and single people, but most are FMs. He finds himself chatting with a divorcee who easily draws him out about his own status; to his surprise, he finds he can say things to her about his recent experiences that he had divulged only to a very few close friends, and then only with considerable difficulty. She in turn alludes briefly to what went wrong in her case, and how it has been with her ever since; he recognizes what she is talking about and finds himself saying, "I know, I *know!*", and wanting to reach out and take her hand. He finds that he begins to think of himself and other FMs as "we," and of married people as "they."

After a few such conversations—not always about marital experiences, of course, but usually involving at least some personal talk—the novice is pleased and proud of himself. He has been able to behave, and indeed feel, not like an unsuccessful husband, but like a single, interesting, and even reasonably attractive man. Not for years has he felt this way; from having been married so long, he had both ceased to think of himself as relating to other women in anything but a neutral way, and had accepted (while fighting against it) his wife's low evaluation of him. But what if it were really not so? What if, after all, he were appealing, a man women might really like? He stands straighter, walks with a spring in his stride, straightens his tie and smiles at the face looking back at him in the mirror. He feels almost as though a lost and forgotten self were about to return; he is as pleased as the patient who walks a few steps after being bed-bound too long.

Before this first plunge, he may have been somewhat ill-at-ease and apprehensive, but at least in his work he has had some chance to meet and talk to unattached women, and perhaps even to flirt in a harmless way. Many an FM woman, in contrast, has been largely confined to the world of domesticity;

for her the first sortie into the World of the Formerly Married is much more difficult. For a while she may avoid every opportunity on one pretext or another. At last, knowing that she must take a try at it, she agrees to go to a cocktail party. She does up her hair carefully, dislikes it and takes it down, then puts it back up again; selects a dress, is dissatisfied, fusses with beads or pins, finally settles on her choice; looks at herself in the mirror, thinks she looks terrible and can't go, sees that she is late—and finally rushes out. She arrives late and stands around searching frantically for a familiar face; finally, she is taken in tow and introduced to three or four people. At first she hardly knows what to say, and feels she is making dull and halting conversation. Then she realizes from something one man says that he too is a recent FM, and she feels better. They make a few wry jokes that establish rapport; soon she hears herself sounding almost gay and delightful, and likes the sound of it. She has the first inkling of the truth about herself—that she is not just someone's cast-off wife, nor an escapee who couldn't endure her marriage, but a person apart from that marriage—a separate, valuable, and whole human being. She glances in a mirror, and this time likes the face that smiles back at her; she is almost pleased to be who she is, finds that it is delightful not to dislike herself, and for the first time dares to think that life may have good things in store for her.

Both for men and for women—especially those who were married and faithful for some years—the discovery that they can meet and relate to people of the opposite sex in this new capacity is extraordinarily heartening. A part of the self that had been discarded many years ago is being rediscovered; or perhaps it is a part that was hardly ever known before. One has a feeling of rejuvenation and youthfulness that is intoxicating but unsettling. A man of forty may be almost embarrassed at having the feelings of a twenty-year-old, and a woman of thirty-five may blush to find herself feeling coy and kittenish; yet it is marvelously restorative to have such feelings, and they cherish them, recognizing that within the World of the Formerly

Married such feelings are accepted as normal. It is only from the rest of the world that they must hide them.

In this way there begins a most valuable and necessary process—the regrowth of self-love. Though moralistic writers often use that term to signify selfishness and shallow vanity, it can also be used in the positive sense, as it sometimes is by psychologists, to mean the fundamental approval and accept-ance of one's self that is the basis of emotional health. Self-love is the law of all life: unless we love ourselves, we cannot thrive, nor truly love others. Clinical psychologists and psychiatrists have demonstrated beyond doubt that people who approve of themselves are apt to approve of other human beings too; those who see themselves as unworthy, guilty, or contemptible are apt to see others in much that same somber light.

And therefore as the FM learns to rationalize his marital failure and has his first minute successes in relating to other people, he begins to like himself again and to repair the damage his ego has suffered. In the first flush of good feeling, the mood of optimism may expand beyond sensible bounds: he feels a wild surge of hope and expectation that he will be the person he always meant to be—successful in his work, sur-rounded by new and better friends, busily playing the field of love for a while and then finding the perfect mate. He feels as though he could work all night, drive four hundred miles at a clip, play two hours of tennis, stay up talking until three A.M.; it seems as though the years have not harmed him, but given him powers he had not dreamed of.

The formerly married woman, when this spell comes upon her, has comparable dreams of glory. She feels as though nothing would be difficult for her: she will change her hairdo, buy smarter clothes, remake herself, do the living-room over, read the current important books, take French lessons, work out a plan for meeting all sorts of new people—she can do it all, she can do anything she wants to. She brushes her hair at night and smiles at herself in the mirror; she lies in bed and finds herself strangely desirous, though not of anyone in particular. The blood throbs in her temples as she envisions scenes and deeds of passion; she is half-ashamed to be dwelling on such thoughts, astonished at the signs of readiness in her loins —and deeply pleased that this side of her is coming back to life. Sleep will not come easily this night, yet in her very sleeplessness there is reassurance and hope.

Thus the newly separated proceed beyond the novitiate toward full membership. They have begun to extricate themselves from the wreckage of love, to deal with loneliness and alienation and seek fellowship in the society of their kind, and to repair their feelings about themselves and rebuild their self-esteem. They are ready and eager to meet potential partners of the opposite sex and see how well they can like them. Their novitiate began in the mood of the Ancient Mariner—

> Alone, alone, all, all alone,
> Alone on a wide wide sea,
> And never a saint took pity on
> My soul in agony

—but closes in the mood of Miranda in *The Tempest:*

> How beauteous mankind is! O brave new world
> That has such people in't!

CHAPTER THREE

The Marketplace

1 · *Where Is Everybody?*

Every society has its own way of matching up its unmarried people. During nearly all of Western history, parents and other elders performed this function, judging for themselves the compatibility of the prospective mates, and using such business acumen as they had to get the best possible terms. Paying only minor heed to the wishes of their children, they shuffled and sorted them, sometimes used go-betweens and marriage brokers to locate prospects, bargained and dickered with each other over money and property, and managed one way or another to pair off most of their young.

This system worked well enough for many centuries. But the new mobility and democracy of American life began to affect it: after the colonial period, most young men and women began to have a good deal to say about the matter, and could refuse someone urged on them by their parents or even choose someone their parents disapproved of. By fifty years ago, parental control was rapidly declining, society was becoming too vast and fluid for families to know all about each other, and love was supplanting practical motives as the reason for marrying; under these conditions, the old method of mate selection finally collapsed altogether, and a new one—dating —spontaneously appeared, in which the unmarried young took over the job of finding partners for themselves. Their market-place was the school, the party, and the neighborhood, where they could freely test out different partners, meet unchaperoned and without commitment or change of status, and make their final choice largely on the basis of emotional needs. Despite all its faults, dating was well-adapted to modern society and, for all anyone can prove to the contrary, has performed its function as effectively as the older methods did in their time.

But while the unmarried young always have been a concern of society, the Formerly Married never have: in the past there were almost no FMs, or so few that little pressure existed for the invention of a social mechanism to bring them together. They have appeared in large quantities only in very recent times; then, because the marketplace of the unmarried young was inappropriate or unavailable to most of them, a marketplace for the Formerly Married began to develop which is still being enlarged and modified every year.

By and large, most newly separated people are unaware of the many opportunities and methods this marketplace now offers for meeting potential partners. Some feel quite hopeless about their prospects at first, and say things such as: "I can't seem to meet any women who are right for me." "How on earth do you get back into circulation after nine years of marriage?" "Where are all those divorced men I used to hear about?" "How do I start? Where should I go? What should I do?" "Where *is* everybody?"

Even if the novice has begun to make a few sorties—to a cocktail party, a country-club dance, an evening at a church social—he or she may still feel powerless to find the right kind of unattached partners to start dating. Before he does, he may know many aimless evenings and interminable weekends filled with bitter envy of couples walking hand in hand, and a feeling of isolation and helplessness. This is true for at least half the men and three-quarters of the women—and, surprisingly, almost as true for the attractive as the plain, the city-dweller as the suburbanite.

But this is before they have begun to discover the many possibilities that exist nowadays for meeting people of their own kind and finding suitable dating partners. Many of these possibilities strike the novice as distasteful, improper, or even degrading; but to judge from the amount of dating activity among the Formerly Married and their high remarriage rate, the marketplace as it now exists is serving its purpose surprisingly well.

II · *Conventional Methods—Standard and Poor*

Most recently separated people, when they first feel ready to date, are aware only of the conventional and conservative ways of meeting potential partners. Of these the most familiar and nearest to hand is the introduction or meeting arranged by friends or, less frequently, by relatives. The FM has been seeing or talking to these people already, they know his or her degree of distress, loneliness, and hunger for new companionship, and it takes only a hint or suggestion to send them thumbing through their address books for a name to suggest. After this first effort, some of them continue for years to ply him or her with names of people they come across from time to time. Professor Goode's survey (the basis of his book, *After Divorce*), and a survey by August Hollingshead, a professor of sociology at Yale, give similar figures: friends are a principal source of new contacts for over a third of the FMs queried, and relatives for about one-sixth.

Unfortunately, a very high proportion of the people met in this fashion are singularly unsuitable—especially when they have been suggested by married friends rather than single ones. Dispensers of advice to the separated and divorced often say that married friends are the best means of meeting potential dates, but many experienced FMs say that married friends have an uncanny knack of choosing the wrong people. Here is the testimony of two witnesses:

[F, age 33] When I told my friends that I was available again, they eagerly thrust men on me one after another—they had me over to meet them at cocktails, or at dinner, or to make a fourth at bridge—and for a while I looked forward to meeting each new one. But they were almost all just *hopeless*. They were either dull, or physically unappealing, or playboys, or old-maidish bachelors still living with their mothers. And two of them were flagrant fairies, though my married friends didn't even suspect it.

[M, age 38] When I felt I had to start getting around, I asked a number of friends if they had anybody in mind. Many of them didn't, but others came up with the damnedest retreads and rejects. Here I was, just beginning to think of taking a chance on myself, and they were pairing me up with women not a bit better than the wife I'd left. After a few months I learned to politely duck those invitations—at least, the ones made by friends' wives—unless I could talk man-to-man with the husbands first. I can't figure it out.

But some do figure it out. The new freedom of the separated person signifies an opportunity to sample the wares available, and to find a better-looking, sexier, more loving, or more successful partner than the former mate. Most married people either consciously wish, now and then, that they could do the same thing, or have such a wish rankling in the unconscious. The FM man therefore causes his male friends, and the FM woman her female friends, to feel envy and anxiety, which they allay by suggesting partners who would represent only a minimal sort of reward for having broken up a marriage. Perceptive FMs sometimes put it like this:

[F, 30] If you're at all attractive or bright, you're a threat to your married women friends, so they want to get you hooked up as soon as possible. But somehow they don't want to admit to themselves how attractive or bright you are or how well you may be able to do, and they have somebody over to meet you who is an absolute creep, or stuffy, or quite unworthy of your intelligence or your emotional capacities. They probably mean well, but they have a weirdly distorted view of what you're worth.

[M, 43] At first, every time my married friends said, "We've got just the girl for you," I'd get excited and hopeful, and think, maybe this was going to be something important. But time and again I'd walk in and my heart would sink at once, because it was somebody too old, or homely, or with no figure, or no sparkle, or no sex appeal whatever. I think my middle-aged friends can't stand the thought of my not living just the way they do, or my having desires and feelings other than those they have settled for.

Nevertheless, introductions by married friends do satisfy at least a minority of FMs, occasionally produce a hit, and are a preeminently "safe" avenue of meeting, since the intermediary friends know each person and are able to vouch for good behavior. This method also avoids the risk—always greater for women than for men—of being thought too loose or too eager; the introduction through friends has the sanction of custom, and fits the mores of the married world.

But it does involve another sort of risk—that of the inescapable evening. For unlike the casual encounter at, say, a cocktail party or on a ski slope, where either party can disengage if he or she feels the need to, the meeting arranged through friends follows a more formal code of behavior. Many an FM goes hopefully to the home of friends for the evening to meet a choice new man or woman, and enters the room full of anticipation; then come the introductions—and the feeling of deflation. This is he or she—but the face is not the right face, the voice is not the right voice; or even if the external façade is agreeable, it often happens that within half an hour or so of conversation one becomes aware that there is no hope here. Then the long evening lies ahead, the forced smile held in place until the face is weary, the mind prodded and cudgelled to think of things to say, and at last the obligatory, seemingly endless chore of the man's taking the woman home.

A certain number of introductions made by married friends turn out better than this and subsequently result in dates, but by and large the method is fairly ineffective—not ony for reasons already mentioned, but because the very presence of the married friends in the transaction has an anti-catalytic effect. Meeting someone at the home of married friends, the FMs feel themselves under scrutiny, their reactions being appraised. They play the game, trying to please the married friends but resenting the new person for not being the right one; later, when the friends privately query them, they lamely say something like, "Yes, I thought he was awfully nice . . . but, something just doesn't quite click between us. You know how it is." And the friend says yes, she knows—but she does *not* know, and is disappointed, a little hurt, even a bit cross.

Unmarried friends or other formerly married people are less demanding and less inhibiting. They are freer of distortions of judgment when they select someone to suggest to the new FM, and more understanding and uncritical if the meeting is not a success. Thanks to their own experiences, and the mores of the world they inhabit, such friends usually avoid setting up an evening in which the man and woman are formally paired off with each other. Veteran FMs know that the important thing is to save face and to guard against unduly trying social situations; the smaller the degree of commitment the better, since it puts less strain on the people being introduced, should they not be attracted to each other. Single people and FMs therefore may tell a man and a woman about each other privately, invite each one to drop by some evening when there are a few people coming over, and leave each one free to pretend that the other is not his or her reason for being there.

Even freer of surveillance and structure is the method in which the go-between friend tells each one about the other, and then lets them make contact by telephone. Almost always, of course, the initiative rests with the man. Such telephone calls are not easy for him to make at first. The man who has been married for years may feel as nervous and awkward when he starts that first conversation as he did when he was a gawky adolescent; the woman receiving her first call may find herself straining for talk to fill up the long pauses. The novice has forgotten the skills he or she once had long ago. But since usually only one of the two people is the novice, the more experienced one soon puts the other at ease, not so much by any specific remarks as by a manner which indicates that such phone calls are perfectly normal and expected among FMs and that two people in similar circumstances need feel no awkwardness with each other.

In one sense, this method of meeting new people is relatively safe, in that both the man and woman have some prior evaluation of each other from a known and trustworthy intermediary, and are likely to be socially suitable for each other in an overall way. Moreover, even in a brief telephone conversation the questing adult can drop many clues about himself and pick up a good many clues about the person on the other end. But in another sense the method is a gamble far more often lost than won. For self-introduction on the telephone, if it goes well, leads to a blind date, a species of appointment with profound drawbacks. For one thing, the blind date is somewhat embarrassing, being reminiscent of adolescence and the overeagerness to date for the mere sake of dating. But more importantly, the telephone conceals as much as it reveals; one may read into a voice, during a ten-minute conversation, all those traits he or she is hoping to find, but when the door opens on the appointed night someone else is there instead— the same person but not the hoped-for person. What sounded like manly confidence may look like windy bravado; what sounded like girlish gaiety may look like overage silliness. We say things to each other not only with words, but with all our gestures and expressions; the telephone carries only part of our message. And perhaps the most important information the phone cannot convey is whether or not the two, when they meet, will experience sheer animal attraction for each other— a reaction as important as it is unpredictable.

For just such reasons most formerly married people—men as well as women, the outgoing as well as the shy—avoid blind dates, or virtually give them up after a few dismal experiences. Nevertheless, the method remains an important, if minor, part of the total marketplace. It seems to be used, along with other methods, by perhaps one out of six FMs, especially those who have learned not to expect too much and to take each new gamble lightly. The workable attitude toward blind dating was expressed by one veteran in his early forties as follows:

> At first I wouldn't dream of trying a blind date—it seemed too much strain. But after a while I learned better—I became a seasoned campaigner, used to the fact that there are dozens of disappointments for every good experience. The key thing is not to hope for too much, and to take the whole thing lightly. After all, an evening is only an evening. The two of you are in the same boat, and even if it's no go you get through it, and laugh it off. But once in a while it turns out quite agreeably— and who knows but what some day it will pay off?

Another conventional source of contacts is the job or professional employment milieu. One-quarter of the women in Goode's survey, and more than one-third of the couples in Hollingshead's sample, reported that this was the most important source available to them. But a far larger number find it of no value at all. Non-working women, of course, obviously cannot use it at all, but even men and women who do work often say that it is a relatively unsatisfactory and unfruitful method of meeting new people. The reasons are familiar: many a job brings one into contact only with persons of the same sex, but even if there are persons of the opposite sex, most of them are married, or already involved, or otherwise unavailable. The work situation is a low-efficiency part of the marketplace; other things being equal, a cocktail party composed of twenty FMs is several times as rich in possibilities as an office with twenty co-workers.

Still other conventional methods of meeting potential dates include church activities and community work; both are comfortable milieux since they involve no surveillance, and there is no problem about breaking away as soon as one wishes to, but both methods are relatively unproductive since only a small proportion of the people present are unattached, and hence potential dates.

The cocktail party is very nearly as conventional and comfortable as these two, but often a good deal more useful in terms of the per-hour yield of brief encounters with potential dates. Cocktail parties come, of course, in all sizes and shapes, but nearly all of them offer a loose, uncommitted milieu which one can enter with little sense of obligation, and in which one can fall easily into conversations and break away when desirable (to greet a friend, refill one's drink, use the phone), remaining pleasantly shielded all the while by the very density and free intermingling of the persons present. One out of five people I queried named cocktail parties as a favorite locale for meeting new dates, and some were quite emphatic about the fact that it was the least demanding and often the most fruitful method, at least in the earlier stages of formerly married life.

For all that, older hands know that the cocktail party has distinct limitations. There is too much noise and smoke, too many interruptions, too superficial a style of conversation, to permit more than a cursory appraisal of a new person. One hopefully makes a few dates on the basis of brief cocktail-party encounters, later discovers that he has misjudged badly, and after a while grows more cautious; he may prefer to jot down a name and number at a party without making a date— only to find the note in his pocket weeks later and throw it away, since he no longer clearly recalls why he thought the person worth dating, and hesitates to squander an evening to find out.

The cocktail party, moreover, is a human smorgasbord: so many delicacies are spread out before the guests that they hardly know what to taste first. The most distressing feature of the cocktail party for unattached people is the roving eye. A woman may engage in conversation with a seemingly interested man, but while he smiles and nods in reply, his eyes are straying off beyond her to see whether or not there is someone better to be investigated. Even the way an FM stands at such a party has a special, semi-questing character: the married or unavailable person advertises by the angle of shoulders or head that he or she is not searching or prospecting, while the formerly married person by his or her posture and glance all but invites other wandering guests to become part of the conversation. The fluidity of the cocktail party undercuts its aim of bringing people together; they are like the microscopic particles of a suspension, undergoing the incessant dance of Brownian movement: darting hither and thither through the fluid medium, oscillating aimlessly, bumping and rebounding, never cohering or clinging.

The conventional methods are, in sum, of limited value; the Formerly Married need exposure to a much wider array of human beings than these can provide. At fifteen, one could view almost any passable-looking boy or girl as a suitable date; even at nineteen or twenty, one was still unformed and flexible enough to make a go of it, for a while, with nearly anyone who met the minimum requirements. But the formerly married man or woman has a wealth of personal history, and an accumulation of cherished tastes and dear experiences; to find some other human being who can fit into one's elaborate matrix of identity, and into whose own matrix one can fit correspondingly, is exceedingly difficult and requires a far wider search than it did in youth. Although a substantial minority of the Formerly Married, either because of inhibitions or the force of local custom, rely entirely on conservative methods of meeting new partners, a majority soon become willing to go beyond them and to try less conventional alternatives that promise better to satisfy their needs.

III · *Grey Market*

Outside the bounds of the strictly conventional, the World of
the Formerly Married offers the newcomer a number of other,
and often more efficient, ways of finding and appraising potential partners. These range from the slightly unconventional to
those which completely ignore middle-class proprieties. The
majority of FMs are torn between their desire to use more
effective ways of finding partners, and a contrary desire to
respect the rules of middle-class society; as a result, they favor
pseudo-conventional methods, which have an acceptable façade
concealing the fact that they offer a chance to shop around
among strangers for new partners.

One important pseudo-conventional mechanism is the club
or association which has some unimpeachable stated purpose,
but also and more importantly happens to serve as a marketplace; in the useful terminology of social scientists, the former
is its "manifest function" and the latter its "latent function."
Parents Without Partners, mentioned earlier, is a fast-growing
national organization of 166 chapters and 18,500 members,
with the manifest function of enabling single parents "to learn
better ways of helping themselves and their children cope with
life in the one-parent or divided family." When it was started
in New York in 1957 by a commercial artist and a writer,
both divorced, its calendar of activities was almost completely
child-centered, consisting of organized parent-child events and
group discussions on the problems of handling the children of
a broken home. Later, other groups were started to discuss
the parent's own personal problems, one of which was the
lack of social life; it was inevitable that someone suggest
having social events for the members, and these, once introduced, rapidly assumed first place in the life of the organization.

To maintain its tax status and its stance of respectability,
Parents Without Partners remains publicly dedicated to educa-

tional and supportive purposes, and in fact does continue to
schedule child-parent recreational events and to give concrete
advice and help to parents having difficulties rearing their children alone. Nonetheless—and this is not to disparage the
achievements of P.W.P.—in most of its chapters the adult
social activities and the chance to shop around for dates are
far more important to the members, and draw far more new
people into the association, than any other benefit. Chapter
presidents and membership directors continually make public
avowals such as this: "Now bear in mind that we are *not* a
marriage bureau, and not basically a social club. It happens
that we do socialize, but that's only incidental. We're here
to help you adjust to life as single parents; we're here to make
you better and stronger than when you walked in that door."
Privately, however, the very officer who makes that pious
statement concedes that the primary motive of nine-tenths of
the incoming members is to look for eligible partners.

The disinterested observer can recognize this at any monthly
meeting. Before the meeting starts, men and women—most of
them secretaries, teachers and housewives, or salesmen, businessmen, and lower-echelon executives—drift into the rented
auditorium in somewhat of a party mood: they mill about,
talking, laughing, searching, speculating, maneuvering themselves a little closer to someone who looks interesting. The
chairman raps for order, but has great difficulty in getting
everyone to sit down and be silent. At last the meeting begins;
there are the usual committee reports, announcements of activities, followed by the speaker of the evening; but during all
this, scores of eyes roam the room, necks crane, whispers
rustle in the background. At last the speech is over, applause
is duly rendered, and the meeting is adjourned for coffee and
cookies; now the real business of the meeting begins. Female
faces don the bright welcoming look, and male ones a studied
indifference or an equally studied air of appraisal. Little groups
form, disintegrate, and re-form; wallflowers stand immobilized
around the margins or wander slowly about, trying to look as

though they were going somewhere; the more daring men cut through the throng to speak to some woman they have spotted, the more daring women openly smile at some man they hope to interest; and those who are neither wallflowers nor daring talk to their own sex, protecting each other against isolation but keeping a lookout on all sides for any better possibility.

"No matter how we fight it," says one national officer of P.W.P., "the major reason behind almost every member's coming to us is social need. Lots of them get other things out of it too, but they wouldn't bother with us if it weren't a great way to reestablish a social life." Many members say that they simply had no access to unattached people of the opposite sex until they discovered P.W.P., and are immensely grateful for the existence of such an organization. On the other hand, many FMs who have heard of P.W.P. either shun it sight unseen, or go to one meeting and never return; the petit-bourgeois flavor, the transparency of the stated purpose of the meeting, and the frenetic shopping around repel the sophisticated and the more desirable, who feel either too proud to use such a marketplace or contemptuous of the merchandise.

The same traits appear even more clearly at some of the social functions of P.W.P. chapters. Parties and dances often have a flavor of their own: a blend of one part Chamber of Commerce, one part Boosters' Club, and one part high-school senior prom in which everyone has unaccountably grown twenty years older. There are name tags for Bill, Babs, Arty, Nancy; hearty but hackneyed conversational openings ("Babs, eh?—I like that name—cute name, cute girl. You new here, Babs? I haven't seen you around before"); records playing too loudly, the chosen dancing with indomitable gaiety, the unchosen watching resentfully or drifting back to the bar to seek analgesia; meetings, greetings, sparrings, breakaways, spilled drinks, platefuls of unwanted food wolfed down for lack of anything better to do. Seen with detachment, it is at once jolly and pathetic, like that famous photo of the aged dowager at the Metropolitan Opera, baring her once-lovely leg and grinning dreadfully at the camera.

Yet perhaps that is only how it looks to one who has no personal stake in the goings-on. To those who do, the parties and dances may be a trifle bleak and somewhat competitive, but at least they do bring together large numbers of people with the same basic problem. There is no gainsaying the value this has for the members, and the various chapters therefore schedule as many opportunities for such interaction as they can. In a typical recent month, for instance, the Manhattan chapter arranged fifteen partly or entirely social events for adults, along with a dozen events for children. This is true not only in the big cities; in the same month a typical Midwestern small-city chapter arranged nine events, six of which were such purely social activities as bowling, a dutch treat dinner, and a coffee hour. Dances, cocktail parties, costume parties, and weekends at nearby resorts draw the large crowds; the discussion groups and group therapy sessions draw far less well.

Numerous other organizations exist whose stated aims have nothing to do with being a marketplace for unattached adults; they thrive, nevertheless, because this is what they are. Sophisticates may, for instance, prefer the cover story of those associations which are supposedly devoted to literary and other artistic matters. In New York City, leaflets printed by The Society of Arts, Inc., state that it is designed for college alumni "with an appreciation and interest in the Creative Arts," although in fact its major energies are channelled into a weekly Friday night dance at a Longchamps restaurant, regular cocktail parties at which members may—or may not—discuss the theater and other meritorious topics, and frequent ski weekends in Vermont.

Without this much formality—without office, telephone listing, or even letterhead—hundreds and perhaps thousands of little groups exist in cities throughout the United States, started by one or more unattached adults (many of them FMs) as a way of meeting others like themselves. It is only a matter of time until they band together in a national organization and perhaps even seek ways to exert pressure on legislators; indeed, this is already happening in England, where a National Federation of Clubs for the Divorced and Separated has recently been formed, its purposes including the coordination of activities, the spawning of new clubs, the applying of pressure to MPs to amend the law relating to divorce, and the like.

Such groups run the gamut of literary discussion clubs, bowling leagues, bridge circles, skiing associations, summer-home groups (cooperative renters), tennis leagues, and the like. Any excuse for gathering the unmarried together will do; often the excuse itself is something worthwhile—but newcomers seldom return for a second or third visit if the people present are not eminently suitable as potential dates. Many such groups are ephemeral and last only very briefly, but others go on year after year, with a membership that changes continually except for a small hard core of the intractably unmarriageable.

Even though all these groups provide a face-saving pretext for their members, many FMs either never hear of them, or resist joining anything that is officially linked with their marital status. But quite a few of these people accomplish the same end as non-joiners by seeking out places where they can receive a given service (dancing lessons, art appreciation courses, lessons in gourmet cooking) while unostentatiously mingling with potential dates. Dance studios are a favorite facility of this sort (in some cities dance studios discreetly advertise "couples and singles" in the classified telephone directory); they maintain the pretext of instruction and contests, as opposed to public dances where most of the guests openly show their disinterest in the dancing and their absorption in the human goods on display. Evening courses and adult classes in many a university have more than self-improvement or extra credits to offer; many of their scholars study one another as much as the subjects being offered. Even health clubs and gymnasia which feature co-ed swims are used as a meetingplace; they have the special advantage, moreover, of permitting a kind of practical appraisal one can hardly make in the discussion group or on the dance floor.

There is, of course, no requirement that a man or woman be separated or divorced to be eligible for any of these activities; they are all used by single people as well as FMs, and for the same duality of purposes. Younger FMs mingle easily with the young singles, but older FMs tend to avoid clubs and dance studios in which the preponderance of members or guests are much younger and have never been married. The same thing is true of such other devices as travel-tours, ski clubs, and resort hotels. Bachelors and single girls use them for the same reasons as FMs, but again the general tendency is for people to seek out the places where they feel most comfortable, and to avoid those where the majority of the guests are not of their own age or marital status.

Whatever the exact make-up of the population, the pretexts of these pseudo-conventional devices often become thin to the point of transparency—and still they are retained in order to save face. But the thinner the pretext and the more evident the real motive, the harder it is for some users to stomach, as one young divorcee makes plain:

I tried a Caribbean cruise last winter. It was a total waste of time and money—seventy-eight girls and eleven men. And what men, at that! My god, they were impossible! Either real drips, or attractive enough but insufferably egotistical—as they could well afford to be. It was so damned obvious why we were all there— it was awful. We girls were just there to be picked over, and most of us ended up on the scrap heap.

Ski clubs which send their members by chartered bus to various ski lodges have become popular with unattached people for the same reasons, and just as obviously. The literature of such clubs stresses the "singles" aspect of the membership (the word is loosely used to refer to all persons not currently married), and although some of the members actually enjoy skiing, most of them know perfectly well that their own, and nearly everyone else's, major reason for joining is something else. One entrepreneur in the East who operates such a club says candidly, "Half of my members have never been on skis in their life, and don't particularly want to be. They go to the lodges for social reasons. The rest is window dressing." When a ski lodge happens to be frequented by more single people and FMs than married couples, a special marketplace atmosphere develops: there is an easy-going camaraderie because of the supposed interest of all in the sport, but as on the Caribbean cruise, the underlying motive is usually evident to all, and embarrassing to the women, except for the very calloused or the very attractive.

The same situation prevails at those large resort hotels which attract mobs of unattached hopefuls on weekends, especially on advertised "singles weekends." Most women who go to such hotels seeking to meet men cannot help feeling almost naked under continual scrutiny; if they are continually passed by, their embarrassment is superseded by shame and depression. But it is not altogether a lark for the men either; aside from a minority who are cheerfully predatory, many men are made uncomfortable by the continual appraisal or hopeful signalling of so many eyes, and by their own fear of entrapment by some undesirable woman.

All this is probably true to a greater degree for FMs than for never-married people. The Formerly Married have lived for years in social tranquillity, away from the turmoil and stress of open competition; it is unsettling to be thrust back into it, and to see one's own needs so transparently mirrored on so many hopeful overeager faces. Most of the formerly married men and women who go to such resorts candidly say that they detest doing so, even though it sometimes proves useful:

[F, 34] I do it because how many legitimate ways are there to meet men anyhow? You have to try. But I hate being on the open market. It isn't fear of competition—I think I'm more attractive than most of the women at those places—but the men are so *awful* in their manner. They're all looking for something quick and easy, and they think all the women are, too. It's really disgusting.

[M, 53] I avoided going to resort hotels for a long while, and when I finally tried, in a desperate period of my life, I found it very unpleasant. The congregation of women—the hungry, eager, slightly shopworn women—at those places seem to me terribly sad. It was a freak bit of luck that I found Audrey [his present wife] there.

[F, 31] I always thought weekends at a resort would be great, but they're a rat race, an auction block.

[F, 38] Resorts?—I'd call them *last* resorts!

Unlike the foregoing, all of which involve an institution, association, or organized event, the World of the Formerly Married also possesses a completely informal, pseudo-conventional mechanism which we might call "the grapevine." This is an invisible spontaneous network of communication along which passes the news that such-and-such a desirable person is now available; the message results in phone calls and other approaches from persons not known to the one being called but known to a mutual friend. This mention of a mutually known name is the nod to convention; where the man phones the woman, it reassures her and makes it acceptable for her to talk to a stranger, and where she phones the man, it gives her some flimsy pretext for doing so (she may say, for instance, that she is having open house next week and heard from their mutual friend So-and-so, that he might be available).

At first, newcomers are astonished by the grapevine, and some view it sourly: "The men just seemed to appear like vultures. I couldn't get over it. It never occurred to me that men would give my name to other men all over the place, and I resented it." Other women either have no objection, or learn to make the most of the situation. Men, though less apprehensive about such calls, are astonished to find women taking the initiative, even under the guise of legitimate business: "Somehow, the word got around that I was separated, and they just came zooming in on me. And this in a Southern town, too! I was amazed, but I soon got to like it. I've met quite a few women that way."

The grapevine is not only accepted as a windfall by some, but diligently cultivated. The newly separated person sometimes starts back into circulation by calling friends, both married and unmarried, and asking them to pass his or her name around. One is not usually this blunt with the married (though it is easy to be so with fellow FMs), but mentions in passing that he or she is getting used to being separated and feels ready to start getting around; or one may say something like, "Know anyone just right for me?" adding a little chuckle, as though it were only a joke, although none but a clod could misinterpret the message. But these obeisances to conventional mores are being abandoned more and more. One veteran man of seven-years' standing says that half-a-dozen years ago a middle-class FM woman would ask her friends if they knew a man for her and suggest that perhaps she could meet him at their place some evening, while nowadays many such a woman says merely, "If you know anyone I might like, please give him my name."

Such boldness and willingness to try new methods are increasingly common among FMs hunting for partners, even though they still cling to some shred of semi-concealing convention. How tiny that shred can become—and yet be retained —is indicated by an unusual communiqué from a divorcee in Scarsdale, New York:

The latest thing is for a girl to make up a list of men she's heard about or seen, and send them invitations to a cocktail party she has no intention of giving. Then she phones each one a few days later to apologize and give some reason for cancelling. And if she's a good conversationalist, she can wind up with half a dozen different dates with new guys.

Even if this particular contrivance is a local idiosyncrasy, it expresses the general need of FM women to take unusual and daring action because they are so much less free to initiate contacts openly.

A more common and legitimate way to take the initiative is to give a cocktail party to swap rejects with other women. On the surface, it is a normal party, but unknown to the men the hostess has told her female friends that each one is required to bring a man she doesn't want and is willing to throw into the kitty. Men sometimes hold similar affairs: one correspondent writes of parties whose invitation lists are made up of names tossed into a hat, share-and-share alike, by a handful of men; the contributors do not even escort to the party the girls whose names they offer up, since to do so might keep them from circulating with complete freedom among the new faces. Gallantry is an impediment, and they will have none of it.

Such parties can be tolerable if the people present happen to be compatible and mannerly; all too often, though, there is a tense, edgy mood of prowling, testing, and appraising ("sniffing around," as one man put it). As a result, some FMs attend only one such party and avoid them thereafter. But others feel that the discomfort is unimportant, and that anything is worth trying for an hour. As one thoughtful and rather unhappy young woman says: "I've decided I have to be willing to look everywhere. The up-for-grabs party has a distasteful aura, but so does Wall Street or the doctor's office. The way I look at it is, how can I tell but what someone else's throwaway may be my big discovery? So I take a deep breath, swallow my pride, walk in gaily, and take a chance on life."

This willingness to take a chance is a key feature of the emergent ethos of the Formerly Married. Though most are unable at first to tolerate any but the conventional means of seeking new partners, the inadequacy of those means and the permissiveness of the subculture cause many of them to adopt new and more venturesome methods and take chances they had not imagined they ever would:

[F, age 37] I've learned to keep my eyes open wherever I am. I now have no prejudice against any avenue of meeting. I even met a very fine man on a subway platform one time. You have a number of disappointments that way, and sometimes I am even frightened, but I feel I must take every chance. You never know when or where.

[M, age 47] You have to be willing to go anywhere, any time, and subject yourself to the company even of people you find crude or boring. If you want to add to your list of suitable women, you have to increase your exposure. It's simple mathematics, nothing else.

One may think that author Marian Champagne (*Facing Life Alone*) is joking when, in addition to many credible suggestions, she urges widows and divorcees on the lookout for men to go on cross-country bus trips, to accept jury calls, and to take their dogs to Obedience Class; but she is in deadly earnest, and a diligent sleuth might well be able to locate people who had found suitable dates, and even mates, in just such unlikely places.

But there is a drawback to the endless multiplication of contacts: a tendency may grow in the far-ranging seeker to rely on instant and intuitive evaluation. If there is no immediate and unmistakable attraction to a new person, he or she hurries on—there is always someone else, so why bother with anything but the brightest prospect? "If it isn't there in a few minutes," says a young woman of wide experience, "you might as well forget it." But a man who has seen much of FM life demurs: "All too many of us fall into the habit of either accepting or rejecting a new contact within a few seconds. We waste potentially good relationships, we fail to explore and develop what could be. We do ourselves a disservice when we so easily reject new people and rush off to meet others."

One might even summarize the effects of all this in the form of a law of physics: the temperature of FM social life is directly proportional to the total number of encounters with potential partners. When there are no contacts at all, the result is absolute zero; when there are too many, the temperature rises to the boiling or explosive point; but in between these extremes there is a zone of benign temperature in which the FM flourishes, experiencing continued emotional recovery and personal growth.

IV · *Black Market*

Although divorce has very different meanings at the different class levels, the lower-class willingness to use it has in recent years been seeping upward to the middle class—a notable reversal of the more usual rule that behavior patterns in America filter downward from the upper levels to the lower ones. This upward seepage of the willingness to use divorce seems, moreover, to be carrying with it certain lower-class ways of adjusting to the divorced state—in particular, the methods used by lower-class men and women for meeting, dating, and experimenting with new partners. These methods, almost all outside the acceptable conventions of middle-class adult life, are currently being used by many of the Formerly Married—most of them gingerly and shamefacedly, a few boldly and defiantly. Perhaps ease of divorce and an imperative need for easier contact simply go hand in hand; perhaps divorce, being moderately deviant and faintly rebellious, breaks the ice and permits the individual to carry out other moderately deviant and faintly rebellious acts. Whatever the reason, a considerable number of middle-class FMs throughout the nation are currently resorting, in their search for new partners, to methods they would have considered common, improper, vulgar, or low-class before they lived with the realities of the formerly married condition.

The outstanding case in point is that familiar way of meeting new partners known as the "pick-up." Although it has long been casually accepted at the lower levels of society as a legitimate and natural way for male and female to meet, the middle class has always frowned on it. The bourgeois girl is taught to shun it altogether; the bourgeois boy, uneasy about it, is more likely to use it to seek a quick sexual encounter with a lower-class girl than to make the acquaintance of a girl he would like to date regularly.

This remains more or less true among unmarried adults; most pick-ups in public places are intended to result in a quick and uninvolved sexual connection rather than a serious relationship. But nowadays many middle-class FMs are borrowing the technique in their search for suitable dates and potential love-partners. Just as a favorite locus of the pick-up among the lower class is the corner saloon, so among the middle class it is the cocktail lounge or bar, or at least those which have spontaneously become known as a rendezvous for unattached adults.

The larger the city, the more specialization there seems to be: in New York's Greenwich Village, and on its East Side, there are bars and restaurants where the younger singles meet, others where FMs in their thirties and forties congregate, and even one where formerly married homosexuals gather. Fashions in these matters change quite rapidly, but to keep everyone up-to-date a newsletter called *In New York* has arrived upon the scene in the past year, in which are listed the bars and restaurants currently used by the unattached as places for pick-ups. Nor is New York unique. Samuel Grafton, writing in *Look*, reports that similar places, catering to definitely middle-class, definitely unattached men and women, exist in a number of cities. Some of them even lend the aid of modern technology to their date-seeking customers: in San Francisco, Los Angeles, and Miami several clubs have telephones at every table to allow any guest to ring any other.

Many a newly separated person, on first hearing about this, is startled at the thought of openly searching for a pick-up date in public places. The first time he visits one of the pick-up bars, or watches the commerce on a busy beach, he may find the whole scene vulgar and cheap—a reaction which helps combat the alarming thought that maybe he ought to try it too. But time, need, and the exposure to the mores of the subculture gradually make the pick-up seem a less crass and distasteful procedure, even to female FMs, and fear of it diminishes with increasing experience of unconventional methods until the pick-up is only the next and not very giant step.

The bar or restaurant, as pick-up site, is not totally outside the conventions; the very woman who will allow a strange man to talk to her in such a place might rebuff him if he tried to talk to her on the street. Even so, the bar or restaurant is used by only about one out of ten women and one out of six men, and then rather infrequently. For some reason, about twice as many of each sex feel that a pick-up in a plane or train is acceptable. Like planes or trains, beaches, museums, libraries, and business or professional conventions have their own small coteries of adherents.

Nevertheless, even some who grow accustomed to the pick-up continue to dislike it and feel nervous about it. A slim, debonair, forty-year-old actor from Los Angeles explained his feelings: "During my years as a divorced man, I found that a much more productive way for me to meet new girls than through friends or at parties was to pick them up on the beach. I did so for years, but I always hated it. I always feared the possibility of being rejected and looking like a jackass. I had to force myself to do it." A few men, however, genuinely enjoy the process; it has some of the excitement of the chase or the hunt, and a choice item, successfully bagged, makes the hunter feel truly triumphant.

Most women seem to accept the method grudgingly, out of sheer necessity. Says an attractive thirty-two-year-old legal secretary from a medium-sized city in the Southwest:

> I thought it wouldn't be too easy to meet men. It turned out to be completely impossible. The people I know don't give parties with single people present, and I couldn't afford to go alone to public events. After nearly a year, I still have found no way other than going to a "joint" alone where I can meet anyone. Pretty shocking for a girl raised as a good Baptist, isn't it?

But surprisingly enough, some middle-class women actually come to accept the practice of pick-ups without misgivings. A successful writer of children's books, thirty-seven years old and quite pretty, says:

> One of the main surprises was pick-ups—conversations begun while walking, travelling, shopping, et cetera, which often turned out to produce some delightful dates. I think it's just a myth that this is not a "nice" way of meeting people. One just has to be careful, that's all.

Basic to all the genuinely unconventional methods is their lack of pretense. As compared with the kinds of parties described earlier, for instance, the more unconventional parties of FMs are open about their purpose. The reject-swapping party mentioned in the previous section has a thin lacquer of pretense over its naked surface; the hostess has presumably invited friends (and their friends) because she likes them. In contrast, there is a species of unconventional get-together that might be called the "open party"; there is no guest list, but by word or mouth all kinds of friends, acquaintances, and strangers hear of it and come—the only requirement being that each man bring a bottle, the only purpose being to prospect for new partners.

Open parties vary greatly, but most are given by people with Bohemian or shabbily furnished apartments (no one with decent furnishings would risk it). While sometimes the guests may be well-dressed and well-bred, more often they are either flashily or ill-dressed, and most of them are manifestly undesirable in one way or another—physically, psychologically, or socially. They are, by and large, the left-overs and discards of the dating-and-mating process. Some watch silently from the sidelines; others bustle around, talking here and there, searching for something elusive. The look on many a face is a compound of hope and disinterest, assumed cheerfulness and actual anger; they have come here to meet Someone, but he or she is not here, and they are exasperated at having tried and been disappointed, at finding themselves trapped into a hot, overcrowded, smoky room, at being stuck in conversation with someone boring and unwanted. Some finally set down their paper cups of warm Scotch (there is never enough ice) and head for the door, pushing through swarms of new arrivals who pour in without the host's paying any attention (who knows who the host is, and what does it matter anyhow?); outside, they troop down the stairs silently, not looking at each other, as though embarrassed at having come there.

Some open parties are run by individual proprietors, "friendship clubs," or non-profit social organizations; they are open in the sense that the only impediments to entrance are a door fee and, sometimes, a suggested age bracket. This degree of organization, rather than making such parties a more conventional source of contacts, makes them even more unconventional: the people who come are paying a promoter or entrepreneur to create a social milieu for them, a practice which is distinctly outside the bounds of middle-class tradition.

Such open parties—which usually take the form of dances, to make meeting and breaking away easier—have recently proliferated like Mayflies. In New York City, on a typical winter weekend, roughly 150 public parties and dances are held, some being advertised in the papers and others by direct mail to "members" (anyone who pays a door admission, at most of these so-called clubs, becomes a mailing-list member). Some of the ads mention age brackets in which FMs predomi-

nate, and some specifically address themselves to those who
have been married. Here are excerpts from listing in one New
York newspaper:

THE DIVORCED SET
  Call _____
  Sundays at 6 P.M.

Dance: The Second Quarter Club—a co-ed group of select
  singles, 25–40. Total contribution $1.25.

Previously Married People. 4 Select Socials.
  Saturday 8 P.M. ages 27–37
  Sunday 3 P.M. ages 25–40
  Sunday 6 P.M. ages 28–45
  Sunday 9 P.M. ages 30–50
  Call _____

Lecture & Ladies Nite Dance, for singles 25–40. "Communication between the Sexes," by Dr. Irving Delugatch. Stan Kaye
  & His Orchestra. Adm. $1.75.

DOCTORS & TEACHERS, you are cordially invited to _____'s
  exclusive HOUSE PARTY, Friday 9 P.M. ages 21–36, Saturday 9 P.M., ages 23–37. Call _____ for invit.

One can pick and choose, according to his own age, pocket-
book, and interests, and according to his preference for dancing
or talking, crowds or small groups, the intelligentsia or the
hoi polloi.

But the idea is far from being special to New York; indeed,
it originated in Milwaukee in the early 1930's with the first
so-called "friendship club"—a public dance, with a modest
admission charge ($.50 at that time, $1.50 to $3.00 today),
where unattached people could meet. Public dancehalls were
nothing new, as far as lower-class people were concerned;
what was new was the application of the idea on a lower-middle
and middle-class level in the guise of a "club." It quickly met
a need of FMs and other unattached adults, and spread from
the Midwest to the West and East.

Open dances and friendship clubs are sometimes run by churches or community organizations, but more often by businessmen hoping to turn a profit. The proprietor usually hires a hotel ballroom or dancehall, engages a small band, puts ads in the papers, and turns away only those who come in improper attire or who are drunk or disorderly. Decor is usually minimal, refreshments are available at concession stands, and the "guests" are left on their own to stand and stare, to talk, or to dance, as they wish. The unwritten cardinal rule of such public dances—as, indeed, of any of the public parties—is that anyone who has paid and been admitted may speak to anyone else without introduction. "In essence," one magazine reporter perceptively observed a dozen years ago, "a friendship club is a dollar pick-up." Even at today's prices of two or three dollars, it is a cheap way to buy exemption from middle-class rules.

To some observers the usual public dance would look quite dreary—the people unimpressive, the conversations vapid, the social interaction graceless and crude, the motives distressingly obvious. To others there might be something touching about it—a candid, hopeful, getting-together of people who are lonely and who need each other. The one thing that seems unarguable, however, is that very few guests find public dances or friendship clubs pleasant in themselves; nearly all those who attend will candidly admit that they do not enjoy the dances or parties, and are even somewhat ashamed of coming to them, but do so because they must.

Yet many FMs, despite such feelings, are grateful that the dances and parties exist. Among the most successful operators of clubs holding such dances on Long Island is a young man named Philip Munson, who, with his brother-in-law, William Echtermeyer, runs three clubs under the overall title of the Universal P & B Clubs, Inc. Their membership has mushroomed in five years from a few hundred to about 15,000, and Munson, reflecting happily on this growth, says, "We have a great appeal to people like schoolteachers—they make up maybe a quarter of the membership—and to men just below the professional level. Evidently there's a great need among these people for a place where women and men can come meet each other easily, on a more respectable level than in bars—and still not someplace expensive for them to go. We stumbled onto it by accident—and then realized how real the need is."

If it is rather unconventional to pay a small fee to make an introduction unnecessary, it is far more unconventional to pay a larger fee to somebody to select a partner for one and to arrange a meeting. Such an intermediary may call himself a marriage advisor, a matrimonial consultant, or a social advisor, or label his business a date bureau, introduction service, friendship service, or matrimonial agency; but no matter what euphemism he uses, he is practicing the ancient profession of the marriage broker or matchmaker. Matchmakers served various primitive societies, and the Arabs and a number of European peoples into recent centuries, although in Europe they gradually disappeared except among the Jews. Matchmaking came to America with lower-class Jewish immigrants—yet surprisingly, today's matrimonial agencies and date bureaus are serving a largely middle-class and non-Jewish clientele. There is no regular census of their numbers; the most recent published figure dates back to 1951, when Dr. Clyde Vedder, a sociologist at the University of Florida, reported that there were eight hundred marriage brokers in the United States. They have an active clientele of several hundred thousand; probably about a quarter to a third of these are FMs.

Some of the matrimonial agencies are highly ethical, service-minded, and dedicated to using the apparatus of modern behavioral science in their matchmaking. The Scientific Marriage Foundation, a non-profit organization based in Mellott, Indiana, was started in 1956 by Dr. George W. Crane, a Chicago physician, and applies contemporary electronic sorting techniques to the ancient task of matchmaking. The literature of sociology is full of data showing broken marriages to be more common among couples of different socio-economic background, of widely varying educational attainment, of dissimilar religions, and so on. The Foundation collects information about its clients—each of whom pays a $25 fee for the service—and codes the data into ten holes punched in an IBM card; the holes indicate such things as age, education, race, religion, marital status, hobbies, and habits. The information is verified by three thousand clergymen all over the country who act as field counsellors. At the Foundation's headquarters in Mellott, IBM operators set a card-sorting machine to correspond to the data on a client's card, and run through the machine cards from clients of the opposite sex who live within a two-hundred-mile radius. If the machine finds a card which matches perfectly on all ten coded items, both the male and the female are notified and given each other's name and address. They are supposed to correspond for a while and then meet in the office of the nearest field counsellor, after which they are on their own. If nothing develops between them, they notify the Foundation and each is sent another name unearthed by the omniscient machine. Thus has Cupid been replaced by an electric motor and a conveyor belt; thus is Love translated into matching holes in slips of cardboard.

According to Dr. Crane, it works beautifully. With an active clientele of about 50,000—many of whom are divorced people—the Foundation manages about 20,000 introductions each year, and Dr. Crane guesses that about a quarter of all the clients eventually marry as a result. It is too bad that there has been no study of the ratio of success to failure in these marriages; one would like to know whether this methodology produces more happiness than human beings have managed to achieve on their own.

Quite different in its approach, but equally dedicated to the good of the client, is a small agency in Los Angeles called Friends Finders Institute. Two sisters, Mrs. Marjorie Richmond and Miss Alice Thornton, both with some training in counselling, founded and operate the organization; they give their clients a good deal of individual personal attention, and therefore restrict themselves to a total caseload of some 350. Each applicant is interviewed for one or two hours, fills out detailed biographical data sheets, and takes a set of socio-metric tests of tastes and attitudes. Mrs. Richmond and Miss Thornton then weigh the results and match the clients to each other according to a method of their own. Having found two people seemingly compatible in most of their habits, likings, and experiences, the sisters introduce them at one of the Institute's socials, and later do some pre-marital counselling with them if they become serious about each other.

Over a ten-year period, the Institute has married off about ten per cent of the enrolled clients. Recently, however, the rate has gone far higher due to a new policy of requiring a long-term (one-year) enrollment, which costs $102; with this much time to work on a case, Mrs. Richmond and Miss Thornton married off nearly eighteen per cent of their enrollees in 1964. Forty-two per cent of all the clients who have gotten married through their services were divorced persons.

Miss Thornton sees the agency as being most helpful to the conservative person who is unable to buck convention in seeking a mate. She writes as follows:

> My sister, Marjorie Tucker Richmond, and I felt there was a need in our culture for the marriage-minded singletons to meet one another in a more efficient way than the usual chance. . . . We are especially geared to the middle-of-the-road, more conservative, conventional type of people. We feel that the unconventional, the more daring who are willing to take more chances on casual meetings, will doubtless meet one another through their choice of activities.

But while respecting her work, it is possible to argue with her interpretation; the use of Friends Finders Institute may be less conventional than casual meetings, and more apt to be looked upon askance by the bourgeois. And indeed, many of the clients come almost unwillingly, nervously, and secretively;

even when gratified by what they find, they are apt to keep hidden from friends what they are doing. As one client writes:

> I myself never hide the fact that I belong to this group, but many people I know there do not wish it known in other circles for fear of people's prejudiced views of this type of organization. I had a schoolteacher friend in her late thirties whom I hesitated to tell about the club, but finally did, and she met a very fine man there—the very second person she met—and married him. But fearing public opinion, she has steered a wide course away from me ever since, afraid that I might spread it around where they met.

A number of marriage brokerages and introduction services are one-man agencies more in the traditional vein. The physical set-up of such an agency usually consists of a small waiting-room and an office, a file cabinet, and the quintessential telephone. The proprietor, unequipped with any specialized training, interviews clients briefly, making notes of age and appearance, income level, education, major likes or dislikes, and a few other salient characteristics. He then sorts through his file cards, trying to find a likely prospect on the same basis as every matchmaking wife who tries to pair off her single friends, the only difference being that the professional matchmaker has greater experience and a much longer list. A few of these people introduce men and women to each other in their offices; the great majority merely give out names, and let the clients arrange their own meetings. A fairly common fee is $100 for a year's service, plus a bonus of another $100 or $200 if a marriage results. Most marriage brokers estimate that each year about ten per cent of clients on their active list get married as a result of the introductions they have made.

On the basis of this figure, plus other available data, one can estimate that perhaps three per cent of all formerly married people who remarry met their new mates through marriage brokers or introduction services. These agencies are thus a very small part of the present marketplace, but as the unconventional aspects of FM life become more and more acceptable and commonplace, it is quite possible that matchmakers or their modern equivalents will become a more important part of it.

It is part of the way of life of the Formerly Married to violate conventions and take risks in order to increase the chances of readjustment and the opportunities for remarriage. Those who accept what the World of the Formerly Married offers and cast aside the proprieties of middle-class life are sometimes rewarded with excitement, fulfilment, and even the discovery of the heart's desire; but they are sometimes penalized by boredom, frustrations, and even the experience of being misused and exploited. The marketplace of the Formerly Married suspends the ancient protective rules of romantic commerce; it is a free-for-all, in which the unwary or unskillful may easily get hurt, the overcautious may come away empty-handed, and the courageous and adept may, with luck, find what they want.

It is therefore characteristic of the Formerly Married to be simultaneously bold and cautious, eager and doubting. *Caveat emptor*, Let the buyer beware, is the guiding principle of this marketplace; and since FMs use not money but themselves in the transaction, they are equally guided by its obverse: *Caveat vendor*, Let the seller beware. As a result, they are quite ambivalent about each other—they are both permissive and judgmental, sympathetic and suspicious, open and guarded. For like buyers and sellers in any marketplace, they must be ready to seize a bargain and yet be wary of being cheated. With this as the recognized but unwritten law of conduct, the subculture tolerates and even encourages a great deal of unconventionality in the search for partners because, in the end, it does far more good than harm.

CHAPTER FOUR

Dating

I · *A Matter of Stage Fright*

What on earth is ailing Raymond Hartwell, Esq.? Three times today his secretary entered his office and found him staring out the window, lost in thought, a pile of briefs still unread in front of him. Two of those times she asked him questions about documents he had dictated yesterday and was met with a blank look that yielded to comprehension only after some effort; the third time he sharply told her to use the head God gave her, and sent her off with eyes brimming over. This past hour he has been thumbing through a little guidebook of some sort and making phone calls; in between times he has played with paper clips, paced the floor in thought, and stared at his reflection in the glass doors of the law-report bookcase, frowning at the grey in his temples and the slight bulge at his waist. His twenty-four-year-old secretary assumes there is some weighty legal problem on his mind, but if she knew what was troubling him, her tears would give way to a fit of derisive giggles; Raymond Hartwell, Esq., is going out tonight on his first date as a formerly married man and, quite simply, he is nervous.

Yet it is nothing to laugh about. Mr. Hartwell was married fifteen years, and long ago lost the confidently male self-image he cherished as a bachelor. It is so long since he saw himself in that light that he has no idea whether he still has any masculine appeal, or any ability to play the part. He cannot imagine how he would seem to another woman if he were to kiss her—or, for that matter, how she would seem to him. After so many years of coming home for dinner (newspaper under arm, weary, husbandly, middle-aging) after routinely going to bed so many thousands of nights (undressing, scratching, yawning, showering, brushing his teeth, reading in bed next to his wife), how can he strut and preen before some strange woman, play the peacock for her admiring eyes, or look and feel like a vibrant and dynamic male? Nor is it only the long conditioning of the years that makes it difficult; he bears within himself the dismaying image of Raymond Hartwell as his wife saw him toward the end of their marriage, hears the words she uttered, recalls her flesh, inert and unanswering to his own.

The formerly married woman may find it even worse. Physical appearance is more important to her than to the man but, by a bitter irony, more perishable; the wear of time makes her even more unsure of herself than the man. A woman in her mid-thirties, though still physically desirable, sees in her mirror the first random grey hairs and little lines around her eyes, and is stabbed by the thought that it is too late already, that there is no hope. Besides, after so many years of being housewife, mother, household fixture, companion of bedroom and bathroom (her every menstrual cramp, her every bodily function known and apparent), how can she see herself as mysterious and alluring, play the girl to some strange man, or look and feel like a tantalizing, responsive female? Nor can she forget the image of herself reflected in her husband's eyes and in the taut pallid face he wore those final months.

For such reasons, the resumption of dating is as difficult and filled with anxiety for the FM as the first shaky steps a patient takes after serious illness and prolonged confinement to bed. Yet such is the recuperative power of the normal psyche that three out of four FMs, despite any practical difficulties they may experience in finding suitable partners, do begin dating within the first year, and over nine out of ten do so before the end of the second.

Those who do not may have been more gravely wounded than the others or, because of special factors, may not be healing normally and properly. One woman in her early thirties was sickened and stunned when her husband abruptly left home to live with a homosexual and revealed that he had actually been a practicing deviant all during their nine years of marriage; more than four years later, she still has not begun seeking or accepting the companionship of other men. A pregnant young woman, divorced by her husband while he was on foreign duty in the Army, moved in with her parents and has lived with them over a year in the hope that he would eventually come back; her situation, and her fixation on that hope, have kept her from dating or even beginning her emotional recovery. A middle-aged surgeon whose sexual capacity withered away during his marriage to a domineering and strongly sexed woman has not dated during his three years as an FM because, as he says, "I feel weary, depressed, old, and much too uncertain of myself to risk trying to be attractive to anyone again."

But these represent only a small minority. Like skin, flesh, and bone, the healthy mind has a considerable capacity to combat infection and to repair damage to itself. The Formerly Married construct relieving explanations of what has happened to them, gradually forget many of the hurtful details, and think or talk about other hurtful details so often that the pain wears thin and disappears; through these and other mechanisms they partially rebuild their egos until it is possible to live with themselves in relative comfort. Yet this is only the beginning of rebuilding and repair; the major part of it will come about through satisfying relationships with other people. It is in search of these that the FM, after the initial stage of recovery, begins to date.

But although dating is the necessary means to a desired end, the FM views his first dates with uneasiness. The very word may make him wince: it sounds so juvenile, so artificial. Dating implies behavior that he thinks would look silly in him—

dancing to records in the living-room, going to movies and a hamburger joint, necking in a parked car, grappling on a couch. Even getting dressed up, going out for a drink and dinner with someone new, and making conversation for a couple of hours may, in advance, seem awkward, unatural, and mechanical. But much of the expected discomfort is due to the fear of not being able to revive and play a youthful role successfully; that fear usually vanishes with a little experience.

Until new FMs acquire such experience, however, they are apprehensive and uncertain exactly how to proceed. Among other uncertainties, the man is unsure what sort of evening to offer the woman. He may think that dinner, dancing, and a round of drinks are almost obligatory, but what with alimony and child-support, he is reluctant to spend $40 or $50 merely to get acquainted. He may want to invite her out just for a drink, as the veteran FM suggested, but is embarrassed to propose it, rightly feeling that his motives will be transparent and wrongly fearing that such an invitation will be unacceptable. He may want to suggest that they spend the evening quietly at her home, talking and playing music, but fears she will think him cheap. He may think of inviting her to come help him make dinner at his place, but wonders if she will take it to mean that he intends to play the wolf.

The woman, as a beginner, is uncertain whether to accept a date for cocktails only or to be offended and refuse. But if she is invited out to dinner, should she let him spend freely, or show a kindly—and perhaps belittling—regard for his wallet? If she invites him to spend the evening at her place, will he assume he needn't ever take her anywhere? And if he wants her to come to his place, would her acceptance be construed as agreeing to seduction?

Once the FM actually starts dating, he rapidly finds that there is great flexibility among the Formerly Married, and that he can arrange the details of his dating in whatever way best suits his own personality, age, means, and tastes. The prevailing philosophy of the subculture, as he soon realizes, is thoroughly permissive. No one need consent to any suggestion he or she dislikes, but it is not impermissible for the other to have made it. If a man wants to invite a woman out just for cocktails it is not improper for him to do so. If he wants to have dinner with her and then go dancing, she, as the early-rising mother of school children, is perfectly within her rights to suggest a shorter evening instead. An invitation to his apartment is allowable, and is possibly—but not necessarily—an advance notice of an attempt at seduction; an acceptance on her part is no guarantee that she will comply—although she well might. But in either case, there is nothing dreadful about his attempt or her refusal. The rule of life of the gallant ladies and gentlemen of Rabelais' Abbey of Thelema was *Fay ce que vouldras*—Do what you like—and it well expresses the dominant attitude within the World of Formerly Married; short of misusing or damaging another person, almost nothing is disallowed. The emotional needs of FMs are so imperious and their haste so great that they have granted themselves and each other the right to discard most of the impediments of middle-class propriety.

The woman neophyte, if she has children, has still other problems to solve when she begins to date. Some are logistical: She must wrestle with the complexities of finding a reliable baby-sitter (she worries more about their reliability than she did when married), feeding the children, issuing instructions about homework and lights-out time, and, despite all, getting herself ready in time. Some are attitudinal: under ordinary circumstances, the children are bound to see her going out with a man, and she will have to explain it to them—but how? If they are very young, she may get away with saying almost nothing, or with a syrupy half-truth ("A friend of ours is coming here tonight"); if they are a bit older, she may try a plea for sympathy ("Mommy needs to have some fun, too") or even appeal to their own self-interest ("I'm going out with a gentleman because I'm trying to find a new Daddy for you");

and if they are teen-agers, she may make no explanations at all, but merely announce it casually at the breakfast table one day, hoping not to be questioned.

The reactions, especially from smaller children, can be disconcerting—especially since they have an uncanny knack of delaying them until the most awkward moment possible. One correspondent writes that although she had explained about her dating to her five-year-old son, he waited until the man arrived before firing off the following barrage of questions: "Won't Daddy be angry? Can I go with you? Are you going to marry him? Is he sleeping here tonight?" Small children also sometimes stage last-minute rebellions, after Mother's date arrives, in the form of temper tantrums, throwing up, or crying spells; older ones suddenly fight with each other or announce a crisis over a missing homework assignment that is due the next day; teen-agers may unsettle their mother's nerves by acting sullen and churlish toward the new competitor for her attention or, conversely, competing with her for *his* attention. (One woman says that her buxom teen-age daughter put on her tightest sweater and openly flirted with the caller when he arrived, thereby making the mother feel at the very outset like an old crone.)

Even with the most careful planning, a woman can never tell what her children may do at the last moment to wreck her composure or destroy any trace of romantic atmosphere. One young woman, about to go on her first date as an FM, went to some pains to make her home look lovely and herself utterly soignée; just as she and her date were about to sweep out, her four-year-old son escaped from the baby-sitter, appeared in the hallway with his pajama pants down, and uttered the unforgettable words, "Mommy, wipe me!"

But men share with women one other problem—stage fright, like that afflicting Raymond Hartwell. The anxiety that new FMs feel before their first dates is so strong as to produce diarrhea, hives, and other disorders in some of them, and to make others call up at the last moment and cancel the date on some pretext. But the great majority, despite their deep discomfort, go through with it because they must—and because, too, they have a feeling of anticipation and hope. A phone call or introduction or some other mode of meeting has sufficed to get the date set up; after making it, the FM feels a glow, a sense of adventure, of youth, of impending success. A man will whistle cheerfully as he walks and laugh heartily at a friend's mild joke; a woman will smile at herself in a mirror and touch her hair. But a while later, apprehension slowly wells up again from somewhere; one feels something ominous and foreboding in the air. As in a dream where we find ourselves on stage and do not know the lines, the FM approaching his first date feels himself about to be nightmarishly exposed to ridicule. How is he to act, how is he to feel, what on earth should he talk to her about? When he smiles, asks questions, or makes little witticisms, will he seem genuine or pure fraud? If he opens the car door for her, strikes a match for her cigarette, or looks into her eyes with interest, will he be convincing or seem like a poor oaf of an ex-husband trying to play a part he does not know?

For the neophyte woman it is much the same. She wonders whether she will project womanliness, charm, and intelligence, or an aura of menus, school lunches, shopping lists, and low-sudsing detergents. She wonders whether she will feel gay and feminine, or will only play-act those qualities while feeling out of place and unappealing. And if by some chance she does act and feel as she would like to, what will happen? Will he think her smile means more than it does? Will he take her hand, or kiss her (she who has been kissed by only one man in a decade), or suggest that she come to his place for one more drink? She frets about her ignorance and unpreparedness, yet she half-realizes that she may feel even worse if, after all, he does nothing, says something about having a batch of papers to go over before bedtime, and brings her home by ten P.M. Fussing with her hair and trying to decide on the right perfume, she wishes she had not accepted but had waited a while longer (though for what she does not know). Suddenly the doorbell rings downstairs and she starts; he is here, she is at her Rubicon, and there is nothing for it but to go down and let him in.

II · *Explorations and Discoveries*

Herewith an extract from my notes of a tape-recorded interview with a highly articulate and willing informant. A thirty-eight-year-old architect in a large Western city, he is a whippet of a man—small, bony, nervous, quick in his movements—and speaks rapidly and without hesitation.

I went on my first date about two months after Joyce and I separated. I'd met Sally very briefly at a professional conference. You wouldn't call her beautiful by conventional standards—her face is too round, I suppose, and her nose is rather snub—but she's small and blonde and very feminine and soft in her manner, and discreetly sexy at the same time. I was greatly attracted to her, but it took me days to get up the courage to phone her and ask for a date. I don't know why—maybe I was afraid I wouldn't know how to talk to her, or maybe I was afraid she might turn me down. But she was warm and pleased, and there was nothing to it.

I was damned nervous before that first date. I got dressed much too early, and perspired so much while waiting around that I had to change my shirt before I could start out, and that made me a little late after all, which made me even more nervous. When I got to her house, there were two boys, one six and one eight, in the living-room with a teen-aged baby-sitter, and I wondered how to act in front of them, but Sally introduced me to them in so easy a way that I fell right in with it, behaving almost as if I were a neighbor dropping in to say hello. When we were outside I began to make some awkward comment about how I didn't know what she'd enjoy doing, and hoped she'd like what I had planned on, but before I could say any more she said that anything I wanted to do was fine with her—she was spending an evening with me, and wherever we went she'd be enjoying herself. She was merely being gracious, but it made me smile and feel pleased.

What did we talk about? Everything under the sun; we never stopped. Surprising, too, because I expected to be tongue-tied. At the bar we sat sipping drinks and asking each other a hundred questions as though we had to know all the major facts about each other at once. I was amazed at how personal and intimate the talk got in almost no time at all. It started when I asked how old her kids were and she told me, and asked about mine, and then asked how they were taking the separation. It was odd, but I didn't mind her asking, and before I knew it I was telling her things about my marriage and the break-up that I would expect to say only to very close friends. Like how Joyce had always been after me to be more commercial in my work instead of being so experimental and artistic, and how whenever she and I would argue about it our sex life would go to hell for weeks. And then Sally was explaining her own divorce to me, and we were comparing notes on how to fight loneliness, and swapping all kinds of likes and dislikes: it turned out we both were mad for Stan Getz and Saul Bellow and Andrew Wyeth, and didn't dig Pop or Op art, or electronic music, or Samuel Beckett. It was remarkable—we just clicked on everything.

She went out to phone home and check on her kids, and I sat there thinking how simple this first date was, after all, and how she made me feel bright and witty and interesting. I sat there smiling to myself and she came back and saw me and asked what I was smiling at. I said, "At my good fortune in having met you," and I was surprised to hear the words come out of my mouth because I never found it easy to say things like that. . . . Later, in the restaurant, I was talking about being shot down over North Korea and trying to make it back through enemy lines, and she put her hand on mine in sympathy. I felt a wave of warmth all through me.

That's the way it went all through dinner. I had to take her home early because her older boy was leaving early in the morning for a picnic, and at the door she turned to me to say goodbye in such a way that I knew without thinking that she would like me to kiss her. I had wondered beforehand how I would know about such things, but suddenly it seemed obvious to me: I really don't know why. Without saying anything I pulled her close to me and kissed her several times, and we got rather passionate in a moment, which I hadn't expected, and were clinging to each other and kissing again and again. Then she gently detached herself and thanked me and popped into the house. I walked away with a smile all over my face, feeling ten feet tall. . . .

Yes, I saw her again very soon, and on our fourth date we became lovers, but meanwhile I had met two other intriguing women and felt like running wild and free. Later I tried to explain it to her, but she was very quiet, and then cried, and then got terribly angry and made me take her home. We made up later, but it was on and off for a couple of months, and gradually sputtered out without ever having been a real love affair. It was my fault, I suppose, but I wasn't ready for anything else at that time, and she was—she'd been divorced for three years. Unfortunate timing. Too damned bad. I sometimes think about calling her nowadays, but you can never go back and really pick it up again—it's never any good that way.

Some FMs have only indifferent, or even distressing experiences when they begin dating—evenings of straining to make conversation, of trying to conceal their boredom or discomfort, of verbal sparring for supremacy—but most FMs, within half a dozen or a dozen dates, have many of the successful and reassuring experiences the architect was fortunate enough to have had the very first time. During an FM's first dates, he gets the chance to experiment with the various roles it is possible for him to play, and to find out which of them feels most comfortable—that of the undaunted optimist or the suffering stoic, the wounded idealist or the witty cynic, the innocent victim or the rueful sinner. This is not a matter of deciding which false face to put on for the masquerade, but of which facet of the real self to reveal or to emphasize. Early in one's life as an FM, he or she hardly knows who or what the real self is or what that self really feels. The role of ex-husband or ex-wife, available man or woman, is brand-new and needs to be tried out in many a different reading. The FM feels both glad and miserable about his new freedom, both guilty about and justified in whatever he did, both disillusioned and anxious to find faith again—and therefore can quite honestly present himself or herself in a number of ways, each of which is real, truthful, and revealing.

Some FMs conceal rather than reveal themselves, hiding behind banter, name-dropping, business talk, or brashly seductive behavior, but this is atypical and disfunctional. The people who hide behind a fictitious façade, showing little or nothing of themselves, seem to be a special subgroup, most of whom are destined for a long, if not permanent, stay in the World of the Formerly Married because they keep themselves emotionally isolated. They may go to parties, talk whole volumes, date a great deal, and even have numerous affairs, but essentially they remain unrevealed, and hence unconnected.

In contrast to this, most FMs are surprised and pleased to find how communicative and outgoing they can be on a date. They freely dwell upon their own and each other's feelings with the unabashed self-absorption of adolescents. They may discuss neutral topics now and again, but gravitate automatically toward themselves and toward a comparison of attitudes and feelings about their state. After a while, perhaps, feeling perilously exposed, they veer off to some other topic— only to return soon, as if hypnotized, to the incomparably fascinating subjects of themselves. Within the first half-dozen dates, therefore, most FMs begin to see themselves as relatively open, communicative, and responsive persons:

> [F, 37] I realized after dating a while that I am much more outgoing and warm than I had thought. I seem to inspire confidence; men really open up to me, maybe because I offer so much of myself without guile.

> [M, 53] What surprised me most was how comfortable and natural it seemed to me to talk intimately with a virtual stranger,

even on a first date. It made me feel not the cold aloof person my wife had always said I was, but someone really *likable*.

FMs like themselves better as they discover latent social skills and personal charm they had doubted they possessed:

[F, 46] What fun it is to adapt myself to each date! I hadn't any idea I could do it, but I can. I discovered that I enjoy making each man feel at ease with me, and regard it as a womanly thing to do.

[M, 40] I found it very exciting that I could seem to interest almost any woman—that I could talk about myself in a way that almost always got through to them. At the same time, I found that I could draw almost any woman out and get her to open up and reveal herself. It was a revelation to me that I could do this. I'd hate to think of the total amount of money I spent in bars that first year charming the bejeezus out of dozens of different new girls.

The exchange of biography between two people on a first date has a special fascination that most conversation between husband and wife cannot have. It is also true that what seems so fascinating and exciting at first may become burdensome and tedious after many a repetition. A supermarket executive in his late thirties says:

For a while I enjoyed the mutual confession sessions with each new girl. But after a while it got to seem to me that I had developed an act—I knew just what stories to tell about myself, how to say who I am and what things matter to me, what questions to ask that would make her do the same. But how many times can you go through all that, and still care? Or still believe in yourself?

And a tart-tongued young advertising woman puts it this way:

I'm sick of the whole business of "explaining myself" to each new man on the first date or two. Sometimes I think I ought to make a résumé for them, listing my college, major subject, de-

gree, favorite composers, favorite books, how long married, reasons for breaking up, favorite foods, attitudes toward sports,
religion, and sex. I could mimeo the whole thing and just shove
it across the cocktail table. It would be a funny bit, but I don't
really have the guts to do it.

But for most FMs the process of mutual exploration and
discovery remains fascinating for a long while, and there is
nothing they more urgently need to tell about than their own
broken marriages. A minority are too reserved or too ashamed
to do so, but the great majority feel compelled to offer each
other an explanation and justification of their status. Sometimes
this is a mere superficial formula, but more often FMs are
likely to talk about their experience in some depth—not necessarily with insight, but with bits and scraps of reminiscence
that evoke sympathy and tenderness, and convey the nature of
their fears and what they hope to avoid in a new relationship:

[M, 38] It's so good talking to you—after eleven years of living
with someone I could hardly talk to. All that interested her was
clothes and money and possessions. Every time I wanted to invite
people over who were interested in books and ideas, she'd find
some way to cancel the party, or she'd say she had a headache
and stay upstairs the whole time, and then be so furious that she
wouldn't talk to me for a week. She thought I was always trying
to put her down, when I only wanted to open up the world for
her.

[F, 31] No, I don't think you and I should play tennis. I don't
know you that well. I've been through years and years with a
man who couldn't stand it if I did anything better than he did.
He got so mad after I beat him once that he picked a fight with
me and hit me in the mouth—I still have a scar inside my lip
where my tooth almost went through. He had to be better at
everything. I've been pretending to be stupid for so long that
I half believe it.

[F, 35] My parents can't understand why I left him, and I can't
tell them. . . . Well, you tell me—you're a man—do you think

a man should insist on it even when his wife isn't in the mood? I mean, insist that she let him *use* her? I think sex is a beautiful thing—but when it was like that, it was so ugly I wanted to scream.

Such disclosures concerning the broken marriages can be viewed as a special form of courtship; they are nearly always meant to show the speaker as a fine, decent, wounded human being who deserves to be loved, and has been wronged. For even those who have some insight, and perceive their marital break-up in terms of multiple causes usually have a distorted and self-justifying view of it. The distortions, some of which are deliberate but most of which are unconscious, almost always enhance the narrator and discredit the ex-spouse; they are not falsehoods, but interpretations of the things that happened. Men tell their dates that their wives were moody, demanding, slovenly, and sexually unresponsive, but those same wives, explaining themselves to their dates, say that their husbands were insensitive, stingy, perfectionistic, and boorish as lovers. And each, naturally, tends to claim that it was he or she who wanted the marriage to dissolve, while the spouse resisted or was obstructive; FMs almost never tell their dates that it was they who were left behind. Behind all these complaints and confessions of one's recent agony is a plea: Listen to my story and pity me, and that will make us love each other. As Othello said, in relating his wooing of Desdemona:

> My story being done,
> She gave me for my pains a world of sighs. . . .
> She loved me for the dangers I had passed,
> And I loved her that she did pity them.
> This only is the witchcraft I have used.

Among the Formerly Married all this happens at a greatly accelerated pace; the result is what we might call "instant intimacy." Since instant intimacy requires a sense of kinship and a fund of common experience, many of the Formerly

Married find that dating never-married or widowed people is far less satisfactory than dating other FMs. Among the people I queried, fellow-FMs were preferred as dates about two to one over the other two categories of unattached people combined; this preference was particularly marked among people in their upper thirties and above.

The formerly married man suspects that the never-married girl of thirty or more has deep emotional problems—fear of men, fear of sex, and so on. Even if this is not the case, or if she is younger, he finds that many of his most significant recent experiences are not particularly meaningful or interesting to her; he may talk about his children, or about married life, or about the strangeness of returning to single ways, but instead of responding with complete understanding as a formerly married woman would, she listens and replies with obvious effort, as though he were speaking in a foreign tongue she had studied but was not fluent in. She does, of course, have the great advantage of being a more convenient date—there are no baby-sitting or scheduling problems, and she can easily go places with him, stay out late, even remain at his place without advance planning; yet even these advantages are outweighed by the sense of fellowship and understanding he finds in women who have been married before. And FM women, in their turn, have equally strong suspicions and reservations about unmarried men in their thirties or older. Most of these men, even if attractive, agreeable, and well-off, seem incomplete or unreachable to FM women who date them. As one thirty-two-year-old woman of considerable experience summed them up:

> Bachelors in their thirties and forties talk and act super-virile, but most of them are mama's boys, and sexually very feeble. They may even act aggressive, but they're all wrapped up in themselves, and either paralyzed or premature in the act. But sometimes they think they're very passionate, and I never have the heart to tell them that they're really nothing. They're so self-centered that you just can't make real contact with them on any level.

In contrast, both FM men and women discover each other, through dating, to be much more responsive human beings, despite marital failures and the resultant emotional trauma:

> [F, 34] Divorced men aren't more emotionally stable than single men, but they're certainly more emotionally aware, and able to understand and respond to a divorced woman's feelings. A personality that has taken a chance on marriage is more open, even though bruised.

> [M, 42] I know what a divorced woman is all about—and she knows what I'm all about. I can count on certain things in her. She's far better able to reply and respond to me and my feelings than the single girl.

Widows and widowers, though they have been married, seem to most FMs even less satisfactory as dates than do the never-married. The formerly married man going on a date with a widow is aware in a matter of minutes that it is a distinctly different experience from dating a formerly married woman. The widow may be friendly and talkative on the surface, but there is an almost tangible barrier between her and the man; she is insulated, and no current of feeling flows between them. Perhaps she is only fearful, like the bride of Solomon: "A garden enclosed is my sister, my spouse; a spring shut up, a fountain sealed." But no: there is something about her that is not so much fearful as hostile. Her eyes look at him rather than into him, but the person who lives behind those eyes cannot be seen. She wears her loyalty to the dead man like a mask over her face; it is as though any show of interest or warmth would be a betrayal of her own love—especially if directed toward a man who, himself, had broken up his own marriage instead of having it broken up, as hers was, by Fate. At best, her attitude seems to be, "See if you can possibly make me like you—I doubt that you can, but I dare you to try." The following comment is typical of many that men make on the subject:

Widows act as if life has done them a great wrong, which maybe it has—but *I* didn't do it, although they act as if in some degree I did. They don't try to relate to me; they look at me like they were waiting for me to prove something, or trying to spot the flaw, or sizing me up and finding me wanting.

Similarly, many an FM woman, upon meeting or dating a widower, finds him to be condescending toward her, emotionally chilly, and passive rather than outgoing. This is a sample comment:

Widowers seem to think there is something lacking, or something wrong, with the divorcee, or else she would have been able to work it out. They have no understanding, and no sympathy. They sit in judgment on you, rather than try to make you feel desirable.

Undoubtedly there are a number of widows and widowers who do not act like this, and it is true that the Formerly Married and the widowed do mingle, date, and enter into affairs with each other. But the fact remains that by and large they are somewhat antagonistic toward each other, and prefer to date their own kind. The preference is neither temporary nor superficial; much later on, the Formerly Married and the widowed will show the same inclinations when they come to select partners for remarriage.

The Formerly Married, in their initial dating experiences, gain new skills, a sense of identity, and a comforting familiarity with the mores of the world they now live in. But even more important than these is the aid and stimulus they get in their task of revaluing themselves and repairing their egos. In a collapsing marriage, a man or woman may feel worthless, unsexed, prematurely old; out of that marriage and beginning to date, the same person may perceive himself or herself as valuable, sexual, and youthful. Most FMs, at this phase of adjustment, have a heady and exciting sense of self-esteem. This is how several of them have expressed it:

A woman of thirty-seven who manages a perfume store:

> Dating as an ex-married person was a whole new experience.
> I learned to enjoy the fact of being a woman—a condition I think
> I had never really appreciated until I met men who really *liked*
> women.

A forty-one-year-old psychologist, male:

> I discovered that I had drastically underestimated my own appeal
> to women, and my ability to be both tender and manly at the
> same time.

A woman violinist and composer, age thirty-five:

> I learned on my dates that I was too defensive and argumenta-
> tive, but at the same time I found I was prettier, sexier, more
> fun, and more intelligent, than I had any idea. Respect and ad-
> miration from men is a wonderful ego-builder, and gave me the
> first self-confidence I had had in years.

A newspaper feature writer, male, thirty-two years old:

> It made me a different man. Or maybe I should say instead that
> I discovered I was *really* the man I had always secretly hoped
> I was but never felt like in the eight years of my marriage.

This regained respect and liking for one's self, though it
may seem somewhat superficial and vain, is a prerequisite for
more profound experiences that are to follow, and a significant
advance toward the recapture of emotional health. Dating,
though it may sometimes look like an adolescent and contrived
form of heterosexual interaction, is an effective way for the
FM to reappraise and reconstruct himself, even while exploring
and testing the qualities he needs in a potential love-partner.
It is a psychotherapeutic experience, invaluable as far as it
goes, though it goes only a part of the way. If it is time-con-
suming, chancy, and often expensive, it shares these characteristics with other forms of psychotherapeutic experience—but
at least it is fun some of the time, which one can rarely say
of the others.

III · *Pass and Parry*

Post-marital dating differs in various respects from pre-marital dating, and nowhere more sharply than in the area of the sexual overture—the male "pass" or the female "come-on." (Since the pass is common and the come-on rare, and since moreover it is the pass that is often regarded as a problem, I will concentrate on the former.) The main differences lie in the far greater speed and frankness with which such overtures are made, and in their permissibility very early in the acquaintance of the dating couple. "Permissibility" does not mean that the woman routinely acquiesces, but that in the World of the Formerly Married it is within the bounds of convention for the man to try.

Most middle-class FMs last dated when they were of college age, anywhere from ten to thirty years ago. The mores of that stratum of American society, though they varied somewhat in different parts of the country, generally allowed the boy to be a mild sexual aggressor and the girl to be defensive but not entirely unyielding. His advances were slow and relatively tactful, her concessions were gradual and based on the development of feeling between them. Usually she held the line at necking for a number of dates, until he and she began to be somewhat emotionally involved; then she might allow him to advance as far as light petting, and still later as far as heavy petting, where she would hold the line much longer; he neither insisted on intercourse nor had much chance of achieving it until they considered themselves to be deeply in love or were actually married.

Today the young are often said by the middle-aged to be uninhibited and virtually promiscuous, but it is an old complaint; adults, throughout the ages, have always thought the young to be on the brink of ruin. Actually, the young are doing much what their parents did, the major difference being that they arrive at each stage of sexual behavior a few years earlier,

and so have more experience; by and large, they are not promiscuous or libertine about sex, but still expect and seek it
chiefly within steady and emotionally meaningful relationships.
Hence, even young FMs who were dating only a few years ago
at first find the general behavior of formerly married men and
women startling; older FMs, of course, are even more likely
to be shocked.

And what is it that startles or shocks so many of the newcomers? First, within the World of the Formerly Married it is
common, almost standard, for the man to make a pass—verbal
or physical, jestingly or seriously—within the first few dates,
and in many cases on the first or second date. Over half the
women I queried said that all or most of the men make a pass
at them on the first or second date, and men themselves con-
firm it.

Second, though it is not standard, it is fairly common for
women to acquiesce to propositions made so early in an
acquaintance; possibly half of these very early propositions are
accepted, without there being any need for the intermediate
stages of necking, petting, and emotional attachment. Of those
women who refuse, moreover, the majority do so pleasantly
and conditionally, indicating a possibility that they will change
their minds in the future.

Women new to the World of the Formerly Married find the
prevalence of these attitudes and practices not only startling,
but frightening and degrading. Even some of those who think
of themselves as sophisticates are not emotionally prepared,
when they first join the ranks, for the sexual expectations and
unabashed approaches of many of the men. A woman copy-
writer in an advertising agency, who had always considered
herself knowledgeable and emancipated, felt as follows when
first thrown into the arena:

> It's kind of horrible. They're a bunch of nuts, all trying to prove
> something. After my first few dates, I wouldn't go out with any-
> one new for a long while—I just didn't want to have to face that
> inevitable try and the inevitable anger that my refusal produced.

A Midwestern homemaker in her earty thirties had this to say:

> I was so shocked the first time that I cried. The second time
> I got mad. The third time I was waiting for it and I got the
> giggles. That was the worst—it made him absolutely livid with
> rage.

Only after a while does such a woman adjust to the climate of
opinion in the world she now lives in, and realize that immediate sexual contact is sought by only a few as a mere opiate,
but by many more as a partial antidote to the emotional poisons
left within them. Once acclimated, she may still choose to be
chary of awarding her favors, but no longer is upset or angry
at the frequency or seeming casualness of solicitation.

Men are less apt to be sharply taken aback; the initiative,
after all, is theirs most of the time, and they are therefore not
often taken unawares or propositioned against their will. Yet
this does happen more frequently than it did in their younger
years, and a man new to the World of the Formerly Married
may well be surprised and rather uneasy when certain looks
or a gentle pressure of the hand seem to indicate that it is high
time for him to make a move. Even more surprising to him may
be the broad hints dropped by the somewhat bolder female
who senses that she is dealing with a slow-moving novice, and
seeks to arouse him in order to reassure herself of her feminine
appeal. She may remark that her new apartment is marvelous,
the only drawback being that the bedroom gets too cold at
night; she may tell him he is puzzling to her because he does
not behave like other men; or she may tweak him more overtly,
as in the following overheard conversation:

> (*The scene: a table for two in a good restaurant. He is on his
> first date as an FM; she is an Old Hand.*)
>
> He: I'm delighted that you like this place. I think the enjoy-
> ment of fine food is important for one's soul.
>
> She: Oh, I agree! And so are other physical pleasures—a good
> game of tennis does so much for my spirits—

He: Yes, and skiing does it for me—
She: And a long soak in the tub—
He: And lying in the sun—
She: *(impishly):* And sex—
        (*Long pause, while he tries to think of something to say*)
He: Say, you were telling me about your older boy—

He may be skittish the first time this happens and nearly spill his coffee while thinking madly what to do, but unless he is one of the very badly damaged, he will soon get used to the milieu around him and feel freer to act according to his own wishes and needs, without undue fear of offending or creating an unpleasant scene. Whether he becomes a "fast operator" or chooses to hold back until he knows a woman well and genuinely desires her, he will cease being overly anxious about the subject; he will learn to handle the come-on with equanimity, even if he continues to prefer a woman who allows him to be in charge.

Thus far I have used the term "pass" as if it meant an overt, verbal suggestion by the male. But this is only one meaning of the word. The veteran FM man, if he is sensitive to a woman's mood, can usually tell in advance whether or not a degree of rapport exists between himself and the woman that will make a pass welcome, and if it does exist, he hardly need put the suggestion in words. One man of savoir-faire explains:

I never suggest sex verbally or try to see how far I can get with a girl. Only boors and bores make passes of that sort. When I am with a woman who appeals to me sexually, I indicate to her by my whole manner how I feel—but only if I really feel that way. And she sends signals back in kind—a glint in the eye, a *moue* at the corner of the mouth, a little pressure of her hand on mine or of her thigh against mine while dancing. Sometimes it's even subtler than that, and I just know from her overall attitude towards me. If I don't see or feel it in her, I don't try.

But if I do see or feel it, I don't have to "ask"—it happens with hardly a word.

The FM woman just beginning to date is lucky if she goes out with such a man; he will sense her unreadiness and will take her home and bid her goodnight with a kiss. But to judge from what women have to say about it, such refinement is not the general rule. The fault is only partly that of the man. Though FMs communicate most marvelously about many things, many women—especially newcomers—hide or disguise their sexual feelings; they are as likely to act falsely flirtatious as falsely reluctant. This makes it difficult for the man to read the message correctly; besides, he is either in the process of rebuilding his self-confidence, or anxious to keep it rebuilt by achieving continued conquests. Many FM men therefore fall into the habit of making a routine pass on a first or second date whether or not they have been getting positive signals. And this disturbs many a woman new to the game; since she felt no willingness, she cannot imagine why he should assume it in her—unless he feels that she, like a whore, should "turn a trick" for her dinner. This is particularly true of the crude no-nonsense type of pass, which is surprisingly frequent:

[F, 29] What a shock it was to have my very first date tell me that he liked me, and wanted to take me out again next week to dinner and the theater—and then say, point-blank, that that was his part of "the bargain" and my part would be going to bed with him. In those very words! I just stared at him, thinking he must be making a joke, but he wasn't.

[F, 38] What surprised me was how things are accelerated for people in their thirties or forties. I found that in lots of cases a man would ask me after only an hour, "Yes or no?" In fact, on my second date as a divorced woman, this man—he looked and acted all right at first—started talking about sex within half an hour, and then said to me, without any preliminaries, "How about it?" I was so green that I actually said, "How about what?"

Even the somewhat more graceful pass, which relies on a "line," may seem crassly dishonest to the fledgling FM woman:

[F, 33] It was a real education. I never knew a self-respecting man could say, "I'm falling in love with you" after one or two dinners, just to justify asking you to go to bed with him. Personally, I would have respected him more if he had just come right out with it.

[F, 35] I got *some* initiation—I first dated a charming man who kept telling me he was burning with desire for me, and when I got embarrassed and asked him to stop, he said, "Tell me, how long is it since you've felt like a real woman? Too long, I'm sure. *I* could make you feel like one." I didn't know whether to feel insulted or laugh in his face. I never expected to hear that kind of line on a first date. What was even worse, he was right—I hadn't felt like one in months.

Whatever form of approach he uses, the man justifies it to himself: the point-blank pass is mere honesty ("She needs, I need, we're both adults, so why beat around the bush?"); the man who dares her to feel like a real woman is playing an agreeable game ("She feels flattered as hell, even if she doesn't want to give in"); the man with a sincere line *is* sincere—temporarily ("I'm not lying when I speak of love on a first or second date—I do feel a kind of love, at the time"). Still other men say that they try to bed their dates on little acquaintance because sex is intensely pleasurable, or necessary to the soul, or because it is the only way a man and woman can really get to know each other. Of all their reasons, this last one touches closest to home; most FM men, whatever they think they want, are desperately anxious to find the temporary reassurance of a few hours of intimacy to replace the lost intimacy of their shattered marriages.

In the next chapter we will see what happens when the FM woman accepts the offer; for now, let us inquire how women refuse it, since the problem of refusal looms large in this new life. Some women, first of all, are too hostile to men or too antipathetic to sexual activity to adopt the tolerant attitude of the subculture in parrying a pass. Whether new to the World of the Formerly Married or accustomed to it, they seek to hurt the man and to express anger at having been propositioned. Here are some of their responses: "Just what sort of person do you take me for, anyway?" "I was hoping against hope you wouldn't start *that.*" "Sorry, but I just don't find you physically attractive." "I couldn't make it with you if I tried." (*Giggling, or trying to stifle scornful laughter*): "You must be *kidding!*"

Reading these assorted rebuffs, one may chuckle—but uneasily, for all of them, especially the last two, are intended to wound. And they do, especially in the case of the insecure FM male, who may be thrown back into a spell of doubt and self-contempt. The woman's response was basically unfair, although the man's proposition was not: he behaved toward her according to the mores of the world they both now live in, but she judged and punished him by the standards of the world they both left behind. He may have been guilty of a want of delicacy or good taste or lofty emotion, but meant her no harm; she, however, was guilty of harming him, and meant to.

A second group of women feel somewhat the same, but recognize that the early pass is part of the FM way of life, and compromise by turning it aside with jokes or smart-aleck replies. But as is so often the case with humor, the motive power is a concealed or unconscious wish to hurt. One can see the wish, though half-hidden, in such replies as these: "Sure, I'd love to—the second Tuesday of next week." "Say, thanks a lot! How lucky can a girl be?" "You'll have to get in line. There are dozens ahead of you." The underlying motive is even clearer when the smart-aleck refusal employs coarse language. One elegant and highly cultured young woman says her favorite answer is, "You can always get laid, but good friends are hard to find," a statement which, she says, has a wonderfully cooling effect. Others make unpleasantly bold jokes about the dangers of sexual activity: "I couldn't do it outside of marriage—I get pregnant too easily." "I left my diaphragm at home and wouldn't think of taking a chance with a man who appears so virile." The last is particularly revealing: it seems to flatter and to be humorous, but the flattery is a transparent fake and the humor is aggressively unromantic. The woman who uses this particular rebuff says it works superbly, and no wonder.

In contrast, the majority of women, having neither a generalized anger against all men nor a moral revulsion against unmarried sex, rapidly accept the prevailing philosophy of the World of the Formerly Married; even if not ready to acquiesce, they are able to adopt a tolerant attitude toward the usual pass. Such women learn how to refuse so deftly and kindly that the men feel almost good about it. Even a very brief refusal can, for instance, be discreetly flattering. One woman says her favorite way is to say simply, "Please, not so fast," which implies that the man's haste, rather than his suggestion itself or his person, is all that is wrong; he is allowed to infer that another time he may get another response. One wit has referred to such refusals as the "bent-elbows" type—the woman resists but does not hold the man at arm's length, and lets him think that it is not his desires, but her own, that she is struggling against. Other and longer versions of this species of reply include the following: "I would very much like to, but I can't just now, and I'd rather not say why." "I'd love to, but my psychiatrist says I should hold off a while." "You're awfully nice, but we hardly know each other yet." "I'm not ready to get that emotionally involved." "I'm terribly tired tonight, but maybe some weekend. . . ."

Even without flattering the man or hinting at future possibilities, a woman may refuse him and still save his ego from damage by offering him a credible reason other than his own lack of appeal to her. Formerly married women have found all sorts of ways to do this: "I'd really like to, but I just can't let myself, because even though I'm divorced I'm a good Catholic and I disapprove on moral grounds." "I'm just getting over being in love with someone else." "I feel that sex should be

saved for marriage. It's too wonderful to be cheapened by in-
dulging in it except with the deepest kinds of feelings." "I'm
very much involved with someone else, and I just couldn't—
could you, if you were?" "The children might wake up and
hear us, and I couldn't risk doing that to them."

Some men take almost any rebuff poorly, even the most tactful; they strike back by charging the woman with being sick,
frigid, neurotic, or "all tied up in knots." They usually disappear for good after one refusal. Other men do not strike back,
but seemingly cannot believe that the refusal was in earnest,
and try again and again, all evening long. They disappear also,
but sometimes only after making such efforts on several subsequent dates.

In contrast, certain others are literally grateful for the refusal. Most FM men, like most chronic bachelors, feel an
obligation to make a pass at every woman sooner or later—
surely by the fifth or sixth time out with her. But those of them
whose confidence in their own masculinity has been badly
shaken may feel relieved by a gentle and tactful refusal, which
obviates the need to go further, and forestalls the possibility
that they would prove inadequate or even incapable in bed.
Occasionally a very perceptive woman will recognize this, as
did one young beauty who has had some training in psychology:

> Most formerly married men seem to need to proposition every
> woman they meet out of concern for their personal image of
> masculinity. But it doesn't represent real sexual desire. Often I
> have realized that men feel relieved when I refuse them gently
> and with a very good excuse. Sometimes we bcome much friend-
> lier as a result. It's a sad commentary on the split between sex
> and tenderness in our world.

But the pressure on men to make the gesture is not wholly
self-imposed. A Los Angeles bank executive nearing middle
age makes this complaint:

A lot of women claim they're sick of men making passes at them, but if you go out with them just for companionship and a pleasant time, and don't make a pass after half a dozen dates because you don't find them sexually arousing, you can see them wondering: What's wrong with him? Is he impotent? Homosexual? Does he have some loathsome deformity? They ask you in for one last drink before you go home, and kick off their shoes, and curl up on the couch, and take their hair down— and then if you don't follow through, to keep their own self-respect they write you off as not a real man.

The result is that some FM men will date a woman three or four times and then, unless they feel genuine desire for her, will drop her before the question becomes embarrassing; others may cling to a woman who makes it plain that she wants no sex relations, and with whom a long-term platonic relationship is possible.

In all the foregoing, it is apparent that although formerly married men and formerly married women find each other suitable companions, they are often at cross-purposes. What pleases the man or enhances his ego often displeases or diminishes hers; what suits her best often seems to him either a rebuff or a challenge. For even in the special world FMs inhabit, they are still male and female. Their desires and their needs are neither identical nor fully harmonious, nor have they ever been so since mankind first walked upon the earth, nor will they ever be.

IV · *The Paradox of Dating*

Formerly married men and women are often plagued by contradictory sets of feelings, and by behavior that belies or frustrates their stated aims: they are creatures of paradox; in psychological terms, they are ambivalent. This was true of their feelings about their spouses during the disintegrating phase of marriage, and their feelings about the freedom of the early weeks of separation or divorce. It is similarly true of their feelings about the purpose of dating, for although its ultimate goal is to find a potential replacement for the missing spouse, many formerly married men and women use dating chiefly for other goals—including even the avoidance of mate-selection.

At first, this may be useful. The majority of newly separated or divorced people face a long period of emotional reconstruction, and the premature effort to choose and to love may result in a poor choice and an impermanent love—the well-known "rebound" effect, rightfully decried by folk wisdom. It is therefore all to the good that dating has so few built-in demands, and can be used to try out emotional relationships on a very shallow level, without any requirement to love or even to care.

An FM may use dating purely as a means of diversion, involving only minimal interpersonal contact. Women—especially those of slender means—sometimes frankly use dating as a way to get out of the house and be taken somewhere at no cost to themselves. "It saves on pocket-money," says one cynical young woman; another speaks of liking casual dates because "they provide a free meal and movie"; a third likes "the occasional wild whirl around town with someone amusing but useless."

Men who are unwilling or unready to risk any close emotional ties have an analogous view, even though they pay the bills. They speak of casual dating as a way of staving off boredom and loneliness, as a ticket of admission to events they can't go to alone, and most of all, as an opportunity to seek sexual outlet. This cold-blooded view of the use of dating was frankly summarized by one businessman in a large Southern city who wrote:

> I think I'd probably be better off most of the time to read a book or work at one of my hobbies, but I find myself calling up this or that girl and asking her to spend an evening with me. Why? Because:
> —I'm gregarious.
> —I like my back scratched and my hair washed.
> —I like to cook for a girl or have her cook for me.

—I don't like drinking alone.
—I don't like masturbating.

But few FMs are so unequivocal about dating, or so one-sided in their intentions. The far more common attitude they have toward dating is a product of contrary motives and desires —the perpetual hope of meeting one's real love versus the chronic fear of making another mistake, the desire to prove one's self through a genuine relationship versus the wish to enjoy variety and freedom. One recalls Saint Augustine's agonized prayer, when he still loved his concubine but was struggling to become celibate: "O Lord, give me chastity—but not yet."

Most fairly new FMs—and some not so new—deliberately "date around" in order to prevent any one relationship from becoming important or exclusive. A public relations man, age thirty-eight, still felt like this after eight months as an FM:

> I hope some day to marry again, but right now I find variety most enjoyable. And safer. The minute some girl starts to close in on me I get jittery and back off. The trouble is that I respond very emotionally to women I like, and they get very involved and possessive if I don't watch out. Dating around is my safeguard. It's much easier to keep things non-committal or to break away if you have several women on the string at one time.

A young mother and part-time schoolteacher had a comparable attitude after a year of FM life:

> I want to care for someone completely and have him care for me, but I just don't feel ready to have anyone possess my soul yet. And I'm not ready to give up all the men who find me attractive and who drift in and out of my life. Loving is a luxury I can't afford yet.

Even when the FM believes that his dating around is an earnest search for a permanent partner, an impartial observer may feel that it is just the opposite. A forty-three-year-old textile importer, separated for close to a year, is a case in point:

You have to keep on the move and meet as many new girls as possible if you want to meet the right one. And I do want to— but meanwhile the business of looking for her is great fun. As a matter of fact, I find dating around with lots of different women is stimulating, intellectually and sexually. It gives me freedom not to have to go along with the desires or personal predilections of someone else; it contributes to better personal development on my part; and it's just plain interesting.

The use of dating as a way to avoid involvement takes many forms. One well-to-do suburban mother says she never turns down any decent offer and tries to keep as many different men on the string as possible. "Sometimes," she says, "I've seen four different men in one day—one at lunch, one for mid-afternoon tea, one at cocktail time, and one in the evening. I can't get enough of it." Other men and women choose married people as their dates; it may take counselling or psychotherapy to make them realize that they are doing so to assure themselves of limited involvement. Some men tell each new woman they date that they consider themselves chronically promiscuous, and though women are not likely to do the same thing, they have their equivalent devices; one tells her new dates, for instance, how much she enjoys meeting and getting to know all sorts of different men, thereby plainly warning him what not to expect from her. Still other people cautiously measure and limit the amount of time they spend with any one date. Too much of one person—two weekend dates in a row, for instance—may be misinterpreted by that person as more interest than one really feels. Such people can reveal their innermost thoughts and feelings to a date, be warm and spontaneous, respond to desire with desire—and then cautiously arrange not to see the same person again for a couple of weeks. People who behave in this fashion are not avoiding emotional involvement, but seeking it in the limited doses they can tolerate. What they want is not truly casual and disengaged dating, but an unlikely mixture of intimacy and freedom from commitment.

Women are less likely than men to continue using dating for any long period as a way to avoid involvement. The horns of the dilemma are not equally sharp for them; their need for financial security and for emotional support—especially if they have children—make "dating around" and all its advantages less appealing than finding someone with whom they can foster a deepening and perhaps permanent relationship. Besides, dating is a great deal more difficult for the woman than for the man: there is a never-ending struggle to find someone to care for the children while she is out, and the alternative—having her date visit her at home—has too many drawbacks to be very satisfactory.

Her dating around, furthermore, troubles the children and therefore makes her feel guilty; at first they are hopeful ("Is he going to be my second Daddy?" a child will ask after her first date with each new man), but later they are bewildered, and finally they are prematurely cynical and blasé. But even when children pretend to be uninterested, they reveal to her in little ways their hunger for the presence of a man in the house. A small boy will bring out a remote-control auto that is not working right and busily try to fix it in front of his mother's date; if the man lends a hand, the boy may plead with him to come back the next day to help with other toys. A little girl will walk through the living-room where her mother's date is waiting, and will seem too engrossed in a book to say more than "Hi!", meanwhile absentmindedly trying out a ballet step or two she has just learned; if he comments admiringly, she may beg her mother to invite him to next week's ballet recital at school. The mother's ensuing guilt makes her all the readier to give up variety in favor of reliability.

And still, for many women as for nearly all men, dating is dangerously capable of becoming an end in itself, self-deceptively used to pursue not a real mate but one's impossible fantasy of a mate. The ever-wider search for The Right Face becomes an ever-wider search for New Faces; the more wildly one seeks for love, the shallower are the emotions one feels.

A rather pretty but high-strung and frequently tearful woman
of thirty-five voiced the despair caused by this self-defeating
obsession:

> I've done everything to get myself into circulation and meet
> new men. I've learned how to swim, play tennis, make cocktails,
> bowl, and ski. I've learned how to really make love—I never
> knew, while I was married. I've joined or visited the International
> League of New York, the Bon Vivants in Westchester, the City
> of Hope, Parents Without Partners, the Minus Ones of Great
> Neck, the Suburbanites of Westport, a Mr. Sword party; I've
> taken graduate courses at the New School; I've gone to dozens
> of weekends at the Concord, Grossinger's, and the Griswold;
> I've been to Europe; I took a course in French at Hunter College;
> I tried a matrimonial agency, tried a year of psychotherapy,
> had plastic surgery, been to scores and scores of cocktail parties
> and dances. I've gone out with at least a hundred different men,
> from a fellow two years younger than myself to a man of sixty-
> three. I try anything and anyone. But I'm frightened—so many
> places, so many men, and I can't *find* it. Where is it? Have I
> lost the way?

If everyone went directly from a dissolving marriage into a
new love that eventually became a new marriage, none of the
ambivalence and the problems involved in dating would exist.
But although a few people do this, the great majority do not,
nor can they. For they must first go through a long process of
healing and rehabilitation, during which they are unable to
love either wisely or well. Dating, for all its hazards, helps
them get ready to do just that. Tissue and bones, after a serious
injury, must knit together before the limb can be used again,
but then the limb must be exercised in order to regain its
strength and mobility. So it is with the feelings: when we have
been damaged in our ability to love ourselves and others, we
need to knit up and regrow those abilities, then exercise them,
so that at last we may use them in a normal and complete
fashion.

CHAPTER FIVE

Sex without Love

1 · *Busy, Busy*

Outsiders are more curious and less informed about the sexual habits of the Formerly Married than about any other aspect of their lives. FMs who are in love and planning to marry are generally assumed to be sleeping together, but the sex life of the FM who is not in love is a matter of wild surmise to his married friends and his relatives, many of whom fear that it is licentious, some of whom fear that it is not.

People who become FMs quickly discover that the society of the Formerly Married does indeed have a busy, varied, and sometimes frenzied traffic in sexual liaisons (most of them not involving love), and that many FMs seem to have sex lives compared to which those of the married are sluggish, if not quiescent. Such is the distinct impression of most new arrivals to the World of the Formerly Married; yet the largest and most widely quoted body of sexual statistics ever gathered seems to indicate otherwise: the first and second Kinsey Reports say that except for men under thirty, "previously married" men and women are sexually less active than married men and women of the same age.

But there are several reasons for this seeming contradiction. First, Kinsey's category, "previously married," lumps the divorced and the widowed together, but from what we have already seen, and from the evidence of other surveys, it seems clear that the widowed are sexually much less permissive than the divorced. The data for the sexual activity of the widowed therefore pull down the average of the "previously married" category; if the Formerly Married were analyzed separately, their rate of sexual activity would undoubtedly be a good deal higher. Second, the newcomer's impression is based on the kind of behavior he sees where FMs meet and interact—in the marketplaces at the very center of the subculture, where there is a continual melee of male-female activity. But the World of the Formerly Married also has an outlying perimeter where many FMs remain isolated and sexually inactive—some because they live in communities and towns in which there is no opportunity for interaction with other FMs, some because their religious or moral beliefs cause them to shun most FM social activities, some because neurosis or sexual incapacity cause them to avoid other FMs and choose a celibate life among friends and relatives. All these people are averaged into the Kinsey statistics; the resulting figures are accurate enough, on their own terms, but they do not fairly represent what the newcomer perceives in the central, most visible, and most clearly identifiable area of the subculture.

Finally, the most important reason for the seeming contradiction is that Kinsey data are entirely based on "outlet" (orgasm frequency), which takes no account of the immense variations in the emotional content of the different activities leading up to the moment of orgasm or following it. Most of the Formerly Married invest a great deal of psychic energy in the quest for sexual satisfaction; the intensity of their search, the time and attention they devote to it, and the emotional meaning to them of their achievements, all give a thoroughly sexual coloration to their lives. If their orgasm count were no higher than·that of the married—indeed, even if it were somewhat lower—their way of life would still, in comparison, seem almost perfused by sex.

My own impressions of the general level of sexual activity

among the Formerly Married, based on questionnaires, interviews, and direct observation, plus consultations with psychologists and social scientists who have studied the matter, correspond with the impressions of most novice FMs, and are as follows:

Of all the people one might meet in the World of the Formerly Married at any given moment, almost none of the men and only about one-fifth of the women have had no sexual intercourse at all since their marriages broke up. Obviously, time plays a part in this: the longer a person remains an FM, the greater the likelihood that he or she will have begun having post-marital sexual activity. But most people start very soon; five out of six FMs begin having sexual intercourse within the first year, most of them with more than one partner. Nearly all of the men and a fairly large number of the women find their sex life more intense, less inhibited, and more satisfying than it was in marriage. A majority of men and women alike say that they found a great deal more sexual activity among FMs who are not in love than they had ever imagined.

So much for averages. It is nevertheless true that even within the World of Formerly Married there is a broad range of behavior, extending from total celibacy to compulsive promiscuity. But it is not a wholly chaotic scene. If we look carefully, we will be able to discern three major styles of sexual activity and to recognize the kinds of people who employ each of them; having done so, we may be able to hazard some informed guesses as to the dimensions, the values, and the dangers of the sexual life of the Formerly Married.

II · *Abstainers*

—An apartment house on Chicago's Lake Shore Drive; autumn, twilight. In the master bedroom a lovely, almost queenly woman in her late thirties has just fixed her long dark braid in a coif around her head, and now slips into a new dress while her six-year-old daughter admires her. Tonight three married couples and a bachelor friend are coming for dinner. They will talk of many things, but especially of her art gallery, the most recent show she has hung there, and her many well-to-do clients; later, one of the couples may play a violin sonata or two; finally, all the visitors will leave together—including the bachelor. For he is only a platonic friend; she has allowed no other kind in her life during her four years as a divorcee. Her friends worry that she has "set her sights too high" and assume that she is lonely and sexually frustrated, despite her busy and glamorous life; she lets them think so, but the truth is that while she sometimes has spells of loneliness, she accounts this a minor price to pay for not having to endure the pawing hands, the invading flesh, the sweat and the slime of man's lust. She sometimes wonders how it is that long ago she used to enjoy it much of the time, and then slowly came to find it rather disgusting. Now she is quite peaceful and without desire, but she delights in being found attractive and having men admire her wherever she goes; she even relishes a bit of flirtatious talk now and then over cocktails, though it never actually arouses her. She thinks that someday she will marry again, but keeps the day sufficiently distant in her fantasies to be untroubled by the thought.

She is representative of the abstainers, the first of the three categories of sexual behavior among the Formerly Married. Although most separated and divorced people are sexually inactive, at least for a short time during the earliest phase of their lives as FMs, a small minority remain that way and never, or very rarely, have sexual activity after the rupture of marriage. Some of them have chastity thrust upon them by external circumstances such as physical illness, old age, or geographical isolation, but most of them choose it deliberately, for one reason or another.

Some of those who choose it do so because they have so powerful a fear of sexual pleasure, or so negative a feeling about the act, that in marriage they found themselves, to their dismay, sexually crippled. Frigid women or impotent men may even regard separation and divorce as a welcome freedom from the demand or obligation married life made of them to engage in sexual activity; they abstain with a sense of relief rather than self-deprivation.

The causes of sexual incapacity are many; in a very general way, most of them stem from unhealthy attitudes toward sex on the part of one's parents, unconscious fears that sexual intercourse is dangerous, unresolved childish sexual longings for the parent of the opposite sex, and the like.

In females, the result of such influences can be anything from disinterest or lack of appetite to intense fear and revulsion such as is voiced by these two FM women:

> I always had this terrible fear of being hurt by it—of being stabbed or torn inside. I always tightened up, when I was married, and it always did hurt. I hated it, simply hated it.

> I'll bet that if the truth were known, most women feel the whole business is ugly, messy, and vulgar. But most of them don't have the honesty to admit it. I do.

But these are extreme cases. A more common type of frigid FM woman has, like the art dealer, known a limited amount of sexual excitement in the past; in an unhappy marital relationship, however, her innate negative feelings about sex gradually gained the upper hand and anesthetized her sexual feelings or even caused her to find the act somewhat repellent. As an FM, she may abstain altogether, without regret, or may experiment a little, unsuccessfully, and thereafter abstain until she remarries—if she ever does. One young career woman assumed her lack of enjoyment of sex was mostly her husband's fault; after the dissolution of her marriage, she deliberately went to bed on three occasions with different men to find out. All three times were "disasters"—she not only achieved no satisfaction, but was horrified at the total "deadness" in those very parts of herself which had, in the past, been at least somewhat sensitive. Rather than undergo this alarming experience again, she has abstained for five years, hoping someday to fall in love and marry a man who will miraculously make everything work properly for her.

With men the cognate difficulty is impotence. It, too, is not a single disorder, but a symptom of any one of several psychological difficulties (it is almost never of physical origin except in elderly or sick men), and can be temporary or chronic, partial or complete. A few men are almost entirely impotent in their marriages, and abstain from sex as FMs in order not to expose themselves to the same catastrophic failure. The more common male abstainer is a man of more or less normal sexuality, who lost potency or desire in the course of a deteriorating marriage and avoids sex afterward out of fear of failure; such abstinence is usually of limited duration, as in the case of this forty-one-year-old textile importer:

> For over two years my wife and I had almost no sex. During that period of quarrelling and hatred I never had any urge. Once in a while we would try, but it was just as likely to fail me as to work. It even seemed to me that my private parts were shrinking up. After we separated, I was afraid that I might have lost the power altogether. I couldn't bring myself to take a chance on it for about a year, and then the first time or two I was just barely successful—and only after an hour or so of trying. Then things gradually got better, and after about a dozen experiences I found myself functioning as well as I had years earlier.

A few others, originally normal but more severely traumatized by prolonged and extreme marital conflict, may so completely lose their belief in themselves as men that they cannot bring themselves to risk playing the part again, or do so in such an apprehensive frame of mind that they are bound to fail. A successful physician was not only crushed in spirit, over a twenty-year period, by a carping and domineering wife, but lost all confidence in his own manhood through the savage mockery she poured upon him whenever he failed to desire sex at the same time she did. His two attempts at sex after the divorce were total failures, and made him feel almost suicidal; in self-defense, he has limited his socializing ever since then to those parties and professional meetings where he is certain not to face any sexual challenge. It is ironic that in so many things that signify masculinity—physical vigor, decisiveness, professional skill—the physician can make himself behave in a manly fashion, and yet cannot will his body to play the male part. For the sex organs are not under voluntary control, but are operated by the autonomic nervous system; they reflect not what a man consciously wants to feel, but what his unconscious mind actually feels. Little wonder, then, that the physician remains an abstainer, comforting himself with the hope that some day "that not-impossible She" will appear who can transform him.

Some formerly married women and a few formerly married men abstain from sex outside of marriage because they regard it as a sinful and sordid kind of pleasure. Within marriage they were able more or less to enjoy sex, even though somewhat ashamed of doing so; they are the people who made love only in the dark, hesitated to caress each other sexually, and hastily washed their hands afterwards to rid them of the scent of sex. The weight of twenty centuries of Christian ascetic thought lies heavy upon them. In the Judeo-Christian tradition, the great original transgression of man against God resulted in the sense of sexual shame; Christian asceticism therefore saw sexual desire as the continuing embodiment of the Temptation, and sexual pleasure as the continuing proof of man's sinfulness. Within marriage it was far less of a disgrace, but Paul offered this concession so grudgingly as to make conjugal sex a kind of shameful weakness ("If they cannot contain, let them marry: for it is better to marry than to burn"); in any event, the primary purpose of married sex was said to be procreation rather than mutual delight. Outside of marriage, sexual pleasure remained wholly unjustifiable, sinful, and vile.

Those FMs who are still under the influence of this tradition today abstain from sex relationships on the grounds that they are disgusting, immoral, or both. A Methodist woman says that she has gone without sex for three years because she would "lose all self-respect" if she permitted herself to sleep with a man outside of marriage. A Presbyterian woman, formerly Catholic, says that "to have sex merely on the basis of physical attraction is degrading; I find it simply intolerable. I allowed it to happen once, and became physically ill afterward. I totally despised myself." A Congregationalist minister in upstate New York goes on dates but practices continence because, he explains, "I consider casual sex sordid and harmful. I am just not interested. I will wait until I remarry." A young Catholic woman in Oregon had two very brief affairs soon after she and her husband were divorced; during the second of them, she felt herself teetering on the brink of lifelong promiscuity and disgrace, and when the affair ended she decided to remain chaste until remarriage. She has rigorously rejected all temptation to "indulge"—it is her word—for the past six years.

Certain other people, though less strongly religious and more liberally educated, feel the influence of the cultural tradition in milder form: they regard married love-making as beautiful, but sex outside of marriage—especially in relatively casual or light-hearted relationships—as "empty" or "meaningless" rather than ugly or sinful. Such people often unwittingly communicate to their dates a suppressed desire for sex, and some women even neck or pet, like teen-agers, but refuse to go further; they are often tormented by their self-imposed abstinence as FMs. It is a difficult dilemma, and some, like this female schoolteacher of thirty-six, never solve it:

> Sex loses its entire beauty and solemnity when performed automatically as a mere relief measure, and I scrupulously avoid it. But I had no idea that the sexual urge, when unsatisfied, could make me so restless, irritable, and upset that I just want to scream. Sometimes I have to work in the yard, raking or digging or pulling weeds, or paint the house, or go swimming, until I'm too exhausted to even move my arms or legs.

Others, like this forty-year-old minister, finally decide that abstinence does more harm than it prevents:

> For nearly a year I was continent on principle. But the frustration of desire got so bad that I couldn't perform my duties properly. My mind wandered, I had continual fantasies of sex acts, I sometimes couldn't fall asleep until three or four A.M., and I felt myself running down physically. I finally gave up the effort, and have had half a dozen affairs in the last three years. I have felt better ever since, and been better at my calling, as strange as that may seem.

Self-denial and working to exhaustion may seem odd ways for mature people, used to normal sexual behavior, to cope with their desires; what may seem even odder is the resumption of masturbation. A certain number of men and women who are racked by desire but cannot allow themselves casual sexual pleasure do return to this form of activity, at least for a time. Kinsey found masturbation accounting for up to thirty-six per cent of the outlet of post-marital men and up to twenty-nine per cent of that of post-marital women; the percentages of those who rely solely on masturbation, however, are probably lower, since a fair number of FMs resort to it only during times when no desirable sex partner is available.

Masturbation is even recommended to FMs by some authorities as better for them than either casual sex or abstinence. Dr. Mary S. Calderone, executive director of the Sex Education and Information Council of the United States, says in her book, *Release from Sexual Tensions,* "Far better to have self-release than to indulge in a temporary and therefore shabby relationship. . . . From the standpoints both of [the formerly married person's] emotional well-being and his social adjustments, I submit that . . . self-release fulfills a necessary function." One could, however, take issue with her. Masturbation may not be sinful in any way, and may relieve tension, but being a return to an early, pre-adult form of release, it may also delay rather than aid emotional reconstruction. Since, furthermore, it channels the sex drive away from interaction with real people, it is hardly likely to advance the individual's social adjustments. As for Dr. Calderone's assumption that every temporary relationship is shabby, we will see this directly controverted by the experience of a great many formerly married people.

Finally, there are some FMs who had a normal sexual life within marriage and who abstain from sex afterwards by choice, without this being the result of emotional disorders or cultural inhibitions. The range of the sexual drive is known to be rather wide; some normal people simply feel the urge far less often and far less urgently than others, or have long periods when the drive is virtually in abeyance. Women seem more likely than men to go for long periods without sexual desire, but there are male FMs whose drive is low and who abstain for months at a time, but not by any particular design.

Other normal men—and to a greater extent, women—have a more nearly average amount of sexual drive, but rarely feel desire in a general way and are not aroused by casual or merely physical contact. Sex and love are so thoroughly fused and inseparable in their emotional apparatus that they experience sexual desire only when they love. Among recently separated FMs this is usually true only of those who have drifted apart or broken away from each other without having done much damage to each other's egos, and who therefore have no need of testing and rediscovering their various capacities one by one before reassembling them. For such people, casual encounters are neither immoral nor repellent, but simply unrewarding. A thirty-three-year-old housewife in Miami writes:

> I had a one-night affair under very idyllic and romantic conditions with a most attractive and pleasant man, out of curiosity and hunger. But for all the sense of excitement and arousal beforehand, I didn't enjoy it. I felt detached and disconnected, and couldn't work up to a climax, not even the second time. I

realized then how impossible it is for me to get really stirred up if there is no genuine emotion. I didn't bother trying again for a year, until I cared deeply about a man. Then it was fine.

An occasional man is similarly unable to enjoy sex except where he feels a deep emotional attachment. This comes from an engineer in his late fifties:

I have discovered that it is simply not possible for me to be sexually involved unless I am also involved in my deepest feelings. I tried it and was an absolute flop, which alarmed me, but a psychiatrist helped me understand it and I decided to wait. Luckily I only had to wait a few months.

That last comment may explain the relative rarity of this type of abstainer: those who so thoroughly fuse sex and love seem to find love-partners rather quickly, and thereupon cease to abstain. Perhaps this is because they are healthier and less damaged than many other FMs, but a cynic might also wonder whether some of them, at least, quickly imagine love where they feel physical desire; the phenomenon is not unheard of in the history of love.

III · *Users*

—The ferry dock at a Fire Island summer colony; a late afternoon in July. The boat has just arrived; people pour down the gangplank and are greeted by a cheerful crowd of children, dogs, husbands, and wives. A young woman debarks and is met by a deeply tanned man in his upper thirties, dressed in shorts and a T shirt. He greets her with a glad kiss and a long hug, and they walk away hand in hand, talking a mile a minute and looking intently at each other, like lovers. Are they? Yes and no. This weekend they will play, cook, and eat together, talk of a hundred things, touch each other in passing and smile, enjoy sex with each other at night and sleep pressed closely together. But there will be no words of love, no demands, no promises; such things will be discreetly unmentioned, as if by agreement. And when they part on Monday morning he will be vague about when they are to meet again, for after each spell of intimacy he becomes uneasy and elusive for a while. He has made it clear that he dates other women, and she suspects that he sleeps with one or more of them. She realizes that having only recently gotten his "freedom" after a long divorce fight, he needs to feel unfettered, and she is baffled and frustrated by his doing with her so many things both tender and fierce, trivial and important, which she always took to mean love, and which now seem to mean much less. Once in a while she cries a little, silently, after they make love; if he notices, he says nothing, for what good could come of it?

This man fits into the second and largest of the three categories—the users. Most formerly married people are either fearful or actually incapable of loving again soon after the disintegration of their marriages, but are unwilling to do without sex until love comes along; yet it is not just that they are unwilling to abstain—they need sex for urgent reasons, and use it as a means of gaining important goals.

This is not readily apparent to the new arrival, who sees only what looks like a great deal of casual and meaningless sleeping around. Some observers of the Formerly Married regard these sexual activities as a sign of moral decay and self-indulgence; others see them as the solace sought by those who have been hurt and are in pain; still others feel that they are only one more symptom of the underlying neuroses which caused marital failure in the first place. These interpretations may be true for certain minorities of the Formerly Married, but the explanation that better fits the great majority is that casual or uninvolved sexual liaisons are another and very important stage in the process of redefining the self, repairing the ego, and rediscovering the meaning of one's manhood or womanhood. The FM's casual sex activities are not so much a denial of love as a step in learning to love again.

The first sexual experiences of the formerly married person are approached with anxiety—greater in the case of women than of men, greater in the case of persons married a long while than those married only briefly. The FM, having met or dated someone, is aware of a mutual attraction; by means of the intense, self-revealing talk so easy for such people, they swiftly develop rapport, and in only a few evenings, perhaps only a few hours, are exchanging subtle signals indicating their desire. At this point the beginner is suddenly filled with apprehension. A man or woman may have disrobed before wife or husband five thousand times, but to reveal his or her nakedness to a virtual stranger is something else. One wants to be found pleasing, and fears to be found displeasing; one wonders whether the other's eyes, when they appraise, will be disappointed and hide the truth behind a forced smile. The very thought is enough to freeze one into immobility.

And even if the first moment goes well enough, how will it be when the mouths meet, the hands touch each other's flesh? For love-making, like speech, is highly individual, and each person's kiss and caress are unique. One is unsure in advance that what he does will seem right to her, and that what she does will seem pleasing to him; the wrong word, sound, or movement may shatter the mood and dry up desire, even in the very moment of finally yielding one's self. But if there is no such mishap, how will it be in the peace that follows—will they laugh together or be solemn, feel close or embarrassed? Will they have seemed good, as lovers, or will they have disappointed each other—and themselves?

Such is the mood of apprehension in which both men and women begin sexual life again, driven, despite their fears, to rediscover themselves and to refurbish their feelings about themselves as males and females. Very little in the FM's life will create as much doubt and turmoil beforehand as these first experiences or, if they are genuinely successful, as much expansiveness and inner calm afterward. And except for the very severely damaged or those who have a prior neurotic problem about sex, the great majority of FMs do have successful experiences, most only after some initial failures, the fortunate few at once.

One of the fortunate few is a young woman who was married for six years to a stolid, inarticulate man who made love athletically and almost without joy. She read and reread the rapturous descriptions of the female climax in literature, and supposed herself deficient; a dozen or so times she felt a sort of flutter, a brief flickering of current, but no more. Now, after three months of separation, she has been dating a bit, and one man greatly attracts her; holding hands with him, she finds herself perspiring and feeling nervous, and to her astonishment there is even an unexpected sense of readiness in her groin that delights her. Finally, after protests and indecisions, many passionate kisses and a few tears, she goes to bed with him, so frightened and ashamed that at first she is rigid and unseeing. But he is unlike her husband; he is attentive, passionate, and a bit poetic, and she feels strangely beautiful and wanted; as if waking from a trance, she begins to perceive him, delight in his caresses, and respond in kind. At the crucial moment, it proves unexpectedly easy to admit him within herself, and she is glad and even proud that it is so. Then in a while she is borne up by an unknown force and loses track of what is happening, is drawn inward and whirled around in the vortex of her being, at last seems to implode, to open inwardly, to dissolve; she hears her own voice crying out some low animal moan that she has never heard before. Then slowly she becomes aware of the room, the man upon her, the pillow, the pounding of her own heart. She is suffused with affection for him, kisses him dozens of times, embraces him with weary arms; but it is only in part he with whom she is delighted, for later when she is alone in bed at home she is aware of her whole body and of the new sensitivity of her parts; she treasures this, and smiles in the dark. Only one word can describe how she feels—*rich*—for she has found a treasure, a jewel beyond price, buried within herself.

A man in his upper thirties was married thirteen years; the last eight of them were marked first by bickering, later by relentless quarrelling, and finally by a deadly calm. Living so, and lying next to his wife at night month after month without desiring or being desired, he grew to feel empty, unattractive, and worn-out. He wondered whether at thirty-nine he was through with sex, whether any other women could ever find him at all appealing, whether he was, as his wife said, a disappointing, clumsy lover who could not manage to arouse a woman but hastily took his own satisfaction and left her cheated and distraught. But now he is divorced and has been dating, and finds that women treat him in a way that makes him feel attractive and youthful. One night, out with a woman he has dated several times and finds very desirable, he hears himself impulsively suggesting that they skip the movie and go to his apartment instead. To his delight, she agrees without protest. Once there, he is as nervous and clumsy as a teen-ager, but she is gentle and patient, and soon they are clinging together, exploring and rejoicing in each other, while in the back of his mind he thinks: This is real, this is happening to me, though I thought it never could. Later, in the calm and quiet after the tumult, a gentle shower of tiny kisses rains upon him; he realizes that she had been as wild and as transported as he, and is now as content; he is astonished and proud, and hardly able to believe it all at once. But he begins to realize, and will realize more clearly in the days and weeks ahead, that he is an alive, hungering, potent male animal and, wonder of wonders, a quite satisfactory lover.

In this or some other fashion, sooner or later, easily or with difficulty, the formerly married man or woman awakens from the nightmare of sexual failure and luxuriates in the reality of success. Everything seems different: one feels younger than in years, sees in the mirror an oddly new and vital face, is filled with a special cheerfulness. The spring of desire, flowing again, seems to wash away time's changes, those depressing intimations of mortality. Bathed in this magical stream, one acquires unsuspected powers: men in their thirties and even their forties find themselves able to make love repeatedly, and women discover deeper and more profound release than they ever knew; both become experimental, daring, and skillful at the variations of passion.

Like a man with a new car, a woman with a new necklace, FMs are enraptured by this new possession and fascinated by their new powers. Not surprisingly, they at first exaggerate the changes in themselves. It seems to them that they are actually younger-looking, more dynamic, and more desirable than ever; they yield themselves to what one psychiatrist has called "the erotomania of the newly divorced"—a high-flying, exuberant, egotistical delight in their new-found sensuality, and an illusion that they can attract and conquer almost any member of the opposite sex.

To feel like this is almost inevitably to act upon these feelings to some degree. After the first sexual relationship they sooner or later try others—perhaps only after the first one has palled, or perhaps concurrently. Some manage to be sexually involved with two or more people at the same time, seeing and sleeping with each one every now and again and yet looking for still others; they become interested in variety, eager to search further for someone or something not yet experienced. Friends or confidantes regularly interpret this as "having a fling," "getting it out of one's system," and "making up for lost time." But although they may be right, as far as they go, the sexual behavior of the Formerly Married means a great deal more than that at deeper levels of the being. FMs who have passed on beyond this phase of erotomania and egotism look back upon it not as a period of folly but one of useful discovery. A tall and very beautiful young woman, divorced at twenty-nine, had great doubts about her own femininity created by five years of unsatisfying marriage:

> I had difficulty seeing myself as a desirable and responsive woman and so did my husband. I felt very inadequate after the divorce, and being sexually active was the cure. A variety of experiences taught me what I needed to know about myself—that I was capable both of giving and of receiving great pleasure. It made me much more secure about myself.

Even rather late in life a woman's entire outlook on herself can be changed by the discovery of her own sexuality. A doctor's assistant, divorced at fifty-five, writes:

> In twenty-four years of marriage I never really became interested in sex. Since the divorce, however, I have discovered that I am a basically "sexy" individual. In these five years I have been intimate with eleven different men, sometimes romantically, sometimes just physically. I love being the way I am now. I feel myself to be a much better person all around.

Men are not as often in need of fundamental awakening, though some do speak of it. A forty-year-old businessman says:

> Sleeping around taught me a great deal. I not only found out for the first time what real women are like, but I found out what I am like. I learned that I have a greater drive than I thought, can satisfy a woman better than I thought, and can let myself go and enjoy sex much more than I thought. My whole attitude toward myself has changed a great deal, and for the better.

More generally, men speak of having suffered paralyzing self-doubt, and of gaining renewal and reaffirmation through sexual success. Says a novelist of thirty-nine:

> I needed reassurance about myself—I thought I was all washed up, in every way. I found reassurance in bed, and all of a sudden I was great again—a man, and a writer. As soon as I found I was sexually okay, I could write better than ever.

People of both sexes, evaluating their own sowing of wild oats, repeatedly speak of it as having changed their entire view of themselves. In technical terms, they suffered an "identity crisis" as a result of a disappointing love relationship and the disintegration of marriage, and used sex in the effort to find an identity and solve the crisis. Psychologists and social critics often point out that this is the fruitless endeavor of the lost, aimless anti-heroes of much modern fiction. But in the case of the Formerly Married it is not fruitless; they are not so much people who have lost their way in the world as people who have lost their way in love and marriage, and for whom a sense of sexual identity is, if not a detailed map, at least a rough sketch of the way to their ultimate goal.

But the use of sex without love has its drawbacks. Even though middle-class FMs almost always have at least a modicum of friendly, affectionate, or even romantic feelings about their casual sex partners, these feelings fall far short of the cultural ideal they have been reared to believe in; this often causes spells of guilt or feelings of self-debasement, especially in women. Even more commonly, most women—and some men—fear that by enjoying casual sex they are eroding their own ability to love and running the risk of succumbing to chronic promiscuity. These fears may as easily occur in those who have only a few long-range affairs over a period of two or three years as in those who have a score of one-night encounters in a season. The desire for promiscuity, deeply hidden within each of us, is brought to light by sexual experimentation; merely to become aware of that primitive self, even though it is still under control, can be alarming.

And a certain element of promiscuity is inescapably present in the use of casual sex. The first time or the first few times with a new partner are more stimulating and more renewing to one's self-confidence than repeated episodes with the same person: what was an exciting discovery of one's desirability and capacity becomes merely a comfort. The act of sex without love is most exhilarating when the partner is unfamiliar and when the first physical intimacy simulates or substitutes for a more profound intimacy; when, in short, sex without love serves as a temporary substitute for love itself.

Even a little touch of promiscuity poses certain practical problems. One must locate appealing new partners and tactfully disengage from the old; one must keep concurrent relationships watertight and totally separate. Many a potential partner will go to bed with such a person, as long as there is no actual proof he or she is sleeping with others, but to keep the truth concealed is not always easy. In the heat of passion, for instance, one may whisper the wrong name, or murmur some giveaway phrase. Or the phone may ring at a crucial moment, and though answering it is risky, letting it ring unheeded shows a chilling degree of self-control.

In contrast to these superficial problems, deeper and subtler ones are faced by those FMs who prefer to stick mostly to one partner for relatively casual sex. Many people who are fearful of, or unready for, anything approaching a deep emotional involvement achieve a species of relationship which brings them the rewards of sex and companionship without requiring real feeling or involvement. Outsiders who see two such people holding hands, talking, and smiling at each other, think them real lovers, but they are seeing only a simulacrum of love, a sham or practice relationship. Even in the very act of passion the two are not united in one rapture but have two parallel and simultaneous moments of rapture. One of my correspondents uses a beautifully precise term for what such affairs offer: counterfeit intimacy. They simulate and partly satisfy the need for genuine intimacy, yet allay the fear of loving and being hurt again; they allow the partners to play at love without having to pay the price of responsibility or lose their freedom; they give free rein to the reassuring sexual side of life, but keep cautious control of the potentially alarming emotional side.

But while such a relationship is being maintained—whether only for a few weeks, or for many months or longer—it is always in perilous balance, threatening either to wither away while it is still wanted or to become deeper and more binding than one partner is willing to endure. Even so simple a matter as how often to meet may become critical: if two people date and sleep together several weekends in a row, it may seem to the more vulnerable or involved one like an undeclared commitment—and the first weekend the other is busy elsewhere, he or she will be hurt or offended.

Even the things they say in bed are a continual hazard to the equilibrium of counterfeit intimacy; the words of excitement and delight they use about each other's sexuality are always in danger of giving way, in unguarded moments, to warmer words, which may alarm and drive away the less involved one. Let the man but whisper "I love you" in the heat of the moment, and the woman, if she is fearful of getting too involved, may for the next week or two be too busy to see him; let her whisper it to him, and if he is the fearful one he may not call her again for awhile, or will offer all manner of lame excuses for not seeing her. It even sometimes happens that one partner lets words of love slip out during or just after passion, and later on actually apologizes or makes a joke of it.

The classic differences between the male and female attitudes toward sex often cause men and women who are casual partners to engage in an undeclared border war. The man more often wants to keep the safeguards of counterfeit intimacy, and is less troubled by its emotional shallowness; the woman more often needs the safety and warmth of a stable, loving relationship. She is fearful of being thought promiscuous, and does not trust him to be discreet; she is fearful of becoming pregnant, and is not confident that he will stand by her if she does. She is less likely than he to want variety, and cannot understand why he is not satisfied with what she has to offer.

Even the problem of where to go to bed together, seemingly a mutual concern, is often a cause of low-level antagonism. It is her children's fault, and hence, in a sense, hers, that they cannot make love at her place, for it would be dreadful to have the children wake and find them—or find a locked door, which is nearly as bad. Circumstances sometimes drive a man and woman to it, but only those of steady nerves can enjoy sex under such conditions.

Where then—his place? Landlords and landladies are chronically snoopy, and even in a large apartment building a woman may quail and blush at the bland smile of the doorman. Even worse, she might have to arise after love-making, get dressed, and leave in the night; it makes her feel a bit like a whore, and even if not, getting out of a warm bed and going home to sleep alone is a hateful business. Motels are even worse: there is something furtive and debasing about an assignation in a rented room; besides, she can always feel the guarded contempt of the desk clerk, the bellhop, and the chambermaid.

If she arranges to stay overnight with him, there are extra costs for a sleep-in baby-sitter—and explanations to be made. Men and women both face questions from their children, but women bear the brunt of them because their sleeping habits are part of their children's lives. The questions may be innocent and artless, coming from the very young ("When you and Jack go skiing for a weekend and it's real cold, do you sleep in the same bed to stay warm?"), or searching and troubled, coming from the child at puberty ("Did Mr. Simpson stay here last night?"). Teen-aged children may ask nothing at all but maintain a gimlet-eyed watch for tell-tale words and actions; a woman has to think twice before changing handbags in front of a teen-age daughter, lest something revealing be seen.

The great majority of men and women strive to conceal their sexual activities from their children—especially in the case of casual sex. Many FMs lie outright, assuring younger children that nice people never do such things until they are married, and maintaining for older ones a pretense of chastity without discussing it. (Very rarely do they seem to ask themselves whether their lies may not in the end be more harmful to the children than teaching them to live with the reality of adult sexual behavior.) Yet a few FMs are able to handle the problem in a more sophisticated and honest fashion. One woman, asked by her fourteen-year-old son whether she kissed her dates or did other things with them, told him that that was her business and that every person—child as well as parent—has a right to certain areas of privacy in his life. One man, stretching the truth only a little, told his eleven-year-old son that he slept with a woman only if he liked her well enough to think he might marry her. A woman with two very mature and wise teen-agers of sixteen and eighteen occasionally stays away over a weekend with one man or another, and tells the children where she is going to be; she offers no excuses or pretenses, but is careful to allow herself the overnight privilege only with men they have met and seem to approve of.

Aside from unusual individuals like these, nearly all FMs have one set of morals for themselves and another set for their children. For the Formerly Married are caught between two cultures; while they permit themselves their present conduct and justify it, they also have a nagging residual feeling that it is not really proper, and do not want their children to emulate them. They remain only partly freed from the standards of the conventional world, and retain dual citizenship, since they mean eventually to quit the new world and make their way back to the one they left. Casual sex experiences help them toward that goal by restoring self-esteem and rebuilding sexual identity, yet at the same time threaten to misdirect them by breaking down the synthesis of sex and love and by conditioning them to enjoy uncomplicated and primitive desire. Until they solve this dilemma, they vacillate between self-love and self-contempt, between bursts of sensuality and periods of self-denial, between delight in their way of life and despair at not living another and presumably better way.

IV · *Addicts*

—The cocktail lounge of a hotel in New York, where a scientific convention has been meeting; early evening of a winter day. A young woman in her early thirties, who works for a national magazine, is taking notes while interviewing a biologist, a husky, strong-featured, but diffident man of perhaps forty. While listening to him and jotting down phrases, she is thinking: He isn't letting himself react to me. She wonders what it would be like with him (indeed, she wonders the same thing about nearly every attractive intelligent man she meets), and smiles at something witty he has just said, looking at him with a directness and warmth that suddenly bring his own eyes into a different focus. He studies her, intrigued but alarmed. She knew this would be the reaction, for she has a great deal of experience with such men; she has a virtually uncontrollable habit of seducing shy intellectual men, and in the diary of her nine years as a divorcee has recorded thirty-nine such affairs, almost all of which she lost interest in very rapidly after the actual conquest. Soon he is gallantly striking a match for her cigarette and making some clumsy little compliment; next he suggests they continue the interview over dinner; and during dinner she quietly puts the notebook away to signify the end of the business relationship, and innocuously weaves into the conversation the fact that she lives alone in a tiny apartment just a few blocks away. Unless he is hopelessly moral—or frightened—the rest should be inevitable, though he may need encouragement along the way. Now and then she worries about her way of life, but each time the mood of adventure comes over her she cannot resist it; she becomes wildly desirous when she meets an intelligent, inhibited stranger, and when at last she has gently led him to conquer her, she feels utterly desirable and womanly, and yields herself so totally that she sometimes almost faints from ecstasy. This never ceases to amaze her, since with her hubsand, who was only intermittently potent, she had no feeling and no excitement whatever, and was only a disinterested spectator of his efforts.

This woman might almost be characterized as an addict. Casual sex, like many sedatives and stimulants, can be helpful to the ailing or suffering FM if used judiciously when needed, and then discontinued, but if used indiscriminately and over a long time it may take hold of the user and prevent his further recovery. (For some people, of course, recovery does not mean a return to conventional ideals and to remarriage; a small minority of FMs regard their sexual liberation as a healthful end in itself, and a permanently desirable way of life.)

Counterfeit intimacy, for instance, can be a most useful transitional relationship for one who means to love again and to remarry, but if he relies upon it too long, he may develop a kind of emotional atrophy. Rather than achieving a sense of sexual identity through it, and then wanting and seeking deeper and more involved relationships, he may grow so adjusted to cool, simple, uncommitted affairs that the separation between sex and love is no longer a temporary safeguard and a convenience, but a fixed pattern. A thirty-seven-year-old insurance executive who has lived like this for five years and has had eight or nine such relationships claims that he is genuinely fond of women but has come to see sexual intercourse as something unrelated to fondness. He terms it "a purely physical thing—a discharge of static. It's very enjoyable—but why confuse it with feeling? I'm happy the way I am now—I don't expect or want to marry again for another twenty years." A telephone company executive found his wife in bed with another man three years ago; ever since the subsequent divorce, he has carefully held women at a distance, emotionally, and grown quite contented with the life he has arranged for himself:

> I've worked out a pattern involving three girls—not always the same three, but the number is what counts. More flexible than two, less complicated than four or five. Each of the present three likes being with me, going places with me, and sleeping with me, all on a free-and-easy basis. Every once in a while one of them starts to get more serious, and then I ignore her for two or three weeks until she cools it. If she doesn't, it's time for me to get out of it and find someone else. I find it a thoroughly satisfactory way of life.

Women sometimes feel the same way. A gentle, sensitive artist, now forty-three, had a long and very difficult marriage with a martinet of a man; having had a long struggle to get a divorce, she has been extremely wary of intimacy for the past four years, and seems habituated to the casual relationship:

> I honestly enjoy not being married—certainly now, and maybe for good. At first I got very lonely, and had to keep busy and go out a lot. But I also found I had to keep men at arm's length —not physically, but emotionally. I was, and still am, terrified of being trapped by the other person's feelings or even by my own. As soon as some man starts getting serious with me, I run. But there are two who make no emotional demands on me, and I enjoy the companionship of each of them, and occasionally go to bed with one or the other.

This pattern, though valuable at first, is so convenient that the FM may never try to discover deeper feelings in herself or himself. Partners are used as conveniences, not people—one phones a date when he needs a few hours of companionship and some sex, and otherwise has nothing to do with her. The comfort and ease of this way of life trap some people; after years of it, they feel it is an ideal answer, and think themselves well off. Occasionally, however, they have some doubts, and wonder what is "wrong" with them or even say things like, "I've become an emotional cripple," or "I've become incapable of caring or ever remarrying."

A more extreme form of casual sex is promiscuity. The term is used in various ways: to one person, it may mean a series of sexual affairs, one at a time; to another, sex with several regular partners concurrently; and to a third, indiscriminate sex with a steady stream of new and almost unknown partners. I shall use it in the third sense.

Some FMs seem to lack the potential for self-healing and re-growth of the self; perhaps in their own eyes they have been failures in their lives, perhaps their work has no meaning, perhaps they are people without self-love for whom the loss of the spouse was proof of their unworthiness. For them, the sexual conquest of a new person produces a brief glow of well-being, and a momentary sense of importance and achievement, but because the basic reasons for their discontent and self-dislike are profound, and because their personalities are too ailing to improve spontaneously, such sexual conquest does not lead to recovery, but serves them only as an anodyne which they need in ever-increasing doses.

Jeanne Knakal, a family counsellor in Sausalito, California, has coined the term "romance addicts" to signify those people —mostly FMs—who continually prowl bars and other market-places in the search for new partners, are galvanized into action by a new face, plunge into romantic play and wind up in bed that same night, and after one or two more dates are dis-enchanted and look for another conquest. Such people, she say, "use their bodies mechanically to produce temporary anes-thesia against the pain of living. Casual and fleeting liaisons have increasingly become the mode in [their] reluctance to face the 'self.' "

A man of this type, urgently seeking temporary relief from self-doubt and self-contempt, often "comes on strong," but after the first night or two of heroic sexual feats and marvelous rapport he starts becoming strangely bored and boring, his sexual enthusiasm and ability rapidly dwindling. He offers some handy excuse ("I must have had too much to drink," or "I've been working too hard"), but the apology is the death-knell; he does not call again, and seeks to ease the hurt of his latest failure with yet another new conquest. Women, too, often begin with great passion but quickly lose sexual responsiveness after the fall. Their failure is not as noticeable as the male's for obvious reasons, but they themselves know about it and invent ways to break up the new relationship and look for another. Like the magazine reporter described at the beginning of this section, such a woman may have a virtual compulsion to seduce new men; she needs constant reaffirmation of her worth, but only when someone new tells her with his body that she is valuable and desirable can she briefly believe it.

Some of those who employ casual sex in this promiscuous

fashion suffer not so much from low self-esteem as from an underlying neurosis in which love and sex, rather than being merely separable, are actually antithetical. We are all forbidden to desire our parents sexually, and this sets up a disjunction between love and sex during childhood. Most of us resolve the problem by partially breaking away from our parents during adolescence, and so being able to love someone else and to desire him or her at the same time, but those who remain too tightly tied to a parent—a son to his mother, a daughter to her father—may unconsciously identify any potential lover with the parent of that sex, and be blocked from feeling sexual desire. So it comes about that certain men are impotent with "good" women (whom they love as they do Mother), but perfectly potent with "bad" women (whom they mistreat, despise, or have no feeling for at all). A parallel disjunction can occur in a woman's feelings: she may be frigid with any kindly and loving man, and be aroused only by a cruel or rejecting one. Such men and women probably failed in marriage because of these same neurotic attitudes, which are deep-rooted and unlikely to improve spontaneously; they are even less likely to remarry successfully, or to remarry at all, than others who are habituated to casual sex.

v · *The Golden Mean*

It is always a little disappointing when truth turns out to be a cliché—and what could be older and more familiar than the idea that the best way is the Golden Mean, the middle course, moderation in all things? Yet although it is old and familiar, it is neither shallow nor wrong; although it has often been said, it is no less true.

The middle course of post-marital sex lies somewhere between rigid abstinence on the one hand, with its attendant frustrations, and habitual promiscuity on the other, with its extinction of the capacity for deep feeling. The great majority of the Formerly Married follow this middle course—or, rather, blunder along it, sometimes veering off to the side of abstinence, sometimes to the side of excess. But they recoil from either extreme, and for good reason: each spell of celibacy depresses them ("I feel dead, finished, old"), each spell of promiscuity makes them feel degraded ("I've become unfit ever to remarry").

Even on the middle road there is always the chance that counterfeit intimacy, so much easier to come by than genuine intimacy, will become a rooted habit. But this seems to happen only to a small number of people; nearly all who have casual sex relationships do, after a while, go on to seek something deeper and more meaningful. One might even suspect that abstainers are more likely than users to remain single; even apart from those with severe sexual disabilities, people who abstain on principle may become chronically wary, fearful, and aloof, unable freely to give or to receive either sexual pleasure or love.

It seems evident that the majority of those who take the middle course do benefit from sex without love—and then come to find it insufficient, or to outgrow it. This is how two of them speak of the emergence of the new mood:

[M, 41] It [casual sex] was enormously restorative to my damaged and bruised ego, and for quite a while I sought it with any and all women. But after four years, I was weary of it, and of its lack of meaning. I even began having a little trouble now and then—I mean, I wasn't always able to make it any more. Then I met a girl I fell in love with, and with her it has been completely different—better than with any of the others, and I have never had any problem about potency with her. I may even marry her, if all goes well.

[F, 39] It was very necessary for me to have intimate relations with different men for a while; one has to reevaluate herself. But there came a time when I felt it was no longer useful, and was making it impossible for me to develop a lasting relationship with anyone. I have become much more aware of what I want—long-term emotional gratification—and I have been going with one man for a year, and ignoring the occasional longing for variety.

Some experts counsel against the use of casual sex (one psychologist refers to it scornfully as a "home remedy for battered egos"), but the evidence is impressive that when used with moderation it does indeed restore confidence, aid the work of repair and growth, and ready the FM for the discovery of his or her own larger needs.

CHAPTER SIX

The Love Affair

1 · *What Is a Love Affair?*

Whatever goals in life an FM may have had before the ending of marriage, they usually become subordinated after separation to the master aim of finding a new love-relationship. Almost every activity, every aim, seems either absorbing or dull, important or valueless, according to its relationship to that central goal. Work and play, eating and sleeping, art and politics, family and friends, all become satellites circling in orbit around that sun. This is true for men as well as for women, for in the modern world a man deprived of love and marriage after being accustomed to them is, despite his work, a displaced person. Gone are castle, courtesan, and gentleman's club; today a man alone is a lonely man. And therefore both men and women, as soon as they are somewhat recovered from the trauma of marital dissolution, begin to seek and to try out relationships that have emotional content.

These range anywhere from sudden infatuations that mysteriously evaporate after a week to profound and passionate alliances that last for years. The searching and testing begin rather soon: most FMs have at least one, and many have more than one, emotional relationship of some kind within the first year, and the majority experience several of them within two or three years. Although these alliances could be loosely called

171

love affairs, FMs themselves are extremely reluctant to use that straight-forward term or to refer to themselves as being in love. They rely instead upon an assortment of cautious euphemisms; instead of having a love affair, they have a *relationship,* an *attachment,* or an *involvement.* They are not in love, but are *involved with, all tied up with, going with,* or *very much in-terested in* someone. A man and a woman are not lovers, but *a thing* or *a pair,* or are *going together, going steady,* or *seeing each other regularly.* Even though they are involved with each other, they may or may not *be committed* or *have a commit-ment.* But when an involvement—especially one with a com-mitment—goes sour, it becomes an *entanglement,* perhaps even a *hang-up,* until the FM manages to detach himself or herself from it.

This semantic legerdemain reveals a good deal about the guarded and qualified attitude of FMs toward their major goal. They are so eager to love again that they act upon their emo-tions impetuously and rapidly, yet they are so mistrustful of those emotions and so unsure of their own judgment that they hold back part of themselves. And not only are they partly inaccessible in the emotional sense, but also in the practical sense: many are still legally married, or are hindered in seek-ing a complete relationship by continuing financial entangle-ments with their ex-spouses and responsibilities to their chil-dren. Finally, unlike the unmarried young who learn to love by loving, the Formerly Married must first unlearn and then learn again, must love anew with the habits of the old still vivid within them; like medieval palimpsests, they are parch-ments written upon more than once, whose original text, im-perfectly erased, may show through and becloud the meaning of the new.

The interplay of these several factors results in a variety of different kinds of love affairs, each the outgrowth of a mix-ture of needs and fears, each representing a special balance between commitment and withholding. Sometimes the mixture is so unstable that love is born and dies in a matter of days or weeks; FMs can become intensely intimate with each other with great speed and yield themselves to a rush of warm feel-ings—which are chilled by quickly succeeding misgivings and fear. Sometimes, on the other hand, an equilibrium is achieved by limiting the intensity of the love feelings, thereby limiting the fear; FMs sometimes manage for many months to main-tain affairs that are more friendly than loving, more com-fortable than compelling.

When FM lovers do permit themselves deep and strong feelings, they often are able to maintain them over a long period only by holding back a part of the self and carefully avoiding any statement or action that constitutes emotional commitment—any avowal or even hint that one loves the other wholly and exclusively. The affair may go on for months with-out there being any clear understanding as to what the lovers mean to each other; the very ambiguity of the relationship is what makes its closeness tolerable to the hesitant lovers. And even if they do gradually make an emotional commitment to each other, one or both may continue for a while to need a certain amount of independence and the right to spend time away from the other, perhaps with friends, perhaps simply alone—a token freedom that minimizes the sense of being en-closed and caged in by one's own commitment.

More so than other kinds of lovers, FMs run the risk of misalliance—of choosing someone who is fundamentally wrong for them, or whose continuing entanglement with a former spouse makes the love affair a hopeless one, doomed from the start. The risk of such misalliance is greater for FMs not only because their lives are more complicated by unfinished busi-ness, but because they are apt to unconsciously choose partners who represent no threat of entrapment: the lover one can never marry is a perfectly safe choice. Such affairs may last quite a while, satisfying some of the needs of the partners while denying others. Usually, however, one of the two comes to want exactly what the affair cannot provide—growth and development toward marriage—and as this want becomes stronger, the relationship falls apart or quietly withers away.

Often, too, one lover or the other unconsciously allows some removable impediment to stand in the way. A man may, for instance, be unable to marry the woman he loves because his divorce negotiations are stalemated; he feels that he cannot agree to the terms his wife is asking, or believes that she will not let go of him, but upon closer examination it is apparent that he has balked at some minor matter or trifling final difference between his offer and her demand. But as long as he considers himself the helpless victim of the process of negotiation, he feels guiltless of keeping himself unavailable for remarriage.

The behavior of the Formerly Married in love thus has a central theme underlying its many different forms: at one and the same time, most FMs are desperately eager to love but afraid of failing at it, adept at finding lovers but equally adept at holding them at arm's length, persistent in their drive toward a complete and binding love-relationship but just as persistent in their stopping off at intermediate way-stations to allay their own fears. Perhaps, as with alpinists, they must rest at these way-stations in order to acclimate themselves to the altitude before climbing farther. It may be only through loving partially that the Formerly Married can become more nearly capable of loving completely.

II · *To Love or Not to Love*

Thirty-six years ago, Willard Waller, one of the most perceptive sociologists who has ever written about divorce, commented in *The Old Love and the New* that "the psychology [of the divorced person] is intricate and contrary, it works and grows by antithesis and paradox." Though much has changed in the world of divorce, his comment remains as true today as it was then, and is nowhere more applicable than to the FM's feelings about loving again. The FM's hunger for love is greater than ever, because to love and be loved again would be the most healing of all experiences, the most positive of all proofs that he is a worthy human being; at the same time, however, he is inordinately fearful of trusting those feelings which have so grievously betrayed him and proven so unreliable. And not only does he mistrust his own feelings, but those of anyone who cares for him, for he built his life upon them once, only to find them not a rock, but sand.

Some FMs feel only a single-minded yearning for love, and some feel only a great fear of allowing themselves to love again. Most, however, feel the pull in both directions, either simultaneously or in rapid alternation. As we have already seen, some men and women limit themselves to superficial relationships in order to keep this conflict under control, but others let the hunger for love break through and are promptly overwhelmed by anxiety, which blights the loving impulses; such must have been the case with the man who briefly came into this woman's life:

[F, 38] A couple of years ago I made a blind date with a lawyer from out of town. I don't ordinarily make blind dates, but a cousin had urged him on me. He walked in, we took one look at each other, and sparks flew. There was something we both felt that was like nothing I had known in two years as a divorcee. We went to dinner but never noticed the food. We couldn't talk enough, we got misty-eyed again and again, and choked up. We went to his hotel room and talked and necked almost all night. I don't go to bed with anyone all that fast, but I would have gone with him without any hesitation if he'd asked me. He told me we would be married, and I wasn't even surprised—it was just that natural and inevitable. He took me home at five A.M., and said he'd phone at nine, when my kids had left for school. I was exhausted, but I couldn't sleep a wink. It had really happened to me at last, and all I could do was paint scenes of the future. I got up with the kids at seven-thirty, and watched the clock—it never ran so slow. At eight-thirty I was excited. At ten of nine I was as fidgety as could be. Nine o'clock, and I was perspiring. Five after. Ten after. My heart was palpitating and I was feeling funny in the stomach. Well, I waited by that phone all morning and all afternoon, and it never rang. Not that night, either. Not ever. I never heard from him. I was shattered. It took months before I got over it, and I still feel a little sick telling about it even now. It was a nightmare. It was like being out of your head, when nothing makes any sense.

Ambivalence about loving seldom takes so extreme and overt a form, but even in milder and half-concealed form it is exasperating and depressing to the one who feels it as well as to the innocent victim. A civil engineer of forty-four says that he has a "natural impulse" to be kind, good, and warm toward women, but as soon as it begins to have its effects on them, he takes alarm and becomes uncontrollably difficult and provocative until he has broken up the budding relationship. A plastics manufacturer of forty-two says that more than anything else in life he wants "a steady and committed relationship," yet he finds himself behaving as though that were what he least wanted. "I'm currently having affairs with three girls at once," he says. "Why?—it must be because that makes commitment impossible. No matter what I think I want, this must be what I unconsciously want." And although this kind of conflict may appear more often, or more clearly, in the male, it also shows up in the female. "I can't understand it," says one young woman who has been separated for half a year. "I was looking forward to running around with different men after my marriage broke up, and here I am sticking to just one man—almost against my will. But I keep getting waves of feeling *caught*—the closer he and I become, the more strongly I feel I *ought* to run around a bit first." A thirty-eight-year-old book editor says that she has fallen in love half a dozen times in the past four years, but that "each time, soon after it becomes serious, I begin to see his faults or limitations, and get a scared feeling that I'm not as deeply in love as I want to be and that maybe it will me hard to get out of it. And I start getting out right then."

The old conflict thus flares up again, within the soul of the

FM, that raged there before marriage—the struggle between the desire for freedom and variety, and the desire for belonging and security. Man (and to a lesser extent woman) is forever torn between the hunger for adventure and the hunger for home. The wanderer, tempest-tossed, dreams of the harbor, the dear face, the snug bed; but as soon as he has had them a while, he dreams of hoisting anchor and setting forth for unfamiliar islands beyond the horizon. So too with love. One wants to belong and to become a part of the substance of someone else, yet one wants to be free and to keep his own soul for himself. To love someone is the goal of one's dreams, but an end to dreaming; it is to be free from yearning, but also no longer free to yearn.

In the bachelor or never-married woman, the inability to resolve this conflict may be a symptom of a chronic neurosis; in most FMs it is a symptom of a temporary neurotic state produced by stress and trauma. When the stress is removed, and the damage done by the trauma is slowly repaired, the inability to resolve the conflict usually disappears. The various expedients we have looked at for preventing full commitment are thus neurotic defenses against the feelings of alarm and entrapment that overwhelm the formerly married person at the approach of love. But unlike the person with a character neurosis, most FMs use these defenses only temporarily; this is, after all, a time of recuperation and new growth. They are merely suffering growing pains—a reasonable penalty to pay for increased stature.

Besides the inner conflict, there are external forces pushing and pulling the FM both ways. Among the former are the opinions of one's relatives, friends, and acquaintances—all those persons whose world he has deserted and to which they hope he will return. Their interest and their good wishes thinly mask their all-too-frequent disapproval and poor opinion of his way of life; it is obvious to him that to regain their approval and good opinion he must fall in love, genuinely and openly.

While remarriage is the only final solution they thoroughly approve of, they will consider him as good as saved if he confesses to loving, and renounces the false idols of freedom and casual sex. Moreover, even if he does not feel that the collapse of the marriage was altogether, or even chiefly, his fault, he knows that the world around him feels he failed in some important way. To love again would prove that there was nothing missing in him; and to have that love result in a successful marriage—*that* would show them what kind of human being he is.

"What's new?" ask one's friends. "Have you met anybody nice yet?" It is a kindly, a hopeful query; but underneath the surface it means (or at least seems to mean) something else: Are you a whole person yet, or are you still an emotional defective? At first, people are solicitous and genuinely concerned about their separated and divorced friends; later, though they continue to ask, there is a subliminal note of impatience and criticism. For no matter how the question is phrased or spoken, the FM squirms, feeling somehow at fault if his answer is no.

Virtually all the leisure activities of adult society are built around couples rather than individuals. Most of the places one would like to go are places for men and women in pairs, not one by one. It is an extraordinary man—and an even more extraordinary woman—who can go alone to the ballet, a play, a country club, or a good restaurant, and be surrounded by people in pairs, without feeling acutely self-conscious and coming away moody and diminished in self-esteem. At parties given by married people, the FM, if currently unattached and alone, may feel conspicuous and ill at ease. He or she may like best the kind of home that exists only in a suburban setting, but in suburbia the formerly married man or woman is an alien who does not fit in. From this anomalous position there seems no way to extricate himself except by remarriage. The social awkwardness of the FM's life thus impels him to try to love better, in order finally to live better. He experiences the social pressures as a desire to love; like the agnostic or doubter who would be saved, heaven may be his goal but what he feels is a yearning to believe.

The pressures brought upon the FM by his children similarly are transformed into a desire to love and remarry. The formerly married woman has an almost continual sense of guilt about rearing her children in a manless home, a situation she could remedy by finding the right man to love. (The formerly married man—except for the rare one with custody—may also feel guilty, but this has less impact on him since his remarriage usually would not change their home life.) When the children meet one of their mother's dates and begin to like him, the pressure is greatly intensified. Let some new man be friendly and competent with her children, awakening a response in them, and she feels something in herself going out toward him; she had not thought to love him, but now, seeing her children enjoying themselves with him, feels herself half-ready to do so. A few men, in fact, deliberately try to "get to" a woman through her children when they cannot succeed with her directly; one FM woman complains that a man she knows and merely likes has taken her sons to baseball games, bowling alleys, and hikes in the woods, until she finds herself resenting the warmer feeling this forces her to have for him. A man reports that he took his children on an outing with a woman he is dating, and, seeing how gentle and warm she was to them, felt in himself a surge of emotion toward her which troubled him because it arose from her relationship, not to him, but to the children.

Children often deliberately try to make their parents care for someone they have met and can envision as a step-parent. Transparently hopeful, they may ask their mothers about each new man: "Do you like him? Do you like him very much? Do you think you might marry him? Aren't you *ever* going to get married again?" Listening to such queries and pleas, she wants to love him in order to make her children happy. The child's desires become truly seductive when he begins to care a good deal for someone in his mother's or father's life. A radio announcer in Florida, whose ex-wife works and leaves their nine-year-old son with a maid, believes his ex-wife would let the boy live with him if he remarried; as a result, he tried to convince himself that he was in love with a girl friend of his to whom his son took a liking:

> I thought myself in love with Sally for a couple of weeks only because of my son. He spent a solid week with me during Christmas and saw a good bit of her. She was wonderful with him— not too sweet, not coy, just natural and adult. One evening at bedtime he said to me, "I know it's very complicated, Dad, but could you please tell me, how much do you like Sally?" I told him I liked her very much. "Do you *love* her?" he asked. I said I wasn't sure; it was hard to tell when liking becomes loving, and I needed lots of time to be sure. I turned out his light, but he said, "Please, Dad, wait a minute. Dad, is there any possibility you and she will get married?" I explained the difference between possibility and likelihood, but he cut me off. "Okay, okay," he said, "but is there any possibility? Because—don't tell her this— but I more than like her. I think I love her. I'd really like her for a second Mommy." I can't begin to tell you all the feelings this aroused in me—first, a resistance, then a feeling of guilt, then the question "Well, why not?", then a great rush of hope and of love for her. I thought, "Maybe this is really the answer, maybe this would be the best thing for me, and for him as well." For about two weeks I really believed it might work out; then she and I had one of those crazy fallings-out that we were forever having, and the whole dream blew apart.

In contrast to all these external factors pushing the FM toward loving are others pulling him away, or at least impeding the way. One such is the lack of a divorce. Some people allow negotiations or a legal separation to drag on indefinitely as a safeguard against new involvement. But others, passionately desiring divorce, are unable to obtain it from a spouse who refuses to cooperate or who sets impossibly harsh terms for cooperating. When one spouse is uncooperative, the other can do practically nothing unless the former has committed some wrong that comes under the state's divorce law—and can be proven despite his denials. Divorce suits on the grounds of cruelty, for instance, are almost bound to fail unless the defendant makes no defense and thereby tacitly admits the complaint. Desertion is another very common ground—but since the deserter cannot sue, he cannot get a divorce unless his spouse is willing to sue. Even if a man deliberately and openly commits adultery to give his wife grounds for divorce, he cannot get free of her unless she chooses to sue him for it —which she may refuse to do until he agrees to her terms. Nor can the would-be escaper go get a divorce in one of the "easy" states unless the other spouse is willing to sign documents submitting himself or herself to the jurisdiction of that state, and offering no contest.

As a result, a certain number of nascent or budding love affairs are choked off by the legal entanglement of one of the lovers with a reluctant spouse. At first, the suffering of the would-be escapee and the intransigence of his spouse are a bond between the lovers: a man pours forth his suffering and his complaints against the unyielding wife to the woman he loves, and his misery and her compassion bring them very close together. But as time goes by and he reports further bitter exchanges, demands and obstructive tactics, she loses the ability to be soothing and understanding, but grows angry along with him—no longer a help, but a duplication of his own anger and frustration. Still later, she begins to urge or nag him to take more desperate actions or try new approaches; she is speaking out of her own need for some resolution and some clear prospect for her own future. But this puts him and her at odds; her need becomes another irritant and burden to him, his inability to get free begins to look suspect to her. They quarrel, forgive each other, quarrel again and forgive again; finally, wearily, they give each other up, sometimes in anger but more often in quiet resignation.

But the divorce, even if completed, can pose formidable obstacles to new love. Alimony and child support take a considerable portion of the income of many a middle-class FM man—the more so if he was the one who wanted the divorce while his wife was reluctant or felt herself treated unfairly. Quite often, alimony plus child-support payments together take from a third to a half of a man's net income, and an even larger fraction is not uncommon.*

The average homemaker and mother trying to get along on a third to a half of her ex-husband's income has a thin time of it, and either must reduce her standard of living, get help from her parents, or go to work until she finds another husband. But the ex-husband, though he can manage to live alone on what remains to him, may well feel a chill coming over his feelings for any other woman when he calculates the dimensions of her need for support. An electronics engineer in Detroit is persuasive on the subject:

[M, 36] Money problems have killed off the two important relationships I've had since the divorce. I can live modestly on what I have left after paying alimony and child support, but I can't see how I could support another woman—especially not one who would want to have more children. The first girl I got in deep with was struggling to keep herself and her two kids; her husband is a gambler and a bum who sends money for the children only when she takes him to court. That looked like a mess for me to get into. I felt guilty, but I didn't want any part of it. The second one had no financial problems—she got good alimony from a well-to-do ex-husband—but she doesn't work, and her alimony would be cut off if I married her. And then, if *we* didn't work out, she'd have to get alimony from me. I felt I couldn't take a chance. I cared deeply for her, though, and couldn't either quit or make a move. Finally, she broke it off for her own sake. I guess I'm not going to want to marry any

* Among the lower class, although child support is commonly ordered by the court, alimony often is not, or is very small. One authority (Jacobson) estimates that alimony is granted in only about one fourth of all divorce cases, but this includes all classes and the childless as well as parents. Among the divorcing people we are observing here, alimony and/or child support is the rule rather than the exception.

woman unless she has a good job and likes it—and anyone like that is liable to be a pretty tough cookie.

It is not only men whose feelings are stifled by financial factors; women suffer the same effect. A highly intelligent and attractive divorcee with three children says, "Most of the desirable men I've met have financial problems due to former marriages, and would probably shy away when they learned that the child support I get really doesn't cover the expenses. So I never let myself get involved enough with them to get hurt." "I want love and companionship more than anything in the world," says another, "but I refuse to let myself get entangled with any man I think can't easily support me and the children. This has put the damper on several very promising romances."

Sometimes it is the existence of money, rather than its lack, that obstructs or spoils a love affair. In most cases, a woman who gets alimony stands to lose it instantly and forever, the moment she remarries. If her ex-husband is wealthy and the alimony is substantial, she is free and independent; with a new love and marriage, she is neither. For some this is not an easy choice, and a certain number of women in such circumstances go from affair to affair, breaking away from each one if it begins to raise the threat of remarriage. A few of them dare to live with the man they love, remaining unmarried in order to continue receiving the alimony, but this is a desperate measure; it is degrading, guilt-producing because of its exploitation of the ex-husband, socially awkward, hurtful to the children, if there are any—and, sometimes, risky, since in certain states it provides the ex-husband with grounds for cutting off the alimony. One may fairly wonder how love came to have the reputation of being a mighty and all-conquering emotion, when so many coarse and lowly emotions seem able to overthrow it.

Children, though they often act as an impetus toward loving again, sometimes act in just the opposite way. Rather often a child will like a new man in Mother's life until the affair becomes serious and the child perceives that the new friend is a competitor; then he may misbehave, act hateful or provocative toward the interloper, and make him seem like an upsetting influence. "When I was seeing a great deal of Bob," writes one woman, "my twelve-year-old daughter grew sassy, threw tantrums, and was impossible to handle. Then I told her I didn't think I would ever marry him, and she relaxed and became herself almost overnight." Again, a man may simply not be able to act like the ideal parent that the children's mother had in mind. "He was gentle and kind to my boys," writes another woman, "in fact, far more so that the man I finally married, but he was so easy-going and so permissive that I could see he would never set standards or be able to exert discipline." "He really didn't like my children," says another, "and I faced the fact that if it was a question of him or my children, I was going to pick them."

On the other side, a man may have misgivings about getting too deeply involved with a woman because of her children. "I'm a pretty good father with my own kids," says one man, "but hers were so mixed-up and wild that I hesitated at the thought of living with them and trying to get along with them. It didn't look like a promising way of life." Some men are drawn to much younger women, but shy away when the latter talk of wanting children. "I thought she was really it," says one man, "until she began speaking about how much she wanted at least one or two more kids. At fifty I've been through all that—I'm beyond it, I don't want to start it all over again. I felt it was a difference of opinion we'd never be able to resolve."

Once again, therefore, it is apparent that the typical FM will probably have to meet a great many potential partners and try out many relationships before finding a new love that can survive and grow. Despite so many reasons to fear love and to doubt it, the formerly married person must learn to cease fearing and to have faith; given the forbidding circumstances, the wonder is that so many finally do so.

III · *Life-Cycle of the Typical FM Love Affair*

The *typical* FM love affair? Isn't every love affair, like every human being, unique? Yes and no; every human being is unique as a totality, yet nearly every one of his major experiences in life has basic similarities to those of many other people. No love affair is exactly like any other, yet if we look closely into one love affair between two formerly married people, we may perceive in it some of the principal components of many such love affairs. No other will be just like the one we look at, but many others will pass through similar stages of growth and decay. The life-cycle of the affair begins, of course, with:

The Encounter. This is very often unplanned and semi-accidental, and probably takes place on neutral ground where each one is free to interact with, or to ignore, the other. Each quickly recognizes the other as a Possibility; each subtly communicates more about his or her status, emotional condition, and interest in the other than any onlookers perceive.

—It began on an October afternoon, two years ago. Two men entered the lobby of a large hospital in Chicago, asked for a room number at the information desk, and then went to the elevators. One of them, Douglas Maclean, was the art director of a small advertising agency—a man of medium height and husky build, with close-cropped curly hair already going grey although he was then only forty-three and still had a youthful, even boyish, face. He recalls the visit:

> I met a friend of mine, who is also divorced, for dinner. He had picked me up in front of the office after work, and asked if I minded stopping off first at the hospital where his cousin, Joan, was in for some kind of check-up. I didn't know her, but I had no objection. Her room was practically jammed—she had five other people visiting her at the time—but in a few minutes she and I tuned in on each other, despite all the talk flying around.

I liked her almost at once. She had soft dark hair and blue eyes, and that kind of wistful look and shy manner that always gets me. She liked me right away, too, because even with all those people there we began tossing clues to each other—we would look at each other for an instant when somebody said something meaningful, or one of us would make an inside remark meant just for the other one's benefit. Before I left, I knew she was recently divorced and not tied up with anyone, had a ten-year-old daughter, taught the piano, and was rather mixed-up about what she wanted out of life. I had a feeling she might be pretty sexy, although controlled and afraid to let go. I was fairly sure that she wanted to see me again as much as I wanted to see her.

The Wooing. A funny old-fashioned word, yet formerly married people do woo each other with their special brand of talk—the pell-mell outpouring of likes and dislikes, experiences and emotions, and, most of all, allusions to, and outright confidences about, their marriages and divorces. The central theme in all the latter is: I have known sorrow—will you comfort me? . . . I am seeking someone again—is it you?

—Maclean phoned Joan Bishop at the hospital the next morning and arranged to visit her. He came the following evening and stayed for two hours; the whole time the two of them talked about all sorts of things in an eager, rapid, darting way as though they had to know everything about each other all at once. They warily circled the subject of their marriages and divorces, came in close, backed away, came in close again; before he left they were fellow-voyagers, virtual strangers who were already strangely familiar with each other. He sat on the edge of her bed and kissed her, took her slender face between his hands and studied her with wonder; she turned away blushing, as if he could read more there than she meant to show. The nurse walked in and he leaped up like a schoolboy; she smiled and said it was time for visitors to leave, and he went home and began considering how and when to tell the two girls he had been seeing most often that he had become involved with someone.

Joan Bishop, thirty-seven at that time and only divorced for two months after a ten-month separation, felt the same hope but without the same degree of conviction:

Ever since the separation, I'd been dating and had even had two brief affairs which were more physical than anything else, but I hadn't *felt* anything for anyone. It seemed as if I had no capacity to care—it didn't matter to me if someone saw a lot of me for a while and then disappeared, as long as there was another to take his place. When Doug came into my hospital room I resented him at first because he was a stranger seeing me in bed and not at my best, but as soon as he began to talk to me I liked him—he was so direct, so vital. Then after he came back for that first long visit, I felt something very exciting —an intuition that I might care. It made me feel *alive* again, just to think that. But I was frightened, too—what if I were kidding myself? Or what if he weren't really serious? I might be letting myself in for a new hurt.

Actually he was far more serious than she, and he had his reasons:

It sounds absurd, but after she got out of that hospital and we'd spent just one whole evening together, I started to imagine how it would be, being married to her. If I'd met her a couple of years earlier, I wouldn't have had such thoughts at all. But I'd been on the loose for three years, and I was ready for it. I was tired of filling up evenings with things to do, tired of dating, tired of having to sell myself to new girls time and again. Tired of living for myself and not having anyone who cared, or about whom I cared. Tired of being an outsider—I felt I wanted to rejoin society.

The Winning. Before having a full-fledged love affair, many an FM has had to pass through a period of sexual rediscovery, a period of limited emotional relationships in which sexual intimacy comes about quickly and easily. But where there is a sense of great potential importance to a new relationship, even the veteran may be hesitant about rushing to bed, wanting it to be different this time—not just sensuous and satisfying, but expressive and deeply meaningful. He or she may hold back for a while, fearing that it might, after all, prove to be just like the others.

—Douglas Maclean and Joan Bishop kissed when they said goodnight, but nothing more, on three successive dates. On the fourth, they had dinner at his apartment, danced a little, lay down next to each other on the sofa, and began to neck like teen-agers. They grew silent and impassioned, and then chuckled at themselves for being so cautious, wondered aloud why they had not slept together yet, and joked about it; talked about whether to do so or not, and trembled as they talked. Finally, he stood up and led her gently by the hand into the bedroom. Hearts racing, they fumbled with their clothing and fell into bed, both of them chilled and nervous, neither of them at all ready. Maclean:

> We clung to each other and admitted how nervous we both were because it mattered so much. Oddly enough, we felt comfortable together even though we weren't ready to make love. Then we *were* ready, more or less, and did it—rather poorly, as a matter of fact, but afterwards we laughed and kissed and felt glad to have gotten past that first time. We did it again an hour later and that time it was better. She had promised her maid, who was baby-sitting, to be back by one A.M., but when she was getting up to leave we started all over again, and then it was really wild. When it was over, we were both saying "I love you" at the same time.

Falling in Love. Adults who are fifteen to twenty years beyond the romances of youth are astonished to find themselves feeling turbulent emotions they knew long ago; they strive to conceal these feelings from the rest of the world, but privately are proud of them and of the minor follies that are the by-product.

—Douglas and Joan both felt a pleasant confusion at their sudden emotions; both displayed symptoms ordinarily seen in the young. Joan:

I was overwhelmed to find myself—the mother of a ten-year-old daughter—feeling like a college girl again. Lying awake at night and thinking about him until all hours. Listening to sentimental ballads and having tears in my eyes, feeling my heart thump if I saw a car like his going down the street. Running for the phone every time it rang, like my life depended on it. Even writing poems again, and sending them to him between dates.

Douglas, for his part, started going to the gymnasium regularly, filled with the zealous intention of making himself perfect for her sake. He would awaken early and lie in bed, revelling in fantasies of what his life with her would be like. At the office he daydreamed a good deal, but turned out great amounts of work in a short time whenever he finally got started. He tried to find little surprises to bring her, and made up pet names for her, some of so saccharine a quality ("fawn-face") that he could use them only in private.

The little scenes and minutiae of love are different for every pair of lovers, and yet universal in their meanings. These are a few which Douglas and Joan later remembered with almost unbearable nostalgia: The evening she first sewed buttons on two of his shirts and her eyes filled with tears; he saw, and, infinitely touched, kissed her hands. . . . The night they romped in the snow like children, came home to her place cold and wet, built a fire and drank brandy, and later stole off to her bedroom although her daughter, Tina, was asleep in the next room. . . . The time they went to a party where all the other couples were married, and late in the evening someone who didn't know them pointed out genially that it was obvious they were the only unmarried couple, since they were the only ones holding hands. . . . The first weekend away together; the moment at dinner when they got giggly, wondering whether anyone else in the dining-room could look at them and know how they had spent the afternoon.

Commitment and Fidelity. Despite the blossoming of love, formerly married people are often fearful of committing themselves to each other fully, either in their emotions or their sexual life. They may continue to see other people for a while, and even to sleep with others; even if they do not, they reserve the right to do so, and admit to each other only after a while that they have dropped all other connections.

—Douglas was ready to commit himself long before Joan was. Time and again she would be overcome by anxiety and a sense of entrapment; usually these periods followed hard upon her having nearly committed herself to him:

> She and I had an absolutely beautiful time, that first weekend away together. We were so close that it seemed to me there were almost no problems left. Yet Monday, on the phone, she seemed preoccupied and a little distant. Same thing Tuesday and Wednesday, and when I tried to find out what was wrong, she got rather huffy. But finally she explained that after coming home from the weekend, she had a delayed reaction—she felt she had made me think she was fully committed to me, but she felt now that she still needed time, and room to breathe, and the right to be alone and free. It was hard for me to accept, but I had to—especially since I had done the same thing to two women the previous year.

Douglas had to pull back temporarily on his own commitment in order to rebalance the situation; he did this by dating other women from time to time, and even occasionally sleeping with one of them:

> When I fell in love with Joan, I had an attack of monogamy, and not only stopped dating anyone else but lost the old itch to be on the prowl. But after a couple of months, when it became clear she was still far from being able to make a real commitment, I'd wonder if I had been smart to cut off all my other connections. I'd sometimes phone up girls I knew, and occasionally go out with one or another of them. But I didn't seem to enjoy them the way I used to. I'm sure I only did it by way of revenge, and not by way of desire. One time I made a routine pass at a new girl and she was willing, and I had a difficult time going through with it, which wasn't like me at all.

Douglas and Joan were, in short, out of phase with each other, a situation common among lovers who are FMs and who are at different stages of their emotional reintegration. Yet Douglas recognized this fact, and even recalled an episode in his own life in which the same sort of thing manifested itself abruptly and destructively:

> A couple of years before all this, while I was waiting for my wife to sign the final papers and go to Mexico, I was seeing a lot of a girl named Bette, who was in love with me. I was fond of her, and during those weeks before the divorce I was nervous and needed her for comfort and reassurance. Then my wife got hepatitis and couldn't go, so I was the one who had to fly to Mexico. I felt strange about the trip and about the freedom I had wanted so long, and I told Bette that I wanted to go and come back, and not be met at the airport but just be by myself for a while. Well, I flew down, and went to court the next day, and then got on the plane, sort of numb and not sure of how I felt. I had two drinks on the plane, and flirted with a stewardess, and gradually felt better. And then when I got off, who was waiting for me at the exit gate but Bette? I knew I should feel touched and grateful, but I was annoyed and almost angry, and she wound up going home in tears that night. The affair was never any good after that. We saw each other a few times, but I found myself wanting to be free of her because she wanted us to be a thing and to get married, and I wasn't anywhere near ready for that.

The phase difference between Douglas and Joan was not this great, however, and after some months she slowly got over her feelings of entrapment. She ceased seeing any other men, and was able after a while to tell Douglas so. Having been the reluctant one, it embarrassed her to admit her own progress toward commitment, and she did so in her own indirect way: she asked him in which closet she could leave some clothes. She let him assume, without her protesting it, that they would spend every weekend together, and she began to use the word "we" instead of "I" in various social contexts. The evening on which she announced, "We've been invited to my folks' house for dinner next Sunday" marked the moment of full commitment.

Obstacles, Large and Small. The love affairs of the Formerly Married encounter more than the usual number of difficulties. For the lovers are not only formed rather than malleable, but are encumbered with the paraphernalia of their previous years and alliances. Some of the difficulties are overcome with ease, some with much pain, but many are not overcome at all—the typical affair, after all, does not end in marriage. Yet marriage is nearly always the implicit goal—and seen in that light, even minor differences or annoyances can easily become big ones as the lovers consider living with them permanently. The neat man can easily put up with the untidy woman until he weighs marrying her; then he may have grave doubts. The party-loving woman may not mind staying at home with the quiet man until she imagines it as a permanent pattern. A permissive parent can tolerate a disciplinarian as a friend and lover until it comes time to think of making a life together.

—Douglas and Joan realized slowly that they were profoundly different types of people; they had sensed something of this in the beginning, but then the differences seemed only intriguing. Douglas, a creative type, was high-strung and impulsive, free-spending, and impatient about details; Joan, despite her gentle manner and soft appearance, was controlled, practical, and conscientious. Their differences, rather than complementing each other, were so considerable as to become a source of mutual frustration. Douglas's view of it:

> At first we teased each other about the differences between us—
> like the way I kick out the covers and roll up in them while she
> likes to sleep with everything neatly tucked in. Or the way I
> throw dirty clothes on the floor while she has to put them into
> the hamper at once. Or the way I'm always late, especially if I'm
> wrapped up in some piece of work, while she's so on time about
> everything that you could set your watch by her. As I say, we

used to kid each other about all this, but after a while I began to think that these little things were the symptoms of two wholly unlike and conflicting philosophies of life. Or kinds of personality, if that seems less pretentious. And then there was a related and still bigger difference—my tendency to blow off in an argument and to be ready to forgive and love again five minutes later, compared to her tendency to close off and go cold, and not come back for a day or two, or even more. If I had married her in a rush, as I wanted to, we might have had a hard time working out our differences. Maybe we wouldn't have been able to. As it was, by the time we'd been going together for some months I began to feel we were so different that it would be a long and difficult fight. It bothered me terribly, because I'd been the one who was so eager all along, and she'd been hanging back, and here I was starting to have doubts and second thoughts.

Joan sees it in somewhat different perspective:

Doug was so persistent that I more or less forced myself to try a real relationship, to see if I couldn't live down my fears. I did get over the feeling of being trapped, but the longer we went together the more I came to feel that we were oil and water, and that we would never really adjust to each other. I could never depend on him to arrive on time—but he'd come full of apologies, and with a flower or something. After a while, you can get sick of that. When he was flying high, because of something exciting about his work, he'd be so charged up that he'd want to drag me around to bars or nightclubs until three or four in the morning, and would always be disappointed in me for not being able to match him. But when he was down, I couldn't get through to him at all, and sometimes he would hardly talk to me except in grunts all evening. All right, he's a creative type—but I'm artistic too, being a musician, and I never let myself act like that. Doug is a brilliant, charming, wonderful man, but he's also somewhat childish and immature, and I don't think he'll ever change. After a long while, I came to think I just couldn't live with that.

The Break-Up. The Formerly Married, having been through the experience of a disintegrating marriage, are already familiar with the process of break-up, and the anguish to be endured when it is prolonged. They are therefore very apt to want to break cleanly and swiftly, although very often one of the pair will not perceive that the break-up is real, and will try to hold on briefly, or will be afraid to let go and may try to continue the relationship in a less binding form. The one who wants the clean break is anxious to get through the period of transition as fast as possible, knowing from experience that he has resources not only within himself, but all around him. The one who tries to hold on, despite the fact that the affair is doomed, is not so much trying to salvage it as clinging to it out of desperation. Some begin looking around and dating other people before finally letting go of the old relationship, some deliberately postpone the break until after a holiday season or the summer, and some make the break but reach out for the other time and again. Joan, who had much less experience and sureness of herself than Douglas, reacted in this way. She explains:

We had more and more arguments about stupid little things, but I think we both knew we were feeling the big differences. One night we really pulled it all out in the open, and got to talking about the things that bothered us in each other. About one or two in the morning, Doug said maybe I'd rather not see him any more at all, maybe the whole thing was hopeless, and I said I thought he was right. We both became sad and tender, rather than angry, and he left. I cried for hours. A couple nights later I just couldn't stand it alone, after Tina was asleep, and I phoned him and bawled my eyes out, and he came rushing over and we sat up very late, holding on to each other and talking it over. For a week things seemed all right, and then we had another argument and another break. This time, I didn't get in touch with him for a week. But I felt lost—I had come to depend on this relationship, after fighting it in the beginning, and I was feeling terrible. I sent him another poem, scented with sachet, telling him how miserable I was, and he came by the next night with flowers. That time it lasted about three days. About

the fourth or fifth time we broke off—I can't remember which—
I forced myself not to do anything to start it up again. Doug
never made a move. I think he began running around with
other women as soon as we first broke up. It was a bad time
for me, but I wouldn't let myself give in any more. I despised
my own weakness for having done so.

Aftermath. Formerly married people usually have a brief
flare-up of the old separation symptoms—depression, insomnia,
loneliness, and the like—at the end of a love affair. Offsetting
the new sense of failure, however, is the recognition that they
have come through it before, adjusted, learned to make their
way, and found new partners and new love. The depression and
misery are therefore short-lived, compared to those which
followed the end of the marriage. And still there are many
things that remind them and stab them to the heart—the
waning light at the time of day when they would meet, the
gifts given during the affair that remind each one of the other.
Almost as trying is the task of telling one's friends and relatives, knowing that in their minds will be the unspoken comment, "What, not again!" Telling one's children can be even
worse; their hope was the greater, their disappointment the
harder to bear. But most of the Formerly Married know how
to live with all this, and recuperate fairly fast. Indeed, after
the first feelings of anger or hurt have subsided, they are very
likely to have a tolerant and kindly attitude toward each other,
and to speak well of each other to mutual friends. They have
learned, through experience, that people whose love does not
last are not so much guilty or imperfect as they are victims of
their own needs, and that the needs of two adult people seldom
dovetail perfectly.

—Douglas and Joan went through just such readjustments.
His was swift and rather easy, hers somewhat slower and more
difficult. She was quite right that he began dating at once and
consequently dulled the ache he might have felt; she, being not
only a woman but the less experienced of the two, languished

at home for two months until word got around that she was available again. But for a long while she would have bad spells; her very work induced them, since she had often played the piano for Douglas, and any Chopin Étude or Prelude that he had especially liked was enough, even when badly played by one of her pupils, to envelop her in gloom.

Half a year later all of that lay behind her, and she was able to speak of Douglas fondly and almost gratefully; late that summer she and he even met briefly at an outdoor concert, and rather than avoiding each other they chatted like two old friends, searching each other's eyes and looking at each other with guarded but unmistakable fondness. For by then each had a lasting respect for the other and for the affair that had ended; with the Formerly Married, the failures of their love affairs are often successes, since they frequently leave the lovers richer, wiser, and more nearly ready for the affair that will lead to marriage.

IV · *Love's Profit-and-Loss Sheet*

Love affairs, in all shapes, sizes, and degrees of intensity, play a central and commanding part in the way of life of the Formerly Married. Not only are they a major interest and aim of FMs, but by whatever name any one of them is called and whatever its limitations or duration, it is apt to be regarded as a meritorious experience. And this is so not only during its time, but afterwards; for the most part, FMs regard past love affairs as valuable and cherished episodes.

For to be in love, or to have been in love, is a badge of achievement. The man or woman who has been an FM for two or three years and not yet been even briefly in love feels embarrassed and defensive about it, while the man or woman who has known anything from a brief infatuation to a serious love will look back on the affair, after the subsiding of pain, with fondness and pride. Regret that an affair ended, or that its ending involved pain for one's self or the other person, is outweighed by a sense of gain; the experience of love, though it did not endure, is viewed as something of value.

In view of the fact that the formerly married person has lived through a failure of love in marriage, and been hurt by it, one would think that every further experience of love that fails to endure, or that dissolves in discord, would reopen the wounds of marital break-up and divorce.

And so it does, for a minority of the Formerly Married. A certain number of them are madly hopeful at the beginning of any new affair, and severely depressed when it falls apart or fails to measure up to its promise. Such people, when they think they have just found the "right" person, burst with the news and cannot keep from telling it to their friends all too soon; later, they are chagrined and ashamed to have to report that once again it was a mere chimera. An FM woman's friends may solicitously ask her how she is getting along with the new man in her life, but if she has already discovered that he is not her answer or she is not his, the question forces her to unmask and once again reveal what they regard as her emotional incompetence. It is the same with a man; he is deeply embarrassed to admit his new failure, and may adopt a tone of cynicism and self-mockery: "Well, I've done it again. Chalk up another mistake for me." After a while, they begin to think of themselves as ruined and beyond redemption; in despondent moments they say things such as: "I'm a lost cause. I give up on me." and "I'm so weary of failures that I don't even want to try any more."

In other times and places—the court of Louis the Fourteenth, for instance, or that of Elizabeth the First—a person who had just come to the end of a love affair would, despite pain, feel enriched for having had it; a love affair was a good thing in itself, and was not felt to be a waste of time and effort simply because it did not lead to something else. For most contemporary FMs, however, it is a means to an end; and especially for that minority of them who most desperately need to prove themselves emotionally competent, or who most seriously doubt themselves, any stopping short of the final goal is not construed to be a partial success but an ignominious defeat and a further descent into the abyss.

Yet this is the minority. A majority of the divorced remarry within five years of their divorces, and since nearly all of these people have one or more emotional relationships before doing so, it is evident that love affairs do not prevent marriage or cause FMs to abandon it as a goal.

On the contrary, for most formerly married people the love affair has important positive values that outweigh the negative ones of its ending. Like dating and casual sex experiences, it is restorative and reassuring, but more profoundly so than either of these. After the failure of a marriage—especially one that lasted a number of years—many a formerly married person feels that he has lost the capacity to love; then along comes a love affair, and he finds that it is possible to care again, that his feelings come to life, that the most treasured of his abilities, though it seemed dead, was really only dormant and can be reawakened. And having learned that he can love again, the FM realizes that there need be no such thing as one-and-only love, and that he bears within himself forever the capacity to care and to care again; once he knows that the springs have not dried up, but were merely blocked, he becomes ever more confident that he can survive future failures and go beyond them to future successes.

But this is only one way in which the personality is repaired by love affairs. Another is in the revaluation of one's self as a love object. The woman abandoned for someone else feels undesirable and unworthy of any man's love; but then, miraculously, some man does love her and desire her, and she rediscovers her own value. Even if the affair ends, she still realizes that she had been able to attract and win a man for a while, and that the self-contempt she felt right after her marriage must have been unwarranted. She knows that much in her is good, and hopes to find the way to make the most of it in the next relationship.

Sometimes the restorative effect of the affair is itself the reason the affair ends. There are FMs who, in the depths of self-doubt, appeal to the parental or supportive side of a potential lover; thus is a lopsided love born which heals the ailing one—and thereby extinguishes itself. A gifted commercial artist was so shaken by the failure of his marriage that he became a borderline alcoholic, lived in a dirty and disordered apartment, and had all but ruined his reputation by turning in poor work, usually late. A young woman who began an affair with him at this point was filled with reforming zeal: she cleaned his apartment, washed his clothes, and laundered his soul with alternating measures of flattery and scorn. After a while he was working well again, paying off his debts, and feeling creative, worthwhile, and successful. But such a man neither needed nor could feel love for a mother-figure, and though he did not deliberately cast her out of his life, his attitude toward her changed; on her side, she no longer had a child to care for, and her attitude toward him altered accordingly. The fire went out of their love, and by agreement they let go of each other with relatively little rancor. Within half a year or so, she had found another down-and-outer to succor, while he had remarried a much weaker and more dependent woman.

The love affair, besides having this healing effect, may also be helpful in a sustaining way. Though FMs think of the goal of the love affair as marriage, many an affair looked at in retrospect appears to have been valuable as an end in itself. To care for someone, even if imperfectly; to belong to someone, even if not completely; to share with someone, even with reservations; to have a warm sexual relationship, even if not a total emotional commitment—all these are comforting, life-enhancing, enriching; they prevent emotional atrophy.

Many FMs recognize this: they speak of past relationships

which "sustained" them, or enabled them to "carry through," or "gave life some meaning," or "supported me when I needed to have support." Sometimes such lovers expect no more of each other than this, but often one or the other expects everything and is disappointed; yet even the latter, when they look back on their lives as FMs at a later date, see the months and years during which they loved and were loved as the fruitful and valuable ones, and those during which they did not as a desert and a waste.

A third and perhaps even more valuable effect of the love affair is that it can bring to the FM emotional capabilities he did not previously have; it may broaden his personality, deepen his self-knowledge, enlarge his capacity for loving. The adolescent does not know how to love until he has tried and practiced loving, and even the adult, if he has known only the one full-scale emotional relationship of his marriage, may discover new dimensions of his being through love affairs. Many FMs testify to this:

> [F, 37] Beginning a short while after the divorce, I had a four-year affair with a man who could never marry me. But he taught me about myself—I discovered my real sexual capacity, my intellectual ability, my whole capacity to be a *woman*. Through him I found out what I could be in marriage—and now am, thank heaven.

> [M, 39] My wife and I had never been very confiding and intimate. She always held back, had something *private* about her. And I thought that was okay, but my second affair was a revelation—I learned how to be completely wrapped up in somebody who was totally open with me, so that everything I did and thought and everything she did and thought belonged to both of us. And I loved it.

When a marriage ends and the FM has an affair with someone very different, he discovers new, or at least latent, feelings and responses in himself that he never knew he possessed—some

of which may be far more gratifying than any he has known
thus far:

[M, 43] She was completely different from my wife—she was a
gentle, womanly, noncompetitive person, an old-fashioned sort
of girl, really. And I found out for the first time in my life how
good that made me feel—how much of an old-fashioned guy I
really was but had never let myself be. In the end, she went
back to her husband, but by then I had learned from her what
I really want and need in a woman.

[F, 39] My marriage was an "ideal" one except that we saw
very little of each other as he got busier and busier. He was
"doing it all for us," but in truth he couldn't stand intimacy.
And I thought all marriages were like that, and couldn't understand why I was so unhappy. Then I met the first of the two men
I have loved since, and learned about a completely different kind
of relationship—one of complete and total involvement with
each other. And that was what I had needed all along, without
knowing it. I would have married him, but along came the
second man, who was the same way but far more dynamic and
strong, and who won me away.

A love affair, in short, is sometimes a form of learning, and
can expand and modify the personality, carrying it far beyond
mere repair to a state of greater readiness for remarriage. The
affair may then end, but instead of turning the person away
from marriage, it leaves him or her further advanced toward
that goal and more familiar with the way. Some remarried
FMs attest to this in the most positive terms; here, for instance,
is a woman of fifty-nine—a researcher in psychology—looking
back a decade to a time shortly before she remarried:

I never flitted from one relationship to another, and each one
felt sound to me in its day. The last one before my present marriage continued for over five years and I believe that it prepared
me for my present marriage in a number of ways, including a
final break emotionally with my first marriage, and some learning about how to appreciate a relationship fairly far short of

perfection. The five-year relationship was ended by my decision to start having an affair with the man who is now my husband. It ended with mutual declarations of affection, esteem, and appreciation for the rewards reaped during those years. My ex-lover thought he wanted to marry me but I'm not sure he really did, and I certainly never wanted to marry him or I would have done so. Yet he gave me the stepping-stone to my present marriage.

Not all affairs have so happy a result. Yet when most of the love affairs of FMs are viewed in perspective, and detached from the tears and solitude, the sense of hopelessness and loss, that so often go with a break-up, they do appear to be generally beneficent. The Formerly Married are basically correct in their opinion about the merit of love affairs; they revivify, retrain, and humanize the FM, and prepare him or her for loving again in a more complete and perhaps more lasting fashion.

CHAPTER SEVEN

Unfinished Business

1 · *Marriage, Terminable and Interminable*

Ask a lawyer when divorce becomes final and he may say, "The moment the judge signs the decree," or perhaps, "One year after he signs the decree," depending on the state in which the court action is taking place. But ask an FM when his divorce will become final and he might well reply, "When I die."

Divorce, though it cancels the partnership of man and wife, never severs their relationship entirely. When two people have once been so joined, it is little wonder they are never fully separated afterwards. The experiences of marriage have created a million microscopic electrical contacts in the brain, and no judge's signature on a piece of paper can undo that multitude of connections; many of them, indeed, will endure until the current itself is turned off. Nor is divorce ever completely final as long as there exist between the ex-spouses practical bonds with emotional meanings—alimony, which continues the woman's dependence and the man's entrapment, and children, who, both in their flesh and in their everyday needs, indissolubly bind their parents.

Nearly all the Formerly Married therefore continue to be linked to their ex-mates—some very closely, others rather loosely—in a variety of ways. One may judge from the follow-

203

ing handful of examples how complicated and curious their unfinished business with each other can be.

—A quiet, dimly-lit Italian restaurant in North Boston; mid-afternoon. A couple in their early forties are finishing a very late and rather alcoholic lunch. Their conversation is low-pitched, but even from a distance the cashier can tell that it has oscillated wildly between damp sentimentality and blazing anger. At one moment they hold hands across the table, at another sit in stony silence avoiding each other's eyes. Three times she has bunched up her napkin and pushed back her chair, only to stay after all, dabbing at her eyes with a hand-kerchief; but at last she leaps up abruptly, almost knocking over her chair, and dashes outside with her coat over her arm, while he, beet-red, hastily pays the check and rushes out after her. A lovers' quarrel after a noontime tryst? Not quite. These two, married for fifteen years, were divorced when she fell in love with someone else—to whom she has now been unhappily married for three years. Her ex-husband, who let go of her only after strenuous efforts to hold on, is finally engaged in a new and promising love affair. They met today to discuss the chil-dren's summer camp plans, but the whiskey sours and the romantic atmosphere (they used to eat here in happier days) carried them back to old love and old anger. At last, having blurted out her unhappiness, she said she thought that they both still loved each other, that she had made a terrible mis-take, and that she would be willing to remarry him; when he tried to parry the suggestion tactfully, she grew pale and rigid, and took the occasion of the next item about the children— some trifle about his helping with their camp luggage—to be outraged and make her stormy exit.

—The living-room of a large colonial house near Washing-ton, D.C.; Christmas morning. Two frisky children and two beaming parents gather around the tree for the opening of the presents. Laughter, glad cries, sounds of admiration; much kissing, hugging, and smiling upon each other. Happy normal family? Not precisely. He and she have been separated for two years, are stalemated in their efforts to reach a divorce settlement, and are furious at each other. When they discuss such matters as alimony and joint property, she becomes glacial and self-possessed, he bellicose and frustrated, and recently they have had to communicate entirely through their lawyers. When he phones to arrange to visit the children, she sometimes even puts the maid on the phone to talk to him. Nonetheless, when they separated they agreed to keep Christmas inviolate, and to stage this peaceful loving scene for the children's benefit. Afterwards he will go home and get drunk, and she will take tranquillizers and aspirin; each will curse the very thought of Merry Christmas.

—A shabby rooming house in Manhattan's Greenwich Village; early evening of a winter weekday. A young woman carrying a shopping bag full of groceries climbs the stairs and opens an unlocked door; in the smoky, disordered room a haggard man lying glassy-eyed in bed waves one hand at her limply. She washes his face, gives him some pills, straightens his bed, makes soup and hamburger, and spoon-feeds him; then she tidies the room, kisses him, and leaves. Old friends? Sister and brother? Lovers? No: alcoholic ex-husband and guilt-ridden ex-wife. He became a chronic drinker during their marriage and she divorced him five years ago for the children's sake. But ever since then, when he has one of his periodic bad spells and is at the point of total collapse she is the one he calls to for help (his relatives live far away, his friends have given him up as hopeless). She struggles, protests, and always gives in, cancelling any plans she may have for the evening and leaving the children with the sitter while she hurries to nurse and feed him. From these encounters she returns home weary and depressed, her pleasure in having been a good Samaritan outweighed by her smoldering anger at being unable to cut the tie by which she is held captive.

—The office of Arnold Mitchell, a Hartford fuel-oil distributor; mid-morning, autumn. Mitchell closes the door for privacy and phones the wives of three old friends; with each one he first makes charming chit-chat, then gradually works the conversation around to the subject of his ex-wife, Nora. He asks each one if they have seen Nora recently (none has); then, in a laboriously jocular manner, he says he is a little worried about her, and asks if they won't call her sometime and try to get her to come out. In the four years since the break-up (which he wanted), he has remarried, and he and his new wife are frequent visitors to the homes of his old married friends; Nora, however, has hidden herself at home and alienated these friends by her chilly and contained manner. Although he feels nothing but a bland friendliness for her, it deeply troubles him that he has kept so many of their old friends while she has lost them, and he is concerned about her isolation and her emotional state. He wishes she would meet someone and remarry, not so much because he wants to be free of the alimony payments (which he can afford) but because he would like to be free of the burden of worrying about her.

An old English folk-song gives the very best of advice on this whole subject:

> It is good to be merry and wise,
> It is good to be honest and true,
> It is best to be off with the old love,
> Before you are on with the new.

But like so much of the very best advice, it is more easily given than followed; many of the Formerly Married have great trouble carrying it out, and some, to their own harm, never do so at all.

II · The Persistence of Love

Fragile as new love may be, old love is a hardy plant; even though crushed and broken, it lingers on and refuses to die. Outsiders have little idea how often the old love endures in one form or another in the hearts of FMs—even those who wanted to escape—and continues, long after the break-up and the divorce, to impede their readjustment to their new lives.

Those of whom this is true try to hide the remnants of the old love not only from most other people but even from themselves, for to continue loving the former mate is to cast doubt on the validity of one's separation or divorce. But love will show itself nonetheless, in many a fashion:

—A man who unwillingly separated from his wife a year ago, professing the deepest love for her, has gradually grown cold and hostile toward her, and has adjusted enough to his situation to have had several brief affairs. Yet when he comes to dinner on his little daughter's birthday, his hands tremble in his wife's presence, his upper lip is beaded with sweat, his eyes meet hers and shift away uncomfortably. Despite his discomfort, he stays on, enjoying his own misery, long after it would be appropriate for him to leave.

—A frail, gentle woman, married to a bully who belittled her unmercifully and sometimes punched her in the face, divorced him at long last a year ago, and believes that she harbors only hatred and contempt for him. Yet when she hears through a friend that he invited a score of people to drop by on New Year's Eve and only one showed up, she is sickened with embarrassment on his behalf.

—A man who broke up with his wife four years ago after a long period of fierce quarrelling sees her one evening at a nightclub, and on an impulse dances with her; that night he cannot sleep for thoughts of her, and is so annoyed at himself that he cuts himself shaving in the morning and tangles bumpers with another car while driving to work.

—A woman whose husband divorced her two years ago now realizes, thanks to psychotherapy, that the marriage was bad, and is glad it ended; each week, however, when her husband brings the children home from their Sunday with him and then leaves, she feels deserted all over again and has a spell of depression and sometimes a fit of tears.

Even these symptoms are trifling in comparison to the most

common one of all: a tendency, on the part of the person who was originally reluctant to separate, to clutch the other afterwards with a drowning swimmer's stranglehold. Some people, in the effort not to fully lose the partner they still love, obstinately refuse to discuss the terms or even the subject of a legal agreement or the divorce suit. Others enter into such discussions but prolong them indefinitely; they delay each meeting, arrive late and argue endlessly over each detail, explode into unwarranted rages and storm out. Popping up with new issues when the old ones have been resolved, they manage to forestall the legal ending of the relationship. A young woman trying to wrest a divorce from her husband speaks:

> Some days I just feel so hopeless about it. A year and a half has passed and he's still making every possible kind of delay. First he ignored my lawyer's letters for a year until we threatened court action. Then he finally showed up and made long abusive speeches about every point. We've had four or five meetings like that over the last half year, and made almost no progress at all. He just won't let go. And at least two or three times a month he hints that I ought to take him back. I suppose you could say that he still loves me in some peculiar way.

Other formerly married people hold on to their ex-mates in pacific and seemingly benign ways; even these, however, are hurtful—especially to the one holding on, whose progress in reconstructing his life is stalemated as long as he clings to the remnants of the old relationship. Some, for instance, reluctantly agree to a *de facto* separation and work out temporary terms without much unpleasantness, but balk at signing a legal separation agreement embodying the very same terms; some sign an agreement but indefinitely postpone the divorce; and still others do go through with the legal divorce, accepting all its external changes without ever admitting that love has fled.

The stigmata of this state of heart are not hard to discern. One woman, long separated from her husband, invites him to have a drink when he brings their children home from a

Sunday outing, shows him the latest dress she bought, coyly mentions that the vacuum cleaner isn't working and perhaps he'd be a dear and look at it since he's so handy with such things. Another, divorced for six years and still unremarried, occasionally borrows her husband's station wagon, asks his advice about her investments, and often calls to pass on news of mutual friends. Men do similar things, though perhaps less often. One man, divorced for a dozen years (and since remarried and divorced again) recently asked his first wife to help him decorate a new apartment. Another, separated from his wife for two years, phoned her when he broke his leg skiing and needed some weeks of nursing; she took him in and housed him in the spare room, where she and the housekeeper tended him until he was able to get around.

Children provide the man or woman who is still emotionally dependent upon the ex-mate with a useful mechanism for holding on. Some women telephone their ex-husbands once or twice a day to discuss the most trifling problems ("There's a special on ice-skates this week, but do you think I ought to put the money into it now or make him get along with the present pair until next fall?"), or to report some minor episode ("I don't want to interrupt you at whatever you're doing, but I simply must tell you the marvelous thing Jenny said just now when I was putting her to bed"), or to confer about some minuscule problem ("How *are* we going to get that boy to keep his room straightened up?"). Others—men and women alike—invent or imagine behavior problems that demand frequent and intimate consultation. Education, from nursery school to college, is a practically inexhaustible source of calls for conferences or get-togethers, and affords the ex-spouse who is trying to cling not only ample opportunity to do so, but the camouflage of a noble motive.

FMs of certain categories seem especially likely to remain bound by unexpired love. Those who assented unwillingly to separation or divorce may be very angry, but they continue to yearn for the ex-spouse longer than those who desired the break-up. Not surprisingly, people who were married a long while generally miss each other more, and maintain more contact with each other, than those who were married briefly. People who have had little chance to meet new partners or who are insecure and afraid to try to meet others, tend to have strong ties to the ex-spouse. The task of emotional disconnection is arduous for everyone, but more so for the insecure and the long-married than for the self-confident and those who were married only briefly. Until that task is carried out, they are likely to remain trapped in the old love and unable to move toward or succeed in a new one.

Left-over loving feelings for the ex-mate frequently include erotic desires. It may not seem remarkable that these should exist for a short while after the break, nor that in a fair number of cases there are actual episodes of love-making between husbands and wives during the first few weeks or months after their separation. But it may seem more surprising that with some FMs this happens over many months or even years. From time to time, a man and his estranged wife may meet privately to discuss, say, sending their child to their grandmother for a month in the summer; if either or both of them have failed to resolve the old feelings and to establish a new love-relationship, the meeting is almost bound to have a faint but unmistakable aura of temptation. One or both may start acting toward the other in an old, long-abandoned fashion: she may be gay, charming, ultra-feminine, he may be courteous, gallant, warm. A bittersweet game gets under way, its moves being fond allusions, private recollections, unwonted compliments, sentimental regrets. There may even come a warm and sympathetic touch which, if more than momentary, can precipitate a sudden embrace and kiss, a jubilant feeling that all is possible, a rush of belief that the past can be recaptured. They know the feel, the smell, the taste of each other so well, have missed it so long, that they savor it all the more now; they fly to bed, devour each other, cling closely for a brief while, and then, in the subsequent calm, discover that nothing has been solved, that they are the same two people they were, and that they have betrayed their own weaknesses and revealed what they meant to hide.

But it does not always turn out that way; some of these moods and episodes lead to reconciliations or remarriages. The chance of reconciliation is greatest when the separation is new; it decreases with the passage of time and the FM's progress toward emotional divorce and readjustment. But for those FMs who avoid the work of emotional divorce or who fear to take active steps toward making a new life, the passage of time makes little difference; a return to the ex-spouse is an ever-present possibility. Even after divorce suits have been filed, one out of four couples change their minds and withdraw them. Of those who go through with divorce, about one out of ten who have not yet remarried would at least consider remarriage to the ex-spouse. According to one estimate, as many as one out of every fifteen pairs of divorced husbands and wives actually do remarry each other after spending an average of three years divorced. But for a majority of these, it would have been better to break the ties and seek love elsewhere: Dr. Paul Popenoe, who studied a group of 200 remarriages to the original spouses, found that less than half of the people were happy the second time.

It is self-evident that wives are more often financially dependent upon their husbands than self-supporting; this necessarily produces, or goes hand in hand with, a feeling of emotional dependency. After separation or divorce, women who are in the midst of raising children usually need alimony as well as child support; it is a rare and gifted woman who can earn enough to support herself and at the same time be an unharried homemaker and mother. But alimony, though it may be necessary, keeps the woman both practically and emotionally bound to her ex-husband. If he should default or be tardy, or unilaterally decrease the payments, she always has recourse to the courts, but this is a slow and disagreeable way to get her money; many a woman therefore tries to keep on good terms with her ex-spouse, and is concerned lest he be displeased with the way she is raising the children, living her life, or spending what he provides, even as if she were still his wife. She may unconsciously regard the alimony as a limited form of love: each week or month when the check arrives she is glad to see it—realistically, because she needs the money, but unrealistically, because it represents a continuing remnant of his former responsibilities to her, and symbolizes the love that created them. To the extent that this is true, the alimony hinders her growth and development toward freedom, and makes her cautious about each new relationship—particularly when any one of them reaches the point of a crucial decision between the sure and reliable ex-husband, and the uncertain future with a new man.

A childless woman, if she wants to escape from the marriage, rarely asks for or is awarded alimony; if it is her husband who wants to get out, however, she can almost always exact up to a third of his income as the price for letting him go and simultaneously as a way of continuing to hold him. But she pays a cost as well as he, for in an era when women pride themselves on being the equals of men, it is demeaning to take money from a man merely because one has been his wife. The ex-wife has to invent or rationalize a need, in order to assuage her own guilt and self-contempt. "Harry and I are very fond of each other," one such woman explains. "He knows I could get only a secretarial job, and would live a hard life. He wouldn't want that—after all, we did love each other for a long while." If alimony can be one cause of continuing emotional entanglement with the ex-husband, it is the law itself that puts this dangerous mechanism in the hands of women. Only two states—Pennsylvania and New Hampshire—make alimony temporary, and in New Hampshire this applies only to childless wives; all the other states allow permanent alimony to be part of the divorce settlement, at least until the woman remarries. In some states, even remarriage does not automatically end alimony; the ex-husband must apply to the court to terminate it, and a few courts have occasionally refused to grant an end to alimony even then.

Whatever the reason for continuing emotional dependency, the spouse who feels it is apt also to have feelings of continuing ownership of the other and wishes for reconciliation, although usually without being aware of the existence of either. Such emotions manifest themselves in many ways. One is a compulsion to intrude upon the private life of the ex-mate: some women, for example, regularly telephone their ex-husbands in the evening on various matters, and some make such calls quite late, as though determined to interrupt any intimate situation that might be developing.

The existence of hidden feelings of proprietorship and wishes for reconciliation often becomes suddenly apparent when the incompletely emancipated spouse hears that the other is deeply involved with someone, or is remarrying. Men are sometimes taken aback by the wave of jealousy or anger that washes over them, but women, their dependency so often increased by alimony, are far more apt to feel it, and in more intense form. On one level, they fear the potential loss of their support: they no longer feel sure of the money, and they worry that their husbands, with other loyalties, will start to delay or hold back the payments, or will apply to court for a reduction. On another level, they feel that some part of their ex-husband's remaining loyalty has been stolen from them—that he has finally become someone else's emotional possession. One woman, writing to her former spouse before his wedding, summarized both feelings in this brief note: "I want to wish you and your new bride every happiness, and since she's taking so much that was mine, I hope you won't let her take anything else that is still rightfully mine because it's all that I have left."

Alimony aside, ex-wives may be quite dismayed at the emotions that overcome them upon receipt of such news:

[F, 43] A note of congratulations to him and his new wife came to me by mistake—that's how I learned he had remarried. I felt great anger, and was sick clear to my soul. Yet as far as I knew I had had no intention or even the slightest wish to go back to him, after what had happened between us.

[F, 34] I was simply furious. I felt I'd been *displaced*. This was really astonishing to me, because we hadn't seen each other in two years, and I wouldn't have had that sicknik back in my life for anything.

Men too have similar feelings, even if not as often:

[M, 48] I ran into her at a big country club dance, where I came alone. She was hanging on this guy's arm and looking up at him adoringly, making a real show of herself. When she saw me, she brought him over and introduced him, and said he was her fiancé. I congratulated both of them, of course, but I felt like all the zip had gone out of me. It was very strange—I didn't want her back, but it made me feel rotten that she was in love and I was not. I belted a few down, and then, not wanting her to see me acting half-stoned, I left the dance early and went home.

Such reactions, though painful, are probably salutary; they are an awakening to reality, a clear call to complete the work of inner rehabilitation that should have gone hand-in-hand with the process of getting legally divorced, and without which a deeply satisfying relationship with someone new is unlikely to develop.

But until such a relationship does materialize, even the liberated ex-spouse is not truly free, for although the bonds of old love in him are severed, he or she is still bound to the other by other bonds of pity and guilt. A happily remarried woman, quoted in Clifford Kirkpatrick's book, *The Family*, poured out this confession:

To go through a divorce you must have no sensitivity, no sympathies and be generally callous. . . . I am sick at heart many times about Tom [her ex-husband]. I feel like a murderer and I worry about him. Sounds idiotic but it's true. We weren't happy the way things were, but tragically, he is the type of man who has no friends, no interests and is too reserved and diffident to do anything about it. Life is a queer complex mess and I guess I'm one of the queerest specimens around. All the same that's the way it is. I hope against hope that he'll find a way to be happy.

But it is more often the male who feels like this, since the ex-wife is commonly less free, less easily able to spend time in new relationships, and generally more troubled by the passage of time and the slow shrinkage of the prospect for future happiness. The man, even though he may be happily remarried, continues to inquire about her life and her mood from friends or the children; he would rather not know, but cannot stop himself from finding out, even as the tongue that should stay away from a sore place in one's gum involuntarily returns to probe it again and again. He hears that she is lonely, or ill, or has been having trouble with the furnace, or is worried about a prowler in the neighborhood; he tells himself it is none of his concern, yet he cannot help feeling he ought to do something for her, and he often does. To the new woman in his life, the former wife is an ever-present specter haunting her marriage. How is she ever to be completely sure of his love? Is there not some private understanding, some secret inviolable pact, between him and his ex-wife that lasts forever, despite his new love? No, not forever; but it may be so until his former spouse is happily remarried. Until then, she is always a threat, or at the very least an emotional tax upon his new love, taking a tithe from the new tenant of his heart.

III · *The Persistence of Anger*

In an earlier chapter we saw that much of the anger felt by man and wife prior to their separation was mobilized to help cut the major ties of habit and affection holding them to a relationship that had grown intolerable. For a minority of separating husbands and wives, anger diminishes rapidly almost as soon as one of them moves out; these are people who were not very thoroughly joined, and for whom the separation marked the virtual end of the process of detachment. They are lucky: it did not hurt very much. Or perhaps they are unlucky: it did not matter much.

For the majority of separating couples, however, there is a great deal of disconnecting yet to be done after physical separation. The need for anger continues, though now they shift its locus; they no longer fight on the field of intimate personal behavior and feelings, but on more externalized battlegrounds —the division of possessions, the question of money, and the terms of control over, or the right to visit, the children. They may have made some temporary arrangements about these matters, but as soon as they begin trying to reach an agreement on final, legally enforceable terms they find themselves—to their own surprise—engaged in a series of nasty and frequently vicious fights over issues they had expected to resolve without difficulty.

Is this inevitable? Cannot sensible, decent people, agreeing to terminate a partnership of love that no longer works, do so without being combative, cruel, or vindictive? They themselves ask the question, almost plaintively: "We *can* be civilized about all this, can't we?" Yes, some can, but all too often such self-imposed civility is a pyrrhic victory over their essential human nature. For anger, if choked back and denied, can poison the heart and produce a host of long-lasting psychological ills, can corrode and sicken the body in scores of ways ranging from migraine headaches to perforating duodenal ulcers.

Thus, to allow one's self to feel anger and to express it in the form of petty quarrels over details of the divorce settlement is more healthful than to deny those feelings or hide them behind a rigidly smiling mask of civility. In nearly every dissolving marriage, each partner is in part the rejecter, in part the rejected; each is therefore bound to the other by guilt and suffering, as well as by residual love. Anger breaks strand after strand of this malignant web of feelings; the barbed words, vengeful acts, absurd little cruelties, all set the two people free. They will be decent to each other later on by virtue of having been temporarily vicious to each other; they will be able in the end to act civilized by virtue of having acted for a while like primitives.

But in the throes of the struggle one does not know all this, or knowing it, feels none the better for it. "How could he be so hateful?" a woman asks her closest friend, "how could he have changed so completely?" "I lived with her all those years," says an embittered man to his lawyer, "and never saw her for what she is." Friends and lawyers, if they have seen all this before, know that in time it will pass, and that some day the two will be unsure just what they found so contemptible and dreadful in each other; if one tells them so now, they will not believe it, or believing it, will still be unable to behave differently.

And they do behave extraordinarily unlike their usual selves —and the more absurd and ugly the behavior of each, the more the other is horrified, enlightened, and curiously pleased. Two who spoke millions of words to each other, ate thousands of meals together, drank in each other's breath and tasted each other's sweat, seem to see each other revealed at last—hideous and abhorrent. Each is not only infuriated by the other's words and deeds, but perversely gratified at the vindication they afford. And no wonder they are amazed and outraged at each other, for see how some of them act:

—A young woman who never even stole candy as a child, or cheated on a test in school, phones the broker while her husband, from whom she has been informally separated some months, is out of town; she orders their entire joint stock portfolio sold and the check sent to her, and deposits the money— the bulk of their savings—in a secret account.

—A scholarly mathematician, who has been unable to get his wife to conclude a legal separation agreement for fifteen

months, uses a pass key to enter the house while she is away
for the weekend, and strips it of a truck-load of costly china,
sculpture, antiques, paintings, and oriental rugs.

—A woman whose husband moved out seven months earlier
gets a call from him; he says he needs to come pick up his
summer clothes, which are still stored in a trunk in the attic.
They argue about money (he has sent neither child support
nor alimony for three months), and he refuses to do anything
about it until she agrees to a divorce. When he calls for his
clothes, the door is locked but a note says that his clothes are
out back; in the yard he finds them lying in a heap beside the
garbage can, every garment slashed with a pair of scissors.

—A bank manager of impeccable upbringing, separated
from his wife for a year, still has her front-door key and sometimes drops by unannounced; if she and the children are out,
he enters and snoops around, reading mail and looking for
clues as to her personal life. She changes the lock on the door;
he thereupon pounds a wooden match into the keyhole, jam-
ming the lock, and tells her he will do it again as often as she
has it repaired until she gives him a new key and stops trying
to lock him out.

Such physical barbarities are fairly common, but because
they involve destruction, waste, or illegal acts, they are generally disapproved of, even within the ranks of the permissive
subculture. Yet the divorce process does require ways of expressing and working off anger, and the subculture has had
to develop an ethic of sorts, setting acceptable boundaries to
irate behavior. It is considered perfectly reasonable to fight
over possessions, for example, but not to destroy them, since
even an unfair distribution is better than total loss. A woman
who threw a diamond brooch down the sewer rather than give
it back to her husband (it had been his mother's) lost the
respect even of fellow-FMs; if she had refused him the divorce
he wanted until he agreed to pay on exorbitant amount of
alimony, they would have felt she played the game hard but
according to the rules. Again, it is held legitimate to fight about

the children—but not let them witness the fights, nor to use them as combat troops. A man who kidnapped his children from his wife's home and hid out with them for a week in a nearby town was condemned by all who knew him; if he had hidden all his assets in an out-of-state bank and withheld alimony and child support from her until she agreed to more generous visitation terms, he would have met little criticism.

But even within such limits, the angers generated during the post-separation period often become too intense for the man and woman to handle by themselves. For it is not enough only to fly apart from each other; the legal dissolution of marriage requires cooperation as well as antagonism. When they lived together, there was still enough love to carry them on beyond each quarrel, and to work out the details of any disputed matter; now there is not, and usually they need outside supervision and refereeing to help them complete the details of dissolution. Enter the lawyers, therefore—in part as experts in framing an agreement and as representatives in divorce court, but also in large part as intermediaries who can transmit hostility at one remove, sometimes damping it down and sometimes fanning it, but always keeping the process of divorce going to its necessary conclusion.

On the surface this process is concerned with questions of law and finances, rights and requirements. It takes the familiar form of conferences between lawyer and client, and lawyer and lawyer, the rough-drafting of terms by one side and the outraged rejoinder by the other, the counter-offer and revised draft, the fresh demands and new outraged replies, the interminable business of haggling over details, quibbling over wording and swapping of quid-pro-quos, and finally the grim meeting of all parties in one lawyer's office to sign the final draft of the agreement. Meanwhile, below the surface something far more important is going on; the legal procedure is achieving the emotional dismantling of the marriage, for the negotiations are a crude therapeutic experience, a mechanism through which residual feelings are worked out and disposed of.

As a therapeutic mechanism, it has distinct defects and limitations: lawyers are not therapists, after all, and the law was not designed to help people with their emotional problems. In nearly every state, the advantage lies largely with the reluctant party; unless both people are equally anxious to dissolve the marriage, the one who is more eager to do so very often pays a heavy penalty because it is the only way he or she can get out. Conversely, where one partner feels vindictive, and has a grievance which is a legal ground for divorce, he or she can take vengeance in the negotiation process.

The negotiations are thus an imperfect therapeutic mechanism, but in the majority of cases, where there is no extreme leverage on either side, an immensely effective one. A large part of the haggling, for instance, involves money and property, and unconsciously using these as symbols, the man and woman carry on their task of emotional disconnection and the working-out of their feelings. A man whose wife undercut his manliness at home gets the chance to play the man with money, by refusing to give her more than the very minimum she would be able to get in a court fight. (Both lawyers always use the realities of court fights as the base on which to argue, though neither wants to go to court.) And a woman whose husband was domineering and belittling gets the chance to assert herself at last by insisting on complete control over money to be spent on the children, and setting very strict visitation terms.

Other people purge themselves of crippling feelings by the haggling process: a man who loves another woman, and is filled with guilt for leaving his wife, is outraged at the alimony she and her lawyer are demanding, and his outrage largely neutralizes and washes away his sense of guilt. A woman still deeply in love with her husband becomes so revolted by his stinginess in the dickering over child support and personal property that she comes to despise him and to feel glad she is rid of him.

Meanwhile, although the major action, during this period, has shifted to the lawyers' offices, the former spouses may continue to engage in a certain amount of hand-to-hand combat, each finding ways to vex the other, each coming to see the vexatious opponent in his or her "true colors." The husband may have been regular all along in sending his wife the informally agreed-upon alimony or child-support payments, but now he may begin to send it late, without explanation, in order to worry her, or may reduce it occasionally by a third or a half with the excuse that taxes are currently due or that he has had a slow month. She, on the other hand, may decide to go in for expensive dental rehabilitation, or to begin four-times-a-week psychoanalysis, or to order a series of repairs to the house or car, for all of which he will have to pay—unless it was she who deserted him—until he is legally relieved of responsibility for her debts by the signing of a separation agreement.

But outside of the negotiations it is the children who offer the richest opportunity for waging the emotional war, since the husband and wife have to be in frequent contact about the children's day-to-day life. This gives them innumerable chances to lash out at each other while maintaining the unassailable stance of selfless parental concern; the wife, in the following telephone conversation, gives a faultless demonstration of the technique:

She: Well, I'd think you'd want your children to go to camp this summer for their health, if for no other reason.

He: But I can't afford it. I'm supporting all of you, and also living in a place of my own, and —

She: Whose fault is that?

He: Look, let's not start that again. I—

She: But you want to penalize your children for something that isn't their fault.

He: I'm *not* penalizing them, I just can't *afford* it!

She: If you shout, I'm afraid I'll have to hang up. Can't you just talk calmly about this?

He: Oh God. . . .

Others play the game even more brutally: One man tells his
wife each week at what hour he will be bringing the children
home, but sometimes gets them back punctually and other
times is anywhere up to three or four hours late; this not only
worries her, but effectively wrecks her plans to use the time
for herself, and no amount of pleading and cajoling on her
part does any good ("But the kids were having such a marvelous time with me—wouldn't you agree that it's important
for them to have a good relationship with their father even if
he *is* the villain?"). Or one may strike at the other with complaints about his or her performance as a parent:

He: I can't understand your letting a child of six stay up so late
watching TV. She looks awful. And are you giving her the
vitamins the doctor suggested?

She: She told me she saw a lady's bathrobe and some dresses
hanging in a closet in your house. I will not have her visiting you if she's going to see that sort of thing. My lawyer
says I can make a case of it.

He: What in hell has that got to do with her getting enough
sleep and food?

She: Just don't forget what I said.

Still other people, in the grip of their anger, lose perspective
so far as to use the children as front-line troops in their combat
with each other. This is tragic because the children very often
know it (more than half of the children of divorce, in one
survey, said they had been "used" by their parents against
each other) and are psychologically wounded by the experience. One seemingly innocuous practice that children perceive
and are often harmed by is to make them act as couriers and
spies. A father may offhandedly question his children about
the men their mother is seeing, or how she is spending her
money, or whether she ever stays out overnight; he thinks he
is doing no harm, but all except the youngest children sense
what is happening and feel guilty for telling him—or for not

telling him. A woman may use her children as a vehicle for transmitting her contempt or anger to her husband, since everything she says to them gets reported to him, but the guiltless messenger is harmed more by the poisoned message than the one it is intended for. One woman, for instance, told her children that their father obviously doesn't love them because he deserted them all and provides her very little money for the family. She succeeded in her purpose so well that his visits with them have been sheer misery ever since because they are so sullen and hostile; what she did not expect is that the children themselves would become self-doubting and insecure, extremely demanding of her, and difficult and provocative in school. Still others set their children against their ex-mates by meddling with or contradicting their child-rearing procedures ("I don't care what your Mother says about bedtime. A child shouldn't be forced to go to sleep. You just stay up until you feel like going to bed, and that's all there is to it. And you can tell her I said so"). Such children look forward with apprehension to their weekly visits with Daddy, sensing the trouble it will cause; they enjoy themselves while with him, but return home tense, tearful, and rebellious, and often it takes a full day before they can again accept life with their mother. She, meanwhile, is made doubly miserable—on one level by their tears and tantrums, on another level by the message of anger which they have brought from him.

All these indignities and wretched emotions might be tolerable if they would run their course and then be done with. But an unhappy minority of the Formerly Married do not seem to use up their anger or hatred; long after the separation, and even beyond the final legal divorce itself, they feel just as bitter as they did shortly after the parting. A midwestern salesman feels this way seven years after leaving his wife:

I hate her more now than ever, because what with alimony and child support I can't live a decent life. Meanwhile she's screwing around and having a fine time, on my money. She's a leech.

She's living off me, and enjoying it all the more because it makes my life miserable.

Three years after leaving her husband, a woman in Detroit still talks about him in this fashion:

He and I despise each other so much that we can't speak a sentence to each other on any subject. We discuss everything through lawyers or through my maid. I only wish I could do something to really *hurt* him. My one consolation is that it must really kill him when he has to write out that check every month.

Such continuing anger is probably more frequent among those who did not want the divorce, but were forced into it, than among those who divorced willingly or even eagerly. Since women are more frequently the reluctant ones (even though in the end they are the plaintiffs in over seventy per cent of the divorce actions), one finds intense unabated anger among FM women more than among FM men. It is also statistically evident that the unremarried feel antagonism toward their ex-mates longer than those who have remarried.

For some of these, the negotiation process failed to dispose of their hostility; the agreement reached only perpetuates their ill-will. A woman who has not worked through her feelings is insulted anew each month when she receives the check from her ex-husband because it is no larger; a man who is still angry at his wife is infuriated each month when he writes the check because it is so large. They use alimony and other elements of the agreement as a device to hurt each other in many ways, year after year; in particular, they threaten each other with changes in the terms, the man holding back money, or the woman going to court again and again to seek more. They continue to harass each other through the children, forever being obstreperous about arrangements for visiting, forever arguing over decisions on education, vacations, or religious training. And some achieve remarkable victories against each other in this endless war:

[M, 49] By now my older boy—he's fifteen—won't talk to me at all. She's convinced him over the past five years that I am a thoroughly bad and selfish man. He feels I did her a rotten trick in leaving her. He has no idea of my side of things, and I can't tell him because he just looks through me when I go there, and never talks to me. He hasn't even said hello to me for the past year. I recently yelled at him and said he couldn't behave like that toward his father, and he just walked out and slammed the door. I've pleaded with her to do something, but she just gives me that thin little puritan smile and says that if you sow the wind you reap the whirlwind.

This is her ultimate retaliation, her final victory; apparently she does not see that the truly punished and vanquished one is not her ex-husband, but her hapless son.

IV · *The Nearly-Final Divorce*

Happily, only a minority of the Formerly Married remain enchained by continuing love or unresolved anger. For most people, the residual love is gradually burned away by the flaring angers—which then die away after their necessary function has been performed. But the difficult period sometimes seems endless, while they are in its midst. It is hard to be content with gradual progress when what one desires is immediate surcease; like the patient having a tooth drilled by his dentist, one simply wants it to be over with. Yet the struggle must continue until the work is done; the intolerable delays and excessive demands made by one partner or the other do not always indicate a malevolence of spirit, but rather an unreadiness to be uninvolved. Yet eventually there comes a turning-point, by which time the more offended one has dealt enough blows to feel somewhat assuaged, the more offending one has been scourged enough to cease feeling unduly guilty, or, if they parted by mutual desire, each has been both scourger and scourged, each has been punished and released.

For some FMs, there is no perceptible turning-point; it seems to them that the longings and regrets slowly dwindle, the clashes gradually grow fewer and mild, and they begin without design, to be civil and even amiable to each other. For most, however, a turning-point does exist, and is the obvious one—the signing of a document ending the legal hostilities; this more or less coincides with and symbolizes the end of the major period of emotional disengagement.

In most states, that document is the divorce decree; in some, however, where divorce law is particularly difficult, or long delays are involved, it may be a separation agreement signed by the husband and wife well in advance of filing for divorce, or while waiting for the court to process and hear the divorce suit. In the difficult states many a husband and wife will sign an agreement and remain in that status for months or years until one or the other can make the trip to Idaho, Nevada, or Mexico, where divorce law is liberal and the time-requirement brief.*

Much newspaper space is devoted to those flamboyant and embarrassing divorce suits in which one spouse makes gaudy charges and the other makes equally gaudy charges in return. But this is really quite rare, occurring only where there is a grave emotional impasse or where a great deal of money is at stake. Similarly, both in fiction and non-fiction there has been much emphasis on the harrowing aspects of the divorce trial, especially the need to testify in open court as to the intimate details of one's married life. This, too, is greatly exaggerated; virtually all the emotionally painful work of divorcing has, as we have seen, preceded the couple's appearance in court, and

* Such use of separation agreements and out-of-state divorces was particularly common in New York, which had the most restrictive divorce law of any state until the enactment of a new one in April, 1966. Idaho and Nevada, as nearly everyone knows, will grant a divorce after only six weeks' residence; in Mexico a single day will suffice. Fiction and drama have, however, exaggerated the frequency with which Americans use "migratory divorce"; no more than three to five per cent of all American divorces are obtained by temporary residence outside one's own state.

what happens there is nearly always a mere formality, exceedingly unpleasant in itself but routine and brief. As already mentioned, in an estimated ninety per cent of divorce suits in the United States the husband and wife, with the aid of their lawyers, have worked out the practical aspects of the divorce privately before coming to court; in court the plaintiff, uncontested, tells the judge whatever the lawyer has instructed him or her to say, adapting the truth freely to fit the legal grounds allowable in that state. The judge, well aware of all this, plays his part in the charade and incorporates the agreed-upon terms in the decree he grants. The fact that all this works, more or less, is no justification for the existing divorce laws, most of which create needless hardships and inequities, and breed disrespect for the law; fortunately, there is now considerable sentiment in legal and judicial circles for divorce-law reform.

For most people, the signing of the decree—the turning-point in the process of emotional disengagement—is slow in coming. The length of time elapsing from the act of physical separation to the granting of the divorce varies widely from state to state, the averages in different areas ranging anywhere from over a year to more than three years. Actually, where the law's delay is long and the terms have already been worked out by the lawyers, the emotional turning-point probably comes well before the actual divorce; a reasonable guess would be that the average time required for the work of emotional divorce is between one and two years.

This is surely a long while to endure such discomforts, but it took time to construct so complicated a relationship, and it takes time to disassemble it. If husband and wife were to agree, in advance to submit to terms decided by an impartial expert, the financial and child-rearing aspects of divorce might be far more swiftly and fairly worked out, leaving the ex-mates plagued with unexpired affections and angers which would make the signed agreement an ineffective instrument of peace.

The painful and protracted process of emotional divorce is first cousin to the process of recovery from a bereavement—a laborious and needful task which an eminent psychiatrist, Dr. Erich Lindemann, has labelled "grief work." One does not recover from grief by distracting and amusing one's self, but by working the grief out of one's system through tears, reflections, and talk, which discharge the feelings and gradually nullify them, slowly modifying one's habits and expectations. So it is with dissolving marriages: there is divorce work to be done, and though it is a wretched kind of labor, it cannot be avoided except at great cost to the rest of one's life. But if one gets on with the work, it is certain that the bad time will come to an end, a healing and forgetting will occur, and a new life will take the place of the old.

Beyond the emotional divide lies final divorce—and yet it is never really final; it is only nearly-final. Over sixty per cent of divorcing people remain involved with one another for many years because of their children and such related matters as alimony and child support; of the other forty-odd per cent (the childless), a fraction—possibly half—are bound by alimony; and even those who have none of these continuing practical ties remain forever linked by the experiences they have shared and the memories which are a permanent part of their personalities.

Despite all this, most divorced persons do achieve near-finality, in the sense of an end to troubled emotions about the dead marriage. The feelings of yearning shrivel away, leaving them free to seek love elsewhere; even more notably, the disturbing feelings of anger fade away, leaving them free to see other human beings as worth loving and trusting again. The dying-away of both hostile and loving feelings yields a nearly neutral attitude toward the ex-spouse, and this brings not only relief but a degree of amnesia concerning the powerful emotions of the past. This is true of those who loved their spouses and were deeply hurt by the break-up:

[M, 34] I was really sick when she told me she loved another man. Sick and terribly angry—that's why I insisted on having custody of our son as the price of giving her a divorce. But today I feel nothing at all, and when I see her I sometimes wonder who this stranger is, and how I could have been so passionate about her. I mean, I look at her and try my hardest to feel something for her, but I can't, and I can't even imagine wanting her sexually.

But it is also true of those who hated their spouses and were desperately anxious to escape from them:

[F, 41] Considering the bitterness and the really miserable things we both did during the first year and a half of our separation, I can never get over the fact that now we deal with each other in a very easy and pleasant way. I know it all happened, but I can't recall the *feel* of the bad days.

The essentially neutral attitude is good not only for the former mates, but for their children; one can infer this from the fact that neutral ex-mates say they quarrel about the children much less than hostile ones, and even less than ex-mates who feel positively or warmly about each other. Apparently, left-over feelings of either kind—even positive ones—cause people to continue to use their children as a mechanism of their own involvement; neutrality permits them instead to consider only the children's welfare. Visiting also becomes simpler and more nearly healthful. Neutral ex-mates are polite, adequately hospitable, and moderately friendly when they meet on these occasions; the neutral father neither scrupulously avoids his ex-wife's house nor spends his visits with the children there in risky amiability. Both extremes are bad for the children—the former filling them with uneasiness because of the hatred it signifies, the latter tormenting them by seemingly giving encouragement to their stubborn hope that their parents will come together again. Only the neutral way avoids both hazards.

In some people, the neutral mood is a species of friendship, based on shared experiences, familiarity, and the comfort of knowing and being known. It is more common among the childless because they have fewer things to differ about, and more common among the unremarried because they often need the friendship of their former mates. Here is how one woman characterizes it:

> [F, 25] Jack and I were good friends and good lovers before we married. We just never should have married—it was too much responsibility for him, and too little freedom for me. The friendship died. We couldn't communicate any more. After the divorce, we didn't see each other for some months; then we met and found we liked each other again. Now we're platonic friends —he's somewhat like a father or brother to me.

Even those who have children and are remarried can occasionally achieve this kind of nearly neutral friendliness. A woman executive quoted by Cuber and Harroff in *The Significant Americans* says:

> My former husband and I see each other a great deal and remain quite friendly. Actually, come to think of it, we're more genuinely and honestly friendly than when we were married. . . . You have to talk together to plan any number of things concerning the kids—but even if you didn't have the kids, you would. When I see him or he calls, we chat at length about things we've read, political events, things that happen to our mutual friends. . . . My fiancé sometimes drops in with me when I have some business with my former husband and we often all have a drink together. [This is four years after the divorce.] After all, we're all civilized people.

But this kind of friendliness is relatively rare, especially among the remarried; the new life and new love virtually erase the old hurt and expropriate the old love. These people are neither enslaved any longer by the past, nor forced to keep repudiating it; yet as detached as they have become in the present, they can see the past in perspective, and appreciate its worth:

[F, 37] We helped each other grow up, parted with little bitterness, had little property and no children to be concerned about. Years mellow one, too, and the feelings of resentment are gone completely. I feel friendly toward him, but my work, my husband, and my children leave me no time and certainly no need to see him. We exchange Christmas and birthday cards, though, and once in a while he or I phone the other just to say hello, as we do with casual old friends, and to see how things are going.

[M, 46] Friends sometimes speak of my long marriage as a mistake or a tragic waste. Not so. Most of it was good, and I would be a fool to write it off. She and I grew away from each other and the marriage ceased to work, but that doesn't invalidate the past. And with the passage of four years since we broke apart, and especially since my remarriage, I haven't any feeling for her but a kind of good will and a sympathetic interest in her daily activities with our children.

Such people have achieved as nearly complete a divorce—without wasting or repudiating what was good in their past—as seems possible. It may be less sophisticated and less romantic than those divorces after which the ex-mates become dear friends and frequent guests in each other's homes, but it is more functional and healthful for all concerned; one cannot, and need not, ask for more.

CHAPTER EIGHT

The Long Stay

I · *The Old Hands*

A sizeable fraction of the society of the Formerly Married consists of Old Hands or Long-Termers—people who, years after separation and divorce, still tarry in this half-world watching others arrive in a steady stream, stay a relatively short while, and then depart. Over a third of all FMs remarry within two years of their divorce—that is, within three to five years from the time of their separation—but the rest remain longer, their chance of returning to the married world becoming smaller each year. Even as long as five years after the divorce—some six to eight years after the actual separation— at least a quarter of all FMs are still unremarried.

Few of the Long-Termers imagined, when they began their lives as FMs, that this would happen to them. Most novice FMs, even if greatly embittered at the time of separation, cannot envision the single state as being satisfactory for any length of time, whether one lives alone or is a single parent running a home; nor do they suppose that they will have to remain single for any length of time. Many expect to stay that way about a year, a span which not only looks quite long at the start, but has tradition behind it (one mourns the death of a husband or wife for a year); only a small minority expect to spend a long while or the rest of their lives unmarried.

Years later, even though they have grown used to the ways

of their world and become both knowledgeable and blasé about the single life, they still feel a certain surprise at finding themselves Long-Termers. A vivacious career woman and mother voiced the feeling of the typical Long-Termer: "It never occurred to me when I started all this that I'd be 'on the circuit' for five years and still see no end to it. I just wouldn't have believed it possible." She and people like her formulate any one of several general explanations for their own failure to remarry. Some regard themselves as lost, unredeemable, or damaged beyond repair, an interpretation which leads them to be either withdrawn and gloomy or frenetically convivial. Others think of themselves as emotional mutants, a special breed with unusual needs—some for privacy and independence, some for variety in their sexual and emotional relationships; they are not apologetic or ashamed, but defiant and almost proud about their inability to fit within the confines of domesticity or monogamy. Still others feel themselves to be too experienced, wise, and disillusioned to accept the terms and promises of married love; their eyes have seen too much, their hearts known too much, for them to love again in the trusting, innocent, credulous way they once did.

Who are all these people? In general, they include very few of the youngest FMs, most of whom remarry quickly; the great majority of the Long-Termers are thirty-five or older. Those who had wanted to divorce tend to remarry sooner than those who had not; among the Long-Termers, therefore, are a good number of people who were reluctant to break up their marriages. People of substantial income are likely to remarry more quickly than those of small means; hence, among the Long-Termers there is a somewhat larger proportion of people with financial problems than there is among FMs generally. Finally, though women are more highly motivated to remarry than men, they are at an economic and social disadvantage in the marketplace, where, furthermore, they already outnumber men three to two; as a result, they are even more noticeably in the majority among Long-Termers.

If Long-Termers are, on the average, somewhat older, more insecure, and less affluent than FMs taken as a whole, there are yet many exceptions: any impartial observer can see that among them are a fair proportion of youthful, confident, and successful people. Indeed, it seems that most of the generalizations one might reasonably expect to make about these people have only a limited validity, there being nearly as many contradictions and exceptions as cases that fit. One might suppose, for instance, that the typical Long-Termer, having been in this milieu for years, has become a coarsened hedonist, accustomed to an endless series of cheap affairs; it is true that there are some like this, but there are also others who have had only long-lasting and genuinely loving relationships, or who, being career-dedicated or inhibited, have had none. One might suppose that the typical Long-Termer would prove glum, cynical, and bitter about being stuck in this status, and unable to return to the world of the married; some do feel this way, but others are still optimistic about their chances of remarriage, or else are quite satisfied with the single way of life. One might envision the Long-Termer as a person who is emotionally withdrawn, avoiding remarriage in order not to be subject again to its demands; there are some like this, but others are emotionally adventurous, and avoid remarriage, not because they find it too demanding, but because they find it dull.

Long-Termers are, in brief, not a type but an aggregation of quite dissimilar types. Many different factors—some of them diametrically opposed to others—can delay remarriage; each, of itself or in combination with others, produces its own crop of long-term unremarried FMs. What all these people have in common is not a single reason for their long stay, but a common status in the subculture: they are the regulars, the veterans who know the way of the world and are adjusted to FM life, even though many of them are neither content with it nor successful at it. They are not unlike convicts who have spent years in a prison and have long sentences yet to serve—an élite of sorts, whose status in their special society is based upon a reversal of American cultural values, whose crime is their achievement, whose sentence is their badge of rank.

II · *Mavericks and Malcontents*

Although the specific reasons for the resistance of the Long-Termers are many and diverse, they fall into two groups: those which account for the contented Long-Termer and those which account for the discontented one. For to the knowledge-able observer meeting a Long-Termer, it is soon apparent that he is either one of those who like this way of life despite its unconventionality and exclusion from so much that they once knew, or one of those who dislike it and have never become sufficiently satisfied by it to give up their hope of remarrying.

Those who like the single life may find it far more agreeable than they found marriage because they cannot endure any great or continued intimacy with another human being. Marriage was too demanding and confining for them; it never let them alone, gave them no peace, required more of them than they could give. Some of them, as FMs, achieve the limited intimacy and emotional rapport they need within the confines of casual sex. As we saw, a great many FMs feel this way briefly during the early stages of their emotional recuperation, and then outgrow it; a small number, however, find this pattern so well suited to their basic psychological requirements that they adopt it as a permanent way of life, and become the chronically promiscuous, the romance addicts, the habitués of counterfeit intimacy.

Unlike those to whom casual sex appeals as a temporary escape and a phase of rehabilitation, these people recognize —usually to their own surprise—that this is what they have always deeply wanted. Such a recognition is more likely to come to a man than a woman, especially a woman rearing children; one resists the realization that is too difficult to live by. But even for men and for childless women, this way of life is so non-conforming that only the true rebel adopts it permanently. The perceptive observer can sense in such a person a fundamental difference from other FMs; though he thinly conceals it, he is the authentic radical, committed to a style of life that others only play at, convinced that his own way is superior to that of the entrenched majority, and bored by the conventionally marriage-minded and the married.

Whatever face he may put on for outsiders, he actually feels nothing but satisfaction in his special way of life. Here is such a mood, as revealed by the managing editor of a major newspaper, a man of fifty:

> For about five years after my divorce I thought I wanted to remarry. But slowly I realized that in truth I didn't want to at all. I'm very much my own man, the way I live. I love the peace and privacy of my apartment after the day at the paper, but whenever I want company or an overnight partner, I have three or four girls I can get in touch with. Usually, I'm a little more interested in one of them than the rest, but never to the point where I wouldn't feel free to chase anything I see at a party or anyplace else. It's my nature. Having tried marriage for almost ten years, I know now that I could never be this happy married again or trying to be true to just one.

A thirty-nine-year-old fuel dealer in Boston feels like this after nine years as an FM:

> Even after all this time I am amazed at how glad I am to be free. I spare my married friends the details of the fantastic joys of bachelorhood because I hate to make them miserable. Still, it's possible I might remarry some day—but only a long while from now, when the fires burn low and I want steady companionship for my declining years. Until then, I'm going to be true to only one person—myself.

These sound like "typically male" attitudes, but one finds the same syndrome in some women, although they are even more careful to conceal it by an acceptable public stance. A woman, herself an FM, who has done much organizational work among the divorced, explains: "A lot of women don't ever want to remarry, but hide their feelings because they're afraid of being labelled bitter, frigid, or hostile toward men. Some of them like having men as friends or lovers, but simply can't stand being tied to any one man. They're 'normal' enough, but society doesn't see it that way, so they pretend to be hunting for a husband." One young woman, a mousy-looking graduate student working toward a doctorate in history at the University of Chicago, most reluctantly gave her husband a divorce in return for substantial alimony and child support. As part of her effort to get over the shock of it, she had herself restyled into an elegant blonde, began buying chic clothes, started gadding about, and within a year dropped out of graduate school. Now, six years later, she says:

> I used to insist, even after I gave up graduate school, that I wanted to find the right man and get married again, but my closest friend pointed out to me one time that I always arrange things so as not to marry—like always going out with several men, or getting a crush on someone new when someone old was getting serious. And you know, she was right. I *like* living like this. I'm an alimony parasite. I read, I visit art galleries and smart shops, I go to many parties, I meet many men and love having them buzz around me, I have various relationships—I love the variety, it's a great life. It's fun. Anybody would take it if she could get it. It's hypocrisy to pretend otherwise—but because people are the way they are, I have to be a hypocrite. But I know the truth about myself, even if most other people don't.

A glamorous appearance and big-city address are not, however, essential to this pattern, though they help; a mother of three children, a round-faced, plain, but effervescent woman of fifty-two who lives in the suburb of a medium-sized city, speaks of her decade of post-marital life:

> I could not accept the idea of remarriage in the beginning because I was afraid of the step-father problems, but after a while

I decided to enjoy whatever life had brought me. And after a few years I found that the carefree life was very good for me, and decided I didn't need to or want to remarry. I can't live without love, but opening your heart to someone, even if for the moment, is a form of love. I have loved many times, and each time is sufficient unto itself. When a man holds me, and kisses and caresses me, I'm in love for the time being, and that's all I need.

All the foregoing are people who function well—even sometimes extraordinarily—in the area of sex, but have only a limited capacity or need for emotional interaction. But there are other Long-Termers who function well in neither area. They are the sexually incapacitated who, though lonely and defeated as FMs, often recognize as time passes that an FM way of life is much better for them than marriage. Privacy, remoteness, and a virtually monastic sexual life are comforting to them, minimizing their anxieties and freeing them from the challenge of passion and emotion. The frigid woman, the impotent man, the man or woman with little or no sexual drive, the guilt-ridden religious fanatic, and the latent homosexual or lesbian, all fall into this category.

Totally abstaining male Long-Termers are rare, and seem even rarer; for social reasons the chaste male strives to hide the truth about himself. A department-store buyer, now fifty-two, explains:

I keep my sex life a secret. I'd be ashamed to have my friends know that I haven't had a woman for five years. I just seem to have lost all desire. It was fading out during my second marriage, and since then I have tried a few times but with very poor results. I don't like living alone—no, that isn't quite true—I guess I often find it unpleasant but it's better than being tied to someone I can't endure. I keep myself too busy and on the move, what with buying trips and business dinners and all that, to feel miserable except once in a while. I let my friends think I have some kind of wicked secret life.

Frigidity is much more common than impotence, as Kinsey and other surveyors have shown. Whatever the reasons for it—religious or sexual inhibitions, the "masculinity complex" of the career-minded woman, the fear of male domination—many women with this problem slowly realize after separation and divorce that a sexless, or virtually sexless, single life meets their psychological needs better than any other, and decide to live accordingly. A book-store manager who was divorced seven years ago—she was then thirty-two—expresses it as follows:

> After the divorce I slept well, worked hard, plowed my after-hours energies into my children and my home, and felt very good. I wasn't interested in seeking dates—I had plenty of contact with people all day long—and I missed sex only in the beginning and then only occasionally. After a couple of years I came to see that I had found a way of life that was right for me. I might remarry, if the right man came along, but it isn't something I am hoping for.

A woman may lead the ascetic life even within a seemingly bohemian framework. An interviewer for a television program obtained these comments from a woman writer in her late thirties who lives in a small studio two flights above a beatnik coffee-house:

> If I stop and compare the life I am leading now to that [she was married for six years] I know I'm much happier now. Maybe I just wasn't meant to be married, I don't know. . . . There are times when I get lonely, and when I do there are always many things for me to do, many interests. . . . I feel the need for sex just before menstruating, but I don't know any men. . . . That is, I don't have any men friends because of my whole attitude. I'm either too busy, or I put them down, or I don't do anything for their egos. So I do without. . . . I don't need the aggravation [of an affair], I just don't want to get involved. It boils down to the fact that I don't want to have a man. That's about it.

Some Long-Termers, though they have neither the psychology of the loner nor the sexual problem of the frigid woman and impotent man, seem reasonably contented with the FM way of life. The psychological and social pressures favoring remarriage happen, in these people, to be just about in balance with those favoring FM life. They lack any definite antipathy to marriage, yet are not rebellious and non-conformist enough to have a definite commitment to the FM way of life. Since there is no clear-cut reason for their long-term status, they are an enigma to their friends, and even to themselves; they simply cannot explain why they have been FMs so long except to say that things have just turned out that way. One might call them drifters, since, having no clear loyalty either to marriage or to the FM life, they are passively borne along by every stray current or circumstance, now having a period of celibacy and then plunging into a love affair, now allowing semi-isolation to envelop them and then letting themselves be carried off by new friends into a spell of promiscuity. Until some new factor comes in to upset the balance, they can go on like this for many years.

A short, thick-set man of fifty-one whose stolid features and slicked-down hair give him the air of an insurance salesman—actually, he teaches music in a large high school—has been an FM for thirteen years, and in all that time has never been particularly unhappy with his single life, yet has never come to view it as the best way for him. A few of his scores of casual relationships have caught fire and become affairs of the heart; three times he might have married but did not, twice because he was locked in interminable divorce negotiations with his wife and once because his fiancee panicked and fled as marriage seemed to draw close. From time to time he has been abstinent from all sexual relationships for a month or two simply out of boredom or the lack of an interesting new face, but he has also had other months in which he has made a number of conquests of women he had never met before and cares nothing about. Although puzzled to find himself drifting along like this year after year, he still pays lip-service to the hope that he may remarry, but he is not so much looking for the right woman as waiting for her to find him—and meanwhile letting the years carry him as they will.

Sometimes it seems that these vacillating people are the passive instruments of any accident or event that plays upon them. They can be propelled into marriage, or converted into permanent loners, almost by chance:

—A woman who thought herself in love, but could not make up her mind to marry the man, got a phone call one morning announcing the sudden death of her ex-husband, who had been paying her both alimony and child support. By that evening, she had come to wonder how she could have doubted her new love so long, or been so indecisive about the idea of remarriage.

—A man who had drifted through seven years of FM life had to assume custody of his two children when his ex-wife became mentally ill. The shift in his practical needs made his former routine impossible; within a few months he had dropped his casual relationships and become engaged to the woman he had been closest to.

—A business executive had made an uncertain way through four years of FM life when, through a buyer eager to please him, he was introduced to a "fast" crowd of hard-drinking, sexually promiscuous people. Despite some initial feelings of alarm and guilt, within a few weekends he felt as though he had found himself; a profound but hidden wish to be promiscuous had been brought to light. He has given up all thoughts of any other way of life, and considers himself lucky to have escaped remarriage.

Other Long-Termers, though they also drift along without commitment to one way of life or the other, slowly change due to an inner and inevitable evolution; eventually they develop a conviction as to what is best for them:

—An actress in her late thirties had been drifting, ever since her divorce seven years earlier. Usually she would have only casual relationships, but at four different times she was involved in love affairs—each of which broke up because of her going on the road in plays, where distance and loneliness each time led her into other and conflicting relationships. She has come to regard herself as incapable of sustaining a real love; her defeats have led her to believe, rightly or wrongly, that she is stuck with the single life and had better learn to make the most of it.

—An airline pilot, after his divorce, meandered through his mid-forties without any long-range aim; he always felt, however, that the age of fifty was somehow crucial: if he weren't remarried by then, he said, he probably never would be. As he approached that age, his lethargic drifting from casual connections to half-hearted involvements and back again gave way to a troubled period of self-examination; he even found himself losing interest in casual affairs. He is now less than a year short of the magic number, but is finally going with a woman he thinks he may marry.

—A young female psychologist wanted to stay free of all ties after her divorce, but time and again drifted, against her will, into close relationships with the wrong men, and then had to break off with them. Her professional work brought her more and more into contact with children, and she gradually began to want a child of her own; as this happened, she started exercising judgment and control over her involvements, and began dating around more widely in order to find someone more suitable. A year and a half ago she remarried, and now has a baby girl.

In contrast to all the Long-Termers we have looked at thus far are those others who are fundamentally dissatisfied with the FM way of life, and have been thinking about or doggedly searching for the right mate for years, but without success.

Sometimes the reason is all too apparent. Among the people we saw haunting open dances, friendship clubs, resort hotels, church socials, and date bureaus, there are quite a few who are physically unattractive and graceless, or boring, or socially inept, or simply peculiar in any of a hundred ways. Some may have highly unpleasant traits of character which caused their mates to leave them, and which have been exacerbated rather than moderated by the failure of marriage; obvious examples are aggressiveness or emotional coldness in men, nagging or childish dependency in women. Such people are quickly appraised by those they meet, and passed by; as an unkind but accurate colloquialism puts it, they are "rejects."

Sometimes, to be sure, they succeed in dating now and then, but the partner quickly perceives his mistake, wriggles away as soon as he can, and does not call again. At other times, however, they manage brief sexual relationships which they hope will lead to deep involvement and marriage; but the hopes fade as they put their clothes back on and disappear altogether during the awkward, silent ride home. Rejects want love and marriage but get only "one-night stands," and not too often, at that. They console themselves with the rationalization that there simply is nothing good around: "What a lot of sad specimens at *that* party!" "The only single men I ever meet are wolves or Mama's boys or queers." "Where are the really *nice* girls?—I mean, girls who aren't gold-diggers, or screwed-up, or dogs to look at."

It is not always physical or character traits that cause an FM to be continually passed over or discarded. Some men are under the severe financial handicap of high alimony and child-support payments; time after time such a man begins a relationship with a suitable woman, only to have her hastily back away as soon as she realizes he can never support a second family. Similarly, some Catholic FMs, even if legally divorced, consider themselves married in the eyes of the Church and ineligible for remarriage; many of them look for love but, when they find it, are rejected as soon as the other becomes convinced that they are unmarriageable. Still other people are denied a divorce for many years by a vengeful or dependent mate; they may fall in love time and again, only to have each affair end badly because of their unavailability for marriage. After a while, they grow weary of being hurt, and settle for casual or promiscuous contacts, without ever being content to stay single. They become grimly resigned to, but never pleased with, the Long-Termer's way of life.

Curiously enough, there are some Long-Termers who are in just as hopeless a position even though they are personable, free from any outstanding impediments, and most anxious to remarry—at least, consciously. Unconsciously, they are terrified of it, being too embittered by their experiences or too frightened of failure to go beyond a certain point in any new relationship, however much they want to. Some remain fixed at the dating level; compulsively and uselessly they seek new partners, date them once or a few times (with or without sexual involvement), and discard them as imperfect. Others enter affairs, one after another, each new and shining at the outset, each seemingly The Answer To It All; inevitably, however, as the relationship approaches the crucial time of decision, they become uncertain or disenchanted, feel trapped, or find things to quarrel about, and break up the affair, dejectedly regarding it as yet another in their endless series of failures.

Sometimes they recognize that what they are doing represents a fear of marriage; the recognition, of itself, is rarely enough to resolve the dilemma, since their fear usually has reasons going further back than their divorce. One woman, after eight years as an FM and half a dozen such affairs, says, "I know exactly what I'm doing each time I do it, but that doesn't help. This last time I started acting bitchy and picking fights with him, and I knew it and even told him about it, hoping he could help me, but it was like someone who is trying to kill himself—you just can't stop him if he really means to do it." To the one rejected, it is also often clear what is happening, yet just as inexorable. A woman of thirty-seven tells how it feels:

I had a really wonderful involvement with a brilliant and dynamic man that had gone on only a couple of months, when suddenly he began to attack me, my children, my opinions, my divorce. He seemed to find fault with everything he had been enthusiastic about. I was bewildered, and terribly wounded, but after a bit I could see that he was simply scared—that it had come home to him that he was heading for marriage, and that he was afraid of being trapped, assuming responsibilities, being the head of a family. I took a deep breath and let him go, and I know he was relieved; I hope he was also a little saddened.

Whether a Long-Termer has been consistently passed by, or has rejected every good candidate, he is likely to be embarrassed and defensive about himself; he feels he is a failure, since the goal he desires always remains beyond his reach even though so many others have grasped it. Both the person who is never chosen and the one who throws away every choice recognize, after a while, that it cannot be only bad luck; they themselves must be at fault in some way. On those rare occasions when they are utterly honest with close friends, they sound bewildered, disconsolate, and either frantic or apathetic. Like the non-conforming rebel, they harbor the knowledge that they are different from most people, but unlike him they are ashamed rather than proud of the secret, and hope against hope that it may prove untrue after all.

At the farthest extreme from those who enjoy being permanent loners are those Long-Termers who are dissatisfied with the single way of life, dedicated to the idea of remarriage, and who, despite the passage of many years, feel neither baffled, defeated, nor hopeless about their chances. They may, to be sure, be occasionally discouraged for a matter of days or even weeks, but more often they are hopeful and expectant. They are forever telling friends about the "new man" or "new woman" they have just met who may prove to be The One, or else admitting in rueful and self-mocking tones that a new and shining hope "didn't work out"—and gamely insisting that they are ready to look around again. All of which is familiar: one sees the pattern in a great many FMs fairly soon after the dissolution of marriage. But why do some people still behave this way many years later? Why are they neither remarried by that time nor trapped in the doldrums of defeat?

There seem to be two answers. Some people, first of all, may have been delayed in remarrying by circumstances or accidents of personal history of a kind which have not killed off hope. The FM may, for instance, have chosen poorly one or more times and been forced to draw back, not because of an unconscious fear of marriage, but because he recognized his own errors in judgment. What keeps such a person from becoming cynical or bitter is the fact that he is not repeating a similar neurotic choice each time, but is making different mistakes and apparently learning something in the process; he has a sense of progress in his unsuccessful attempts. A portrait photographer in his upper thirties spilled out the following story almost in one breath:

After the first year or so I felt anxious to remarry, and I had a brief wild affair with a girl who seemed great but who turned out to be so temperamental and violent—she actually threw things at me, including a pair of shears—that I backed out fast. After a while I found a girl with one child, very sweet and level-headed and very beautiful, and I thought, Oh boy, this is it, this is what I need, but after three or four months I was bored and embarrassed because she was no real companion, intellectually, and I should have known it earlier. That was a tough one to get out of, but at least I won't make that mistake again. And then last year I started getting involved with a woman who seemed exactly right for me, but I should have known better than to let myself start caring about anyone who isn't divorced yet and is still hung up on her husband. After half a year she decided to go back to him and I was left with nothing but a little new wisdom, and a black-and-blue soul. That was rough. But I'm over it now, and I think I learned something. I've learned something each time.

Others have been delayed by almost accidental impediments: one man was sent abroad by his firm for a short trip which stretched out to a foreign tour lasting nearly four years; his search for a suitable mate was stalemated all that time and began in earnest only after he came back to the United States. A woman, now five years divorced, says that after two years of FM life she fell in love with a man who would have been ideal for her; just then, however, he developed leukemia and tried to break off the affair for her sake, but she clung to him until he died, a year later. Since then she has avoided anything but dating and occasional light affairs; only in the past few months has she been able to permit herself the first deep involvement in three years.

The second answer as to why such Long-Termers have no sense of defeatism is that some of them simply take longer than most FMs to go through the various stages of emotional and social readjustment. The immature, for instance, need to grow up; they may have to progress slowly through the various relationships we have seen, not so much recapitulating youthful development as living through it for the first time. The severely traumatized—the people badly damaged by their marital experiences—may need much longer than most to work out their anger, cautiously test out new relationships, and slowly reassure themselves about the opposite sex and about their own capacity for love.

A thirty-four-year-old woman, part-time assistant to a home builder, is a good example of the slow-developing type:

Eight years is a long while, but I feel that I'm ready now for remarriage, and that I never really was before, even though I thought so. After the divorce, the first thing I did was take my two sons and spend a couple of years working in Paris, where I ran a bit wild. Finally I got enough of that and started cultivating closer relationships, but I must have been scared—first I picked a married man, and then a homosexual who was trying to go straight. Then I came back to the States, and after a while began a relationship that lasted nearly three years. It meant a great deal to me, but oddly enough neither of us was sure we ought to marry—we comforted each other in all sorts of ways, without ever being truly in love. It faded away at last, but I feel it has left me ready to give myself, and to be a real woman to a real man.

The married friends and relatives of such Long-Termers sigh for them frequently, counting them lost and irrecoverable; but they sigh for themselves only now and then, being sure much of the time that they are proceeding toward the goal they seek. When they remarry after five or ten years, their friends and relatives are astonished, regarding it as a stroke of unexpected luck, but hedging their enthusiasm with caution, lest the happy outcome prove impermanent. But the FMs themselves know better: for quite some time they had felt they were going somewhere, and while the journey seemed long, they were neither surprised to arrive at the destination they had in mind nor unduly apprehensive about the outcome.

III · *Friends and the Long-Termer*

At the time of separation and for a while thereafter, most married friends of the FM are sympathetic and tolerant, supportive and helpful. But underneath all this, as we saw earlier, there is disapproval, uneasiness, and a sense of threat to the established order—especially their own personal established order. It would be worrisome enough if the FM merely got divorced and immediately remarried; this is a limited uprising against marriage. But for the FM to flourish and expand, to adjust to unmarried life, and to find a considerable number of rewards and pleasures in it over a long period—that is a major, full-scale rebellion, a desertion of the true faith.

Among the Long-Termers, therefore, only the chronic rejects and a few abstinent loners pose no threat to the married person's peace of mind; all the others seem, in varying degree, to be getting a good deal of forbidden pleasure from FM life, without the burden of responsibility that marriage entails.

And therefore the early encouragement and even approval of the FM's activities give way, before long, to criticism and disapproval. One man illustrated the shift as follows:

I met an old friend of mine from out of town for dinner about five or six months after my separation. He's had a good marriage for eighteen years, has four kids, and is a settled man, and was very upset about my situation. But he was surprised to see me looking well, and when he asked about my life and I told him how I was beginning to go out a lot and have a bit of a fling, he seemed delighted for me, especially because I'd had some frustrating sexual problems in my marriage. I didn't see him again for over two years and this time he looked at me quizzically and said, "Tell me, are you still running around the way you were a couple of years ago?" Like, okay, you had a little fun, but cut it out now and get back in here with the rest of us!

It is dismaying and painful to the FM to find even his oldest and dearest friends losing their sympathy and tolerance, and growing cooler as he becomes more adept at living and enjoying the FM life. The same couple who applauded his dating and early involvements slowly change over the years; the smile becomes chilly, the enthusiasm turns to condescension, the message in the eyes is, "We see what you've become—or maybe what you always were." They ask questions, sound interested and amiable, but the FM feels a prickly discomfort; he searches for other words and moods that will placate them, shifts from the cheery tone to a discouraged one, then tries to be amused and self-critical, then serious and searching. They like it better when he seems to be miserable, but they are not convinced; he has plainly gone over to the enemy camp, and they are no longer his allies.

Some writers on divorce and some FMs say that the growing distance between the married and their separated or divorced friends is largely the result of the realistic temptations the latter offer: the unattached woman is seen by wives as a potential home-wrecker, the unattached male as a bad influence on their husbands. Both fears have some justification, but well-adjusted Long-Termers actually offer a far subtler and more dangerous temptation—namely, to consider the short-comings of one's own marriage and the possibilities for a more satisfactory life as a divorced person; this is the major reason for the growing disapproval and disaffection felt by FMs as time passes.

Married women have a number of indirect ways of showing their disapproval of their FM women friends. One is to inquire solicitously about the children's health and state of mind, the unspoken implication being that life in a fatherless household —especially over so long a period—must be seriously harmful to them. Another is to invite the FM woman over only when having a large party, thereby indicating that she has become someone strange and distant, and no longer a companion for quiet evenings. The married woman who wants to convey to a long-term FM friend that her way of life is bordering upon promiscuity, or must be the result of neurosis, has many seem-ingly kindly ways of putting it: "Aren't you getting tired of it yet?" "Don't you just hate it?" "Do you ever think of a recon-ciliation? Maybe it would be best, after all, since you haven't found someone else." "Who's the latest?" She isn't very likely to make such remarks to an FM man, but will tell her husband what she thinks and let him transmit it. Sometimes he does so with a candor that would irk her, if she knew about it. A man who has been divorced half a dozen years tells how the message is delivered:

> I invited an old friend and his wife to spend a Saturday with me and my date at my country club. He said, "I'd love it, but there's a little problem. Last two times we were with you, you had girls who were fifteen or twenty years younger than all of us. My wife felt kind of strange about it—she thought it was odd for you to be chasing after such young ones. Besides, she probably feels that she's being compared to them, and it makes her feel middle-aged. And maybe she thinks it gives me ideas, too."

And perhaps it does. As sociologists have pointed out, divorce itself is a cause of divorce: it is an example, a challenge, a dare—particularly when the FM has made significant discoveries and shown distinct growth as a result of his choice. A forty-year-old business executive tells a fairly common kind of story:

> I was having lunch with an old friend who has known me for most of my life. In the four years since my marriage broke up, I'd never spoken to him about it in any detail. This day, he asked me what had happened and I started talking. I told him about the frustrations of my marriage, the terrific impact sex had on me when I found it outside of marriage, the marvel of finding myself capable of deeper and more powerful feelings than I'd ever known before. "I hear you," he finally said, "and I understand your words, but it's like Greek to me—I can't imagine those feelings in myself." I went on a while, and then he said, "Maybe we ought not continue this—maybe I oughtn't know. It might not be good for me to know." Half a year later, he's beginning the whole routine—and I feel partly responsible. I'm almost sorry I said so much.

Ordinarily, however, it is only the relative newcomer to FM life who talks too much; the Long-Termers have long since learned better, or been blocked in their efforts at communication by the chasm that has opened up between them and their married friends. Both sides stand to be hurt by overly free communication—the FM by the disapproval or depreciation of his way of life which he would hear, the married friends by the description of a life that would imperil their own hard-won equilibrium. Many an FM learns that speaking too openly to his married friends has unfortunate consequences:

> [M, 34] A friend of mine is married to a girl I've known since I was five. After my marriage broke up, I used to see them a lot and tell them my troubles, and they were always on my side. That was long ago. Last year, at their house I got stoned and started spouting some cutting remarks about marriage as an outmoded

institution, and how it hardly ever works well, and how a man is better off the way I am now. She blew her stack. She really gave me hell. "We're like two little people who have been struggling fourteen hours a day for years to make their corner candy-store pay off, and get rid of the mortgage, and you come along and tell me capitalism stinks and you're going to try to lead the revolution. Well, *that* stinks!" I sobered up and apologized, but they've been chilly toward me since then. I guess I haven't seen them since that night.

Much of the distance that separates most married people from their long-term FM friends is therefore needful and self-protective. But there is no need for self-defense or distance when either the FM is thoroughly unhappy or the married people are thoroughly happy. Indeed, the latter phrase suggests an intriguing hypothesis: If a long-term FM reveals the more rewarding and positive aspects of his life, those of his married friends who are truly happy will be pleased, those who are not will show stress, envy, or disapproval in proportion to the degree of dissatisfaction in their marriage.

It is also true, however, that the alienation of Long-Term FMs from their married friends is partly the result of the differences in their interests and habits. The long-term FM is chronically fascinated by his or her own feelings, by the appeal of new persons of the opposite sex, and by the growth and decay of relationships. Married people have closed off their own feelings behind the barrier of conjugal privacy; through habit and reliability their love-lives cease to have priority in their thinking, and they have long ago stopped viewing other people as potential love-partners. Their reactions to people, things, books, plays, are all shaped by this orientation: they go with an FM friend to a show, but laugh at different lines than he does, or come away with an impression of what they have seen that differs radically from his (*Who's Afraid of Virginia Woolf?* and *Luv*, to name but two fairly recent examples, could almost be used as projective tests to distinguish the married viewpoint from the divorced viewpoint.) At social events, married people talk to other people in order to discuss mutual interests; FMs talk to other people in order to interact with them, to test, to sense the potential. Married people feel that the divorced people they meet never really listen to what they are saying, but are always trying to tune in on something else; FMs—especially Long-Termers—find that married people speak but without revealing themselves, communicate but without having anything happen. Here are comments by two long-term FMs, both made during large gatherings:

> [F, 35] I think marriage is on the way out. Single life is so much more alive and daring. You take chances. You are in love or out of love—but never are you just nothing. You're way up or way down, but never bored. Look around us—how many of the married people here tonight can say that? They've lost something—they're so prosaic and dull. They never have anything interesting to say.

> [M, 36] I have changed greatly and my life today is incomprehensible to them. But then so is theirs to me. Theirs is so stifling, so lacking in the unknown, the about-to-happen—how can they stand it?

The result is that the long-term FM and his or her married friends draw apart, circumscribe their areas of contact, and lose the freedom with which they used to speak to each other. But both sides do so with regret, and time and again make some gesture at coming together—they exchange Christmas cards, talk on the phone, occasionally meet in each other's homes after one or the other has issued the familiar challenge, "We never see each other any more." But given the nature of modern marriage—which exists almost solely to provide emotional satisfactions—the satisfied divorced person will continue to be a bad example, a temptation, and a challenge to people with unsatisfying marriages. It is therefore likely that the Formerly Married who have found contentment in that status, especially over a long period, will become more and more alienated from many of their old married friends, for the partial insulation of one world from the other is a needful safeguard for each.

How, then, do formerly married people satisfy their own need for intimate friendships? Must the whole carefully woven fabric of their lives be thrown away because one part of it came unwoven? Fortunately not. Most FMs do remarry within a few years, and for them the old friendships are still salvageable, though somewhat rusty from disuse. As for the Long-Termer, he or she does lose some friends through attrition, but holds on to others; after half a dozen years or so, a few married friends may have disappeared completely from the scene (they probably did so very early), a majority have become now-and-then friends with whom he or she interacts as if they were old acquaintances, and a handful have remained close to him, perhaps becoming even closer than before because they are confidantes who can listen to the details of his or her life without feeling endangered. In that handful are the happily married, plus married people who, having themselves been through the divorce experience, remain tolerant, and finally some never-married friends whose outlook is more akin to that of the FM than of the married.

Some long-term FMs also find themselves closer to certain relatives than they had been during marriage. Parents, brothers, and sisters are concerned about the divorced person, and try to see that he or she not be alone on crucial holidays or forgotten on birthdays. But there are defects in these relationships: parents and older siblings tend to revert to thinking about the FM as they did when he or she was young and unmarried; they are protective but condescending, full of well-meant but useless advice, impatient with behavior they find adolescent. The FM, as a result, welcomes their warmth but hides most of his or her deepest feelings, and conceals most of the non-conformist aspects of his or her daily life. One dare not let relatives know even as much as one lets married friends know. Mothers and fathers of men and women in their thirties

or forties are chronically unable to understand or accept the
fact that their sons or daughters are having sexual relations
with virtual strangers or have had several affairs that did not
proceed to marriage and were not meant to. A twice-divorced
woman in her early forties epitomizes the problem thus:

> Dad is such a sweet man, and so concerned about me since my
> second divorce. He always asks me how things are going, and
> whether I'm lonely, and why I don't just pick someone nice and
> "settle down before it's too late." But he hasn't the faintest
> glimmer of an idea about my feelings about the men I've been
> involved with. I'll bet he doesn't even think I actually do any-
> thing with any of them. He doesn't want to think so, so he
> doesn't. And I wouldn't shock him with the truth for anything
> in the world. I think one has to protect her parents even more
> than her children.

Even the FM's ex-relatives—the former in-laws—often remain fairly friendly with him or her. This is usually a matter
of need: a woman with children may welcome the chance to
leave them with her ex-husband's parents for a day or two;
a man on bad terms with his ex-wife may use her parents as a
way of finding out how his children are, or as intermediaries
to arrange his visits. A number of FMs report being on such
friendly terms with their ex-in-laws that it seems obvious the
latter approve of them more than they do of their own son or
daughter. Perhaps people who have felt the lash of a son's or
daughter's rebellion later feel that that child, in getting a divorce, has once more flouted their standards and failed to be
what they hoped for; the tendency then is to see the ex-mate as
a fellow-sufferer, whose distress they sympathize with, whose
efforts to compensate they understand and condone. An occasional young woman is taken, children and all, into the household of her in-laws, at the time of separation, and made part
of the family until she is able to establish a home of her own.
And not only FM women are befriended by their ex-in-laws in
this fashion. One man's ex-mother-in-law comes with the chil-

dren to his summer bungalow for a month, minds them while he is in town each day, and helps him with cooking and other duties. Another man, whose beautiful and vain wife was won away by a very wealthy man, granted her a divorce at the price of her giving him custody of the children. Her parents commiserated with him, taking the attitude that poor Jean "was just too beautiful for her own good, and really couldn't help the way things happened to her"; the older people offered to move into his house temporarily to help him with the children, and he gladly accepted the offer. After a year, he asked them to sublet their own apartment and stay with him indefinitely, and three years after the divorce they are still there.

Finally, of course, there are the new friends one makes after beginning life as an FM. Many of those who have studied divorced people report that FMs seem to seek, or at least to drift into, circles of new and mostly divorced friends.* Though they by no means associate exclusively with new FM friends, they do seek them out in order to compensate for the loss of some old ones and for diminished rapport with many others; they find among these new friends, more than anywhere else, the tolerance, understanding, and support they need.

The fairly new FM may find that these friendships grow exceedingly intimate in a very brief time; it is the same as with friendships of the trench and foxhole, the closeness of which is beyond those of ordinary life—until ordinary life is resumed. Even the Long-Termer, despite his adjustment to his life, continues to need—or perhaps needs more than ever—friends around him who do not question, criticize, or feel endangered by his way of life, and who understand how he feels.

How could it be otherwise? For among the reasons for the existence of friendship none is more important than a mutuality of interest and feelings. A friend is another I, a second self.

---

* William J. Goode, in *After Divorce*, finds this to be true of only a minority, but his sample consisted entirely of women with children; probably they are less likely than childless women and much less likely than men to drift away from married friends with children.

Companionship, wrote C. S. Lewis, blossoms into friendship when two people discover that they share the same treasures or burdens which each had thought uniquely his own, and when they say to each other, in effect, "What? You too? I thought I was the only one." If it is a sorrow of the divorced life that many old and dear friendships become cool and remote, it is a joy of the divorced life that new ones appear which are both warm and close at hand, and that for every pair of eyes that look at one uncomprehendingly there is another pair whose look says, "What? You too?"

IV · *Children and the Long-Termer*

Mrs. Yvonne English, a slender, titian-haired beauty in her upper thirties, is sitting up late tonight in her living-room, smoking and worrying. Her delicate face, usually serene and smooth as a lily-pond on a summer evening, is strained by dark and troubling thoughts; she has a problem concerning her fifteen-year-old daughter—and it is one for which she has seen no answers in books or articles on handling teen-agers. The problem is what to tell Lucia about what happened ten minutes ago. And what did happen? George left, and will not be back —George, who has been Yvonne's latest involvement, and whose tenure was five months. He is the seventh man with whom, in the five years since her divorce, she has had an affair. Not that she is flighty or fickle; she passionately yearns to find lasting love and to remarry, has been deeply in love with each man in turn, and cannot understand why her enthusiasm wanes each time, making her feel she has committed herself hastily and unwisely. The final scene with George was bad enough, but now at least he is gone. Lucia, however, will be at the breakfast table in the morning, and Yvonne will have to tell her then, or very soon, that George will not be back; what disturbs her tonight is the look she expects to see in Lucia's eyes. For Lucia has watched the men come and go ever since she was ten years old; she has learned to care for each one in turn—but more unwillingly, each time, as she gradually came to suspect that none of them would be permanent. Each time, when the man who came nearly every night has disappeared from their lives, Lucia has seemed more hurt and withdrawn, and has asked fewer questions, and last time there was something new in her face and manner—a look that said to her mother: It's you, isn't it?—it's not them—it's you there's something wrong with. That is what Yvonne dreads; that is why she is sitting up late tonight and trying to think of something to say that will exonerate her in her own child's eyes.

Yvonne English's problem is typical of the special difficulties that often exist between long-term FMs and their children. Very early in the divorce process, both the parent with custody and the absentee parent go through a transitional period, during which they adjust their parental behavior to the new circumstances: in accordance with the mores of the subculture, the father gradually ceases trying to be the omnipotent *pater familias* and settles for something closer to the role of friendly visitor, while the mother takes on the additional duties of authority figure and dispenser of justice. For the time being, these modifications take care of the primary group of problems created by the change in the family; when, however, it becomes clear that one or both parents are going to remain single a very long while or permanently, certain additional problems in child-parent relations appear for which the subculture has not yet devised standard solutions or consensual answers, as it has in the area of the FM's social life.

This is not surprising; until recently there were relatively few such people around. Now, however, the rapid increase in the percentage of divorcing people who have children is changing the picture. Today about one and a half million families with children are headed by unremarried FMs—nine-tenths of the time such family heads are women—and roughly four hundred thousand of them are Long-Termers. Within the next decade or two this considerable body of people will probably generate some fairly reliable techniques for dealing with their common problems.

The "problems of the single parent" have, to be sure, been closely studied by family counsellors, social workers, and others, but their attention has been directed chiefly toward the practical difficulties of running a household, caring for children, perhaps even working part-time or full-time, and having twenty-four-hour-a-day responsibility. The occasional man who has custody has much the same burden of practical problems—perhaps greater, since he is bound to work, and even if he can afford a full-time housekeeper, it may be harder for him than for a woman to find one willing to sleep in. Yet for all these problems, difficult as they are, certain known and reliable answers are already available: servants or baby-sitters for those who can afford them; help from relatives and ex-in-laws, either in the form of money or part-time child care; the use of nursery schools, day-care centers, community centers, YMCA's and the like; and, of course, the aid of the oldest child, as soon as he or she is able to do some of the household work, cooking, and child-care.

But for a subtler, less immediate, and yet even more disturbing type of problem there are no good answers: this is the lack of emotional and social support for the long-term single parent. The FM woman may have learned how to redefine her status vis-à-vis unattached men, made a satisfactory personal life for herself as a divorcee, and worked out the logistical problems of running her household, but her position in the community remains unclear. Her neighbors find her social status indeterminable, her motives in remaining single obscure, her private life alien and suspect. She feels all this even in the beginning, but as time passes she finds that it is becoming a problem not just for her, but for her children, who are simply not as welcome in neighbors' homes as they would be if she were not a divorcee. The children can hardly put this into words, but they feel the difficulty even as minority-group children do; they know that they are subtly and mysteriously held at arm's length.

The neighbors want their child to associate with children who come from *good* homes, whose parents are *fine* people—children, in short, who will *amount* to something some day—but who can know about the children of divorce? The child who spends many years with a single FM parent becomes both resentful toward, and defensive of, his divorced parents for putting him in this position. There seems no solution to this difficulty except remarriage—the very boon the long-term FM seems unable to provide her children; she not only feels guilty about this, but is angry at them for making her feel so.

A problem which involves both of the ex-mates, especially if they are Long-Termers, is that of the conflicting styles of life to which they expose their children. As the years go by there is less similarity in the way the former spouses do things, more expression of their individual choices in food, furniture, and recreation. People of very dissimilar tastes temper them somewhat while they live together, but divorced adults deliberately give free rein to their own preferences, whether they be for slovenliness or fastidiousness, play or work, poker or Shakespeare. The children are exposed, year after year, to two differing styles of life and sets of values—each of which belongs to a parent. Sometimes the children use the father's ideas and tastes as weapons of rebellion against their mother, sometimes they are inwardly torn by the impossibility of living by both parents' standards. The child with, say, a dry, strict mother and a sensual, easy-going father may passionately yearn to be approved by the one and yet live like the other. For years he may oscillate wildly in his feelings and actions, sometimes abjuring one way of life or the other; if he is unlucky, he may never solve the problem as long as he lives.

But why should this be more of a problem for the long-term FM than for those who remarry? Do not remarried FMs continue to have values unlike those of their ex-spouses? Of course —but remarriage moderates the effect of the conflict on the children: if the absent parent—usually the father—remarries, he generally becomes absorbed in his new life and more remote from his children, thus reducing the force of his way of life; if the mother remarries, she gains a powerful ally in the form of the new man in the home.

But as long as both parents remain unmarried—certainly as long as the one with custody does so—the children will not only be affected by the differences between their parents, but will play upon them. If Mother never lets them have a snack close to dinner-time, that is just what they beg Dad for—and since he is only a Sunday parent, he tries to please them as much as possible. If Mother never lets them watch horror movies on TV after dinner, that is what they most want at Dad's place; he innocently tries to make them happy, and delivers them to their mother afterward, high-spirited, fractious, and unbeddable.

Yet children are usually anxious to be loyal to each parent and to be loved by each. "Dad," says a nine-year-old after a particularly good weekend visit, "don't ever say I told you this, but I love you more than I love Mom." Later on, of course, he will tell Mom he loves *her* more—not because he is a chronic liar and manipulator, but because this is the only solution he has been able to devise. It is the best adaptation he has been able to make to his dilemma, and it may remain so until the marriage of one parent or the other tips the balance.

In the same way, children often agree with each parent in his or her estimate of the other, but privately agree with both or neither. One man, in the course of a disagreeable conversation with his former wife, was dismayed to hear from her that their fifteen-year-old son "felt nothing but contempt" for him because he had "walked out on" her and the children years earlier. Before he next saw his son, he rehearsed an eloquent statement of his side of those by-gone days, but the moment he brought up the subject his son dismissed the matter with a sentence: "Oh, come on, Dad," he said as one man to another, "you know I *have* to say things like that to Mother."

One problem that is uniquely the woman's concerns the sex education of her sons. It is not only awkward for her to explain

the mechanics of sex to them, but even more difficult for her
to prescribe and give force to rules of sexual conduct. In a
normal home, the father would do so, or would lend his masculine authority to the mother's code. But a woman without
a husband seems to her son to be a spokesman not for his side,
but for the girls' side; from his friends and from older boys,
however, he hears the male viewpoint, and finds it more agreeable than his mother's code. His father's moral instruction
might seem more compelling than his mother's, but he sees
his father too seldom and under too special conditions for the
subject to come up or, even if it does, to receive any serious
and consistent attention.

Besides, most long-term FMs have trouble imposing morally strict standards upon their sons and daughters for the
simple reason that their own behavior has become unconventional. They try to inculcate traditional morals in their children,
but if their own sexual unconventionality is obvious, they look
absurd playing the moralist, and if it is concealed, they feel
hypocritical. Despite the lip-service they pay to conventional
morality, therefore, their effective attitudes are distinctly more
permissive toward their children's sexual behavior than those
of married parents, according to a recent national survey. Although the survey does not distinguish between recent divorcees and Long-Termers, permissiveness is very likely to be
especially marked in most of the latter.

Permissiveness does not, however, solve the touchiest problem of all—what to say to the children about one's own way
of life. Newly separated or divorced people explain the marital
break-up to children as best they can, presenting themselves
as people who believe in and deeply desire happy and lasting
marriage. But as the years pass, and as potential partners
come and go, it becomes more and more difficult to maintain
that one simply has not found anyone suitable—all the more
so because the children are likely to have found several of the
potential mates quite suitable from their point of view. Gradually the children stop indicating their approval, and no longer

ask the questions that arise in their minds, though like Yvonne English's daughter they seem to be saying: Why haven't you ever remarried? It's really your fault, isn't is?

Those Long-Termers who are discontented with FM life and want to remarry may feel, like Mrs. English, that in their children's eyes they are failures, unable to win what they desire, even though so many others have been able to do so. But those Long-Termers who are contented with their non-marital way of life have an even more uncomfortable situa-tion: they cannot bring themselves to justify and extol it to their children. Sexual rebelliousness suits them, but they are apprehensive at the prospect of having their children discover how they feel, and approve; the only worse thing would be to have their children discover how they feel, and disapprove.

In view of all this, how adequate a parent is the Long-Termer? One way to find out is to ask him. A minority of women feel they are not doing well with their children because of excessive burdens or frustrations which make them irascible and explosive, and a minority of men say that they have be-come too far removed from their children's lives to have any real effect upon them. But most women and many of the men feel that they are doing a successful job, and very definitely a better one than they did when married. As reasons for their improvement, they cite the absence of conflict and tension, better feelings about themselves, and a greater ability to give themselves to their children. But these statements have to be taken cautiously; they are subjective judgments, probably somewhat biased in the parents' favor.

Social workers, family counsellors, and psychiatrists, on the other hand, often talk or write about the many shortcomings in the parental performance of the separated and divorced. They speak of the mother who overprotects her children in order to atone for her guilt at having deprived them of normal family life; they speak of the father who becomes a mere entertainer and gift-giver, buying a little affection and relief from guilt by providing fun and presents. But these comments are based on observations only of those people who come for help with their problems; healthy and successful parents have no reason to.

The truth, as it so often does, probably lies in the middle. Most FM women, despite all the practical burdens and emotional pitfalls of single parenthood, seem to rear their children reasonably well—possibly not quite so well as happily married women, but probably better than unhappily married ones. Fathers, usually being the absentee parents, may be warmer and more relaxed with their children than they were during the stressful period of breaking up; but they see so much less of them, and then in so special a context, that they exert far less influence for good or bad.

Of the several kinds of Long-Termers already described, the real rebels against marriage—the loners who are cheerfully and permanently wedded to FM life—probably make the most indifferent parents. They live in a state of chronic alienation from the society their children are growing up in; moreover, being self-centered and self-sufficient, they are no more child-oriented than they are mate-oriented. The sexually incapacitated, on the other hand, have so few personal and emotional satisfactions that they are often overparental; in addition, they are apt to be severely puritanical about their children's sexual feelings. The Long-Termers who are merely drifting through their post-marital years, without any strong pull one way or the other, are probably rather good parents; being content as FMs without being rebellious against marriage, they are at peace with themselves and yet are not self-centered. But there is little stability in their ways, and the changes wrought by chance sometimes make the children insecure and anxious about the future.

Among those who are not content with being Long-Termers, the rejects are probably the poorest parents; they need love badly and may try to wring it from their children in sufficient quantity to make up for what they cannot obtain elsewhere.

They become suffering parents, controlling their children through their own martyrdom. The rejecting kind, who think they want to remarry but unconsciously prevent themselves from doing so, are sometimes able to give their children the love they cannot give to adults; as time goes by, however, and they enter into, and then destroy, one new relationship after another, they may instil in their young a sense of impermanence and hopelessness concerning adult love. The Long-Termers who are discontent to remain FMs and yet optimistic about the future are sometimes good parents and sometimes poor ones, depending on whether they feel they are proceeding in the direction they desire or are being carried away from it. Those who have been slowly but consistently evolving toward emotional health probably improve as parents with the passage of time, for as they become increasingly whole and balanced people, it is natural for them to be increasingly effective parents.

All in all, it is no easier to be a single parent than to be a good lover or good friend outside of marriage. Only to a small number of people is the FM way of life permanently satisfying and preferable to remarriage. The reports that the institution of marriage is dying or dead are exaggerations; it cannot die as long as there is nothing to take its place.

CHAPTER NINE

Return of the Expatriates

1 · The Marrying Kind

In the first throes of loneliness, most FMs see remarriage as the only possible solution, while later on, having discovered the compensations and privileges available within the World of the Formerly Married, they may be tempted to remain there indefinitely. Yet that world is not so much a substitute for marriage as a training ground for remarriage. Two generations ago, when this subculture scarcely existed, or existed in far less developed form, only one out of every three divorced people ever remarried; today, although the FM's life has become easier and socially more acceptable, six out of seven do so. Despite the possibilities of comfortable long-term adjustment to divorced life, remarriage still seems to most FMs the best solution to their problems.

We have already observed the social pressures—estrangement from married friends, alienation from most social activities, an ambiguous and isolated position in the community—that motivate FMs to commit themselves to remarriage. Yet almost no one ever remarries primarily for such reasons; at least, it hardly ever feels that way. For these are "sensible" and practical considerations, and Americans feel it improper to marry on that basis. Even the divorcee who desperately needs financial support would feel she was selling herself if she married only for security; even the father with custody, who urgently needs someone to run his home and mother his children, has to feel another and nobler motive before making some woman his wife.

And that, of course, is Love—the one reason for remarrying in which all can take pride. Even though ours has been described as the Age of Cool, love is still the *sine qua non*, the major motive for remarrying. And marriage, in return, is the *sine qua non* of love; we live not in close-knit communities or large families, but in closely packed isolation; the only sure source of comfort, companionship, and love is one's spouse. As time passes, therefore, and the FM becomes better able to function sexually and emotionally within the World of the Formerly Married, he or she also becomes readier to attempt to satisfy deeper needs through marriage.

Most of the Formerly Married are not only capable of such a relationship, but have an innate preference for it rather than for the limited and casual kind. Despite previous marital failures, FMs remain marrying people: at every age level they are more likely to marry than people who have never been married at all, and this difference becomes greater as the age levels progress. Ninety-nine out of one hundred women who are divorced by twenty-five will remarry sooner or later; only eighty-eight out of one hundred single women of that same age will ever marry. Two out of three divorcees who are forty will eventually remarry, but only one out of seven single women of forty will do so. The odds favoring marriage are higher for both single and formerly married men at every age, but show a similar divergence.

All of which indicates that FMs and never-married people tend to have somewhat different kinds of personality—the more so as time filters and separates them. Except for the very young, most never-married people either do not need or cannot tolerate the intimacy of married love; FMs, despite the failure of their marriages, do need such intimacy, and either can tolerate it or mean to try their best. Nearly all FMs did love their mates for a while, even if imperfectly, and were loved in return; knowing something of that experience, they remain unsatisfied by the substitutes and the partial loves of unmarried life. For most of them, the mistake was not marriage itself but the particular marriage they made; only the "loners" were, at heart, non-marrying people who misjudged themselves and then learned better.

Yet few of the divorced are either clear or consistent about the kind of person they now believe they need and can love well enough to marry. Some think they know the traits they are searching for, but most are much more specific about the traits they want to avoid. Some are more exacting in their requirements than they were before; others are less so, and expect to find and tolerate many imperfections in anyone they love. Young and middle-aged FMs dwell upon the emotional and sexual characteristics they hope to find in a new mate; older FMs more often say they want someone companionable and easy to get along with. Nearly all believe they know themselves better now, and have a clearer notion of what sort of person they need; virtually all mean to avoid the sort they chose before.

Whatever it is they are seeking, formerly married people far more often find it among other FMs than among never-married or widowed persons. Divorced people marry other divorced people about sixty per cent of the time, single and widowed people only forty per cent of the time. But their preference for each other is even stronger than these figures indicate, for the proportion of FMs among the people from whom they are free to choose is less than half as large as the proportion they marry. To put it another way, since divorced women make up approximately one fourth of the total population of unmarried women from among whom divorced men are free to choose new mates, one might expect about one out of four remarrying men to select an FM woman and the other three to select single women or widows. But similarity of experience and social status draw FMs to one another so powerfully that divorced men actually marry divorced women two and a half times as often as chance or random choice would account for.

To the divorced person, another divorced person is knowable, familiar and, in a sense, dependable: the broken previous marriage is taken as an earnest of his or her intent to have an unbroken one, the wreckage of love is proof that love existed and can be rebuilt. The customs and social mechanisms of the World of the Formerly Married not only maximize the exposure of the divorced to other divorced people, but help them ready themselves to try to make good those hopes and promises.

II · *Return Trip*

The course of true love never did run smooth and, as we have seen, it is especially bumpy for the Formerly Married. Unlike the young, who come to each other relatively empty-handed, the divorced man and divorced woman come with all the acquisitions of the years—their individual histories, habits, and tastes, their children, friends, and chattels. Love can be a rickety vehicle, loaded with so much of life's baggage, and the trip back to the world of the married is often interrupted by slow-downs, halts, and backsliding.

Nor is the way itself well-marked. Young unmarried people of the middle class follow a well-established route whose signposts are, usually, dating and necking, petting, going steady, talking about marriage, heavy petting or intercourse, formal engagement and, finally, marriage. FMs ignore this orderly progression: they rarely linger for any time at the dating and necking stage, but proceed swiftly to full sexual relations—in advance of most of the development of feelings of love. As for marriage, the woman very likely thinks secretly about the possibility of it the first time they make love, much as she did in any previous affairs; the man may refuse to let himself do so that soon, or may think about it but wrestle the thought into submission. Yet if it is an affair with marriage potential, both of them openly begin to refer to it far sooner than unmarried people would, but usually in a bantering manner; humor keeps the subject from being alarming. He may, for instance, grumble that what will finally force him to get married again is the pain of getting up in the middle of the night and dressing to go home; she may retort that for her it is the need to have someone who can open stuck windows.

And soon they deliberately act the part of man and wife without discussing it—they may pile his children and hers in the car for a day at the beach, and play the father and mother for each other's benefit even more than that of the youngsters. Or perhaps he will come over for dinner one evening, wearing old clothes, in order to fix things for her—a couple of doors that will not close, a lamp that needs rewiring; seeing him do this with her two excited boys as helpers, she glows, feels protected, and is filled with affection. Or perhaps they spend a Sunday afternoon together reading the paper and loafing, and later leave the children with a baby-sitter and visit friends for the evening. "Pretty domestic kind of day, wasn't it?" he says—and abruptly switches to some other subject; but both of them know he liked the thought more than he feared it.

The unmarried, having never been man or wife to anyone, may need signs and symbols to mark their progress; the Formerly Married mark theirs instead by ever more daringly testing out the roles of man and wife. Yet many of them omit the conventional gestures of courtship: half of those who finally remarry do so without ever having announced an engagement, and even those who do have an engagement announce it more quietly and keep it briefer than do the never-married. In part this probably reflects the greater experience and more realistic outlook of the Formerly Married: they have been through one or more affairs already that have fallen short, and know how many complications there are in their lives, how many possibilities exist for disagreement or disenchantment, how many habits and tastes they must try out on each other, how many situations they need to see each other in before committing themselves and their children to what they hope will be a permanent relationship.

Even after they have begun to love each other in earnest, and to feel genuinely committed, any one of a hundred difficulties may make them suddenly waver and briefly doubt that it can ever work. Perhaps at first he likes her children, but later becomes jealous of them, or impatient or too stern; he and she argue about it for hours; then, growing gentle and sad, they hold hands and talk long and softly about whether or not they are wrong for each other. Or perhaps she seemed soft, womanly, and gentle at first, but later shows a strength and obstinacy that exasperate him; after a series of angry interchanges, they fall silent until she comes over to him, tender and contrite, and they cling to each other like weary swimmers to a float; they kiss and forgive, but each wonders whether they have solved the problem or only postponed facing it squarely. Or perhaps he has a series of business problems, and is preoccupied and impatient; she tries to understand, but needs more of him than he is giving her, says as much, and instead of making him warmer and more attentive only makes him feel guilty and angry.

Yet in the love affair which does proceed toward marriage, these problems are resolved in one way or another, and love grows. For some, that growth is relatively easy and spontaneous; for most, it requires a great deal of work. Perhaps she is ready to be reassured of his affection five minutes after a spat, while he needs an hour or two to simmer down; either one or both of them must change, or they must get used to their differences and learn to allow for them. Perhaps she chokes back anger and fumes quietly, when he has hurt her feelings; he may have to draw her out, make her talk, and teach her to discuss it with him rather than bottle it up. Each finds innumerable ways to please the other a little with certain words, special smiles, tiny deeds. Each learns which things they both like and can enjoy together, and which they must let each other enjoy alone. Each makes dozens of compromises and bargains with the other about their tastes in food and sex, their ways with children, their needs in friends.

Unmarried young people go steady but continue to act like dates who are in love; the Formerly Married go together and act like lovers who have just been married. Dating becomes a thing of the past; they evolve into a couple, seeing each other as much as they can, growing so comfortable that they can sit quietly in the same room, reading and not feeling obliged to talk. But they do talk a great deal: each is eager to share with the other the experiences of the day, each devours the other's words so as to live the other's life vicariously. Waking or sleeping, working or playing, in each other's presence or apart, they become intertwined and enmeshed, until they are no longer lonely when alone, no longer single when solitary.

And now a change in allegiances comes about almost by itself. They meet or visit married friends, and find them indulgent, warm, approving; the married people welcome them with a slightly annoying largeness of spirit, as though they had strayed from the True Church and now are penitently returning. At the same time they are beginning to feel themselves drawing away from their FM friends; it is not a matter of a deliberately created distance, but of an inevitable decrease in the number of shared feelings, a loss of identification, a regrowth of privacy. If the man still has a couple of drinks or spends an evening with another formerly married male, or the woman meets another divorcee for lunch, each smiles and talks as always, but something is different; an inner barrier, invisible but almost tangible, separates them and blocks out certain confidences and intimacies. For they no longer want to share their intimate feelings with others, now that they love. The same man who could talk volubly to a friend about a sexual fling or even a new and promising affair can hardly bring himself to say that he feels a deeper and richer love now than ever before; instead he relies on simple clichés: "I think this is really it" or "This one's different."

It is at once marvelous to feel one's self rejoining all that from which one had felt alienated, and rather sad to feel one's self becoming alienated from all that to which one had been joined. Like seniors at graduation, the lover and his FM friends are effusive when they meet but ill-at-ease; already it is clear they are going different ways, that each is holding back part of himself and guarding some of his thoughts while pretending to pour them out freely. They know with regret that the promises of continuing friendship are well-meant, but that the friendship will not continue as it was. The FMs are glad for the lovers but a little jealous; they wish the lovers well, but feel almost deserted, almost betrayed.

Somehow the word is finally given out—perhaps in the form of an informal, verbally announced engagement, perhaps merely in the form of a casual mention to friends about a wedding date. It is at this very point that some FMs suddenly become alarmed at the multiplicity of adjustments they will have to make in the future, or belatedly discover some seemingly insoluble problem in the marriage they had planned. One or the other of them may grow panicky and call a halt to everything, postponing the wedding indefinitely; then the panic recedes, they rush together again, the wavering one is forgiven, the plans are renewed. Despite shilly-shallying, they move rapidly toward their goal and arrive there soon: FMs spend less than half the time in courtship that never-married people do. For though the Formerly Married have so many bits and pieces to fit together, they are adept and knowing about it; moreover, being adult, they are impatient to live within marriage again, and not content to play at it from the remoteness of engagement.

Many an FM is apprehensive when the time comes to tell the children about the future marriage, and with good reason. No matter how eagerly children had besought their parent to remarry, their ambivalence usually became obvious as the courtship progressed. The more absorbed the man and woman became in each other, the more rivalry the children showed, even though they also showed increasing fondness and trust. In view of their conflicting feelings, one never knows in advance just how they will respond to the news. Small children may burst into happy tears, or they may have a tantrum; older ones may be warmly congratulatory, or outspokenly critical and cold. Strong reactions of one sort or another are more likely on the part of the woman's children; happily, they are positive more often than not. In the case of the man's children, the limited amount of contact they have with their father and his daily life tends to make their reactions milder; they are about as likely to be indifferent as delighted, and are only rarely hostile or upset.

The wedding is usually far simpler than the ceremonies of people marrying for the first time. Only about half of the remarriages are held in churches, as compared with four fifths of first marriages. The bride does not wear white, and rarely wears a long gown; she appears usually in a cocktail dress or even sometimes a suit. The minister, rabbi, or officiating justice keeps the ceremony short, and eliminates from his customary wedding speech the glowing promises that have already once proven false for both bride and groom. Even the cake, if there is one, is plain; a bakery in New York has, for instance, tactfully designed a special model for remarriages, featuring white sugar bells on top in place of the usual figures of bride and groom. Offsetting these simplifications are a few special complexities: children of both sides underfoot, excited and noisy; relatives and old friends who have known bride or groom in the previous marriage, and who have to exercise special care not to say anything inappropriate; married friends and FMs, an occasional ex-in-law or ex-lover, sometimes even an ex-spouse, all intermingling, putting on their best smiles, and trying to take each other's measure; and throughout, amidst the prevailing atmosphere of good will and good wishes, the unspoken, almost palpable thought in the minds of most of those present: "I hope it works out this time"—at once a wish and a doubt. Then it is over. The newly married people have left the World of the Formerly Married; they are no longer rebels, dissidents, non-conformists; they have rejoined the flock and made peace with their society.

III · *Will It Work?*

What chance is there that this remarriage, or remarriages in general, will do well? It is a subject about which experts have widely differing opinions.

A number of psychoanalysts, marriage counsellors, and psychotherapists whose views derive from Freudian psychology hold that human personality is formed in its essentials by childhood experiences, and is not capable of significant change in adulthood except through deep psychotherapy; they therefore feel that the experiences of marriage, divorce, and life as an FM cannot modify the individual in any important sense, and that in remarriage he will only make the same mistakes and encounter the old problems again.

One of the best-known exponents of this view was the late Edmund Bergler, a psychoanalyst who set forth his opinions in a book entitled *Divorce Won't Help*. Dr. Bergler stated that divorcing people believe they have learned a lot from their mistakes and are sure they will be more successful in their next marriage, but that this is pure illusion; they are wholly unaware of the actual reasons for their choice of the wrong partner, their behavior within marriage, and their decision to flee via divorce. For these reasons, which are part of their neuroses, are thoroughly hidden in the unconscious; and since adult experiences do not modify the individual's neurosis, divorced people are bound to fall in love unwisely again, and to fail again in marriage. "Since the neurotic is unconsciously always on the lookout for his complementary neurotic type," wrote Dr. Bergler, "the chances of finding conscious happiness in the next marriage are exactly zero. . . . The second, third, and nth marriages are but repetitions of previous experiences."

On the other hand, a growing number of psychoanalysts and clinical psychologists believe that human nature remains much more plastic after childhood than Freud realized, and that it is capable of change and growth even in the adult years, if exposed to significant experiences or to a new environment. It follows that marriage, divorce, and FM life can importantly add to the individual's emotional capacity, self-knowledge, and judgment, and that most divorced people should do better in their remarriages than they did in their first ones. Apart from psychological grounds for such a belief, a number of sociologists hold that the statistics on remarriage indicate that faulty first marriages must be not so much the result of neurosis as of normal errors, misjudgments, and incompatibilities. The late Dr. Abraham Stone, an expert on sexual problems and a marriage counsellor of vast experience, concluded from his own observations that "the majority of bad marriages are those in which the individuals are quite normal and average, but are wrong for one another, though each might have been right for somebody else." Professor Jessie Bernard found in her own extensive study of remarried persons that the majority of divorces are caused by "team factors"—normal misjudgments, based on inexperience, as to how two given personalities will fit together in the partnership of marriage. "The experience of an unhappy first marriage," she writes, "although it may constitute a high tuition fee, may nevertheless serve as a valuable educational prerequisite to a successful second marriage."

"Who shall decide, when doctors disagree?" Perhaps the divorced themselves; at least they should know whether they are making the same mistakes, even if they fail to understand why.

A certain number of FMs do admit that they are still often attracted by the same type of persons they were married to, but claim that they hastily back away as soon as they recognize the similarity. Others take longer, and get themselves into trouble. One man writes that he fell in love with and married a pretty little girl whose tart tongue and witty manner delighted him; as her husband, however, he found that she was a belittling and hostile woman. After divorce, he tried to avoid her type, and eventually became involved with a tall, earnestly intellectual college instructor; it took several months before he realized that he had changed only the unessentials; she often used her intellectuality to express the same kind of hostility toward him, and toward all men, as had his first wife. He got out of the affair with some difficulty, and probably saved himself the pain of a second divorce.

A few FMs admit that they did not see the similarities soon enough and ended up, as Dr. Bergler said they would, with the same unhappy results. A young businesswoman who was married to an architect for four years, and to an industrial designer for two, explains:

> I did the same thing in my second marriage that I had the first time—I chose someone insecure and undeveloped, and tried to make him mature. Believe it or not, I actually financed *both* of these men all the way through their graduate education. I played mother and teacher and big sister to each of them. It works fine but only for a while; then I get frustrated, because I want somebody to lean on, and they get difficult because they don't want to grow up. I finally went into psychotherapy, and once I understood that the problem was of my own making, I never let myself make the mistake again.

But without requiring psychotherapy, most divorced people seem determined to avoid the same kind of relationship they had the first time. Some say they still feel a certain pull toward the same type of person but have learned to recognize and deny the impulse, and to react more positively to quite different types. Others find themselves actually repelled by the traits they once liked. A forty-five-year-old securities analyst speaks:

> My first wife was a real bohemian—zany, sloppy, always going off on the spur of the moment and leaving things on the stove to

burn up, spending more than we had on a wild impulse to fly to Mexico—things like that. It seemed exciting and magical when I was twenty-five, but after six years of it and a divorce I found it loathsome. Instead, I found myself liking other kinds of people with qualities I used to sneer at. My present wife is sensible and competent and even-tempered. She loves fun but has a sense of responsibility to me and the children.

Though such testimony does not constitute rigorous proof, it does suggest that many of the Formerly Married have learned to avoid choosing the same sort of person they were married to before. Yet this is no absolute guarantee that they will do better in a second marriage. The all-important question remains: Is the chance of happiness in the second marriage "exactly zero," or is it reasonably good?

One kind of evidence often brought to bear on this point is the divorce rate of the remarried. A few studies of this rate have been made at various times in different parts of the country; the figures differ somewhat, but are always higher than those for first marriages. One of the most recent and careful studies, based on Iowa records for the early 1950's, shows that remarriages are twice as likely to break up as first marriages. Those who marry a third or subsequent time run a still greater risk of further divorce: if both spouses have been divorced twice or more, the chance of a later marriage failing is nearly five times as great as it is for a first marriage.

Such figures are often used as proof that divorced people lack the capacity to make successful marriages, and are bound to fail again and again. But this conclusion is unwarranted. At least sixty per cent of second marriages do endure until death. Moreover, some divorce-prone people become chronic repeaters and reappear again and again in the remarriage and divorce data, making the chance of divorce for the mass of remarrying FMs look greater than it actually is.

But even those who do get divorced a second time are not all neurotics and marital incompetents. Some—perhaps even most—are acting upon what they have learned: that divorce is not as dreadful as they had once thought; that the life of the FM is not necessarily unhappy or unrewarding; and that even the distressing aspects of divorce are less destructive of the personality than remaining in a bad marriage. Their second divorces do not show an inability ever to make a successful marriage; they do show an increased readiness to give up an unsuccessful one.

Another kind of evidence is the survey in which remarried people, or people who know them, are asked to evaluate the happiness of their second marriages. Of the handful of such studies, the two most important are in close agreement, even though they used different methods and were based on people in different parts of the country. Psychologist Harvey J. Locke, in his book *Predicting Adjustment in Marriage,* presented the results of his survey of 146 chiefly middle-class people, all remarried, some of whom lived in Indiana and some in California. He found three-quarters of them to be happy or very happy, and only one out of nine unhappy or very unhappy; the remainder lay in between. Dr. Jessie Bernard based her study, *Remarriage,* on some two thousand middle- and upper-middle-class remarriages in a Northeastern state, two-thirds of which involved at least one FM, the other partners being widowed or never-married persons; these marriages were evaluated for her not by themselves but by others. Seven-eighths of them were rated anywhere from satisfactory to extremely satisfactory; only one-eighth were said to be unsatisfactory or extremely unsatisfactory.

Although neither of these researchers asked how the second marriage compared with the first, the answer would seem perfectly obvious; nevertheless, Dr. William Goode, as part of his study, *After Divorce,* asked that question of all the remarried women in his sample. Nearly ninety per cent considered their second marriages much better than their first ones; the rest found them only a little better, or no better, or worse. Dr. Goode cautiously points out that all of these women had been remarried two years or less, and may have been somewhat more enthusiastic than they will be later on; even allowing for this, however, the evidence strongly contradicts the opinion of Dr. Bergler and his allies that the remarried are bound to fail again and that their chances of doing better the second time are nil.

So much for the bare bones of statistics—but how does it feel in the flesh? Even if a majority do better the second time, is the difference great enough to warrant all that they had to go through? Three remarried people—one unhappy, one moderately happy, and one very happy—may help us decide for ourselves. First, a Midwestern business executive, now forty-eight, represents those who are unhappy the second time around:

> I married my second wife on the rebound when I wasn't ready for matrimony, and ruined all my hopes of a better life by picking even more poorly than I did the first time. For these past six years, I've been trying far harder to make a go of it than she is willing to make. She turned out to be a lousy housekeeper, which bothers me no end since I am compulsively neat. She is continually dissatisfied with her lot, and accuses me all the time of either holding money back from her or not earning enough to provide properly for her and our children, even though I make nearly $20,000 a year. The worst thing is that she got the German measles when she was pregnant with our second child, and though I begged her to get a legal abortion, she refused, and gave birth to a Mongolian defective. Since then her shrewishness has been unbearable. I can't think how to improve the situation. She won't consider marriage counselling. There is no real communication, and what love we had once is completely soured. But if I can't salvage this marriage, and have to go through divorce again, I will feel really like a hopeless case. In fact, I feel like one right now.

Next, a striking redhead of thirty-four, brisk and saucy in manner and a highly efficient personal secretary, represents the great majority who consider their remarriages average or somewhat above average in happiness:

Tony isn't an ideal husband—that's an understatement. He can be a damned difficult man when his writing isn't going well—sullen, nasty, unwilling to do anything around the house, drinking too much, sitting up all hours and smoking, sometimes going out without saying a word and staying out until I'm worried sick. And in any kind of crisis he's no help at all—when the maid doesn't show up, for instance, or the landlord won't come fix the furnace, you'd think it was the end of the world. But he's got a fabulous mind, and when things are going well he's funny and kind and gay. In fact, even when he's being difficult he's never dull. And he's masculine through and through. I never feel the lack of that, as I did with my first. He's a pretty good father, at least when he's in a good mood. All in all, it's not as good a marriage as I myself once hoped for, and promised myself to make, but I think it's at least as good as most. Maybe better. I'm not complaining.

Finally, there are the minority whose remarriages are extremely satisfactory or very happy; a woman in her early forties who teaches history in a small New England college can serve as a model of this group:

My first marriage was sociologically ideal—similar backgrounds, income level, tastes, education: all the factors were beautifully matched. But we were friendly strangers from the beginning. He was always unromantic, cool, fair-minded, rational, but he was never really involved with me as a human being, and he became less and less so as time passed and his business interests multiplied. It was a very smooth organization that we ran and called a marriage. We didn't have fights—that wasn't the trouble—it was just that there was nothing happening between us. Even when he finally came home from his many activities for a weekend, he wanted to sleep and rest, and read in bed, and be left alone. There was no companionship, no communication, little sex. I felt unimportant and purposeless—and I thought all marriages were like that after the honeymoon period. But in contrast, my present husband, though he is a whirlwind and a hard worker

—he's a gynecologist—is warm and intense, and I come first in his life and he in mine. It is more beautiful and exciting after four years than I could have imagined. We spend every possible moment together because we want to. We have travelled to Asia and Australia together, lectured together, cleaned the barn and hunted and fished and skiied together; we sleep rolled in one tight ball together. Each of us wants to make the other feel secure in our love. Ours is a genuine *union*.

Not many remarriages—and not many first marriages, for that matter—can match this one; yet a considerable number of those who do have successful remarriages speak, with some of the same sense of wonder, of the discovery of a more satisfying and different kind of love. Such people would have no trouble at all answering the question as to whether there is enough difference between the first marriage and the second to warrant all that they had to go through; in fact, the question might strike them as somewhat absurd.

IV · *Is It Worth It?*

But however emphatically the question might be answered for themselves by the very happily remarried, or even by those who have achieved only an average degree of happiness, we need to ask it in another and broader sense: Is divorce, generally speaking, a morally valid choice—that is, by and large does it do more evil than good, or more good than evil, to all concerned than remaining in an unhappy marriage? For non-divorce, like divorce, involves a host of consequences for man and wife, for children, and for society; and since these may be either healthful or noxious, it can be morally as bad or as good a choice as divorce itself.

Let us, therefore, consider non-divorce for a moment. Almost no one will take issue with the premise that if poor marriages could, of themselves, turn into good ones, or be remade into good ones by outside influences, non-divorce would be the preferable alternative—definitely so where there are children, marginally so where there are not. What, then, is the likelihood that improvement in a poor marriage will take place spontaneously? Folk wisdom tells of the newly married couple's "period of adjustment," during which all sorts of conflicts and difficulties are ironed out until marital happiness succeeds the post-honeymoon let-down. There is at least some sociological evidence to back up this popular belief. Professor Judson T. Landis once studied 409 long-term marriages and found that in six major activities of married life (friendships, finances, sex, and so on) anywhere from one quarter to one half of the husbands and wives felt there had been maladjustment at the outset; in each of the six activities, about half of these people felt that they had arrived at a state of adjustment with their spouses, the time this took ranging anywhere from several months to many years.

But this is less encouraging than it sounds. It is one thing for two compatible, but new, partners in marriage to have their initial maladjustments dissolved by familiarity and time; it is quite another thing, and far less likely, for there to be a spontaneous remission of any severe, deep-rooted conflicts that emerge as two people come to know each other intimately. Ersel E. LeMasters, director of the School of Social Work at the University of Wisconsin, studied a group of marriages which had had serious conflicts in them for a number of years; later on, he did a follow-up and found that although only one-fifth of them had broken up, not one of the four-fifths that remained intact had improved by itself. In most of these intact marriages, furthermore, one or both spouses were paying heavy penalties in the form of alcoholism, psychosomatic disorders, neurosis, work troubles, depression, and the like. Many other studies of troubled marriages made by caseworkers and other experts in family life have reached the same conclusions: the spontaneous improvement of marriages with profound conflict is extremely rare, and continued living in such a marriage can be seriously damaging to the personality of one or both spouses.

If there is little hope of spontaneous improvement, what are the chances that a disintegrating marriage can be held together and made into a good one by means of outside help? It is a truism among marriage counsellors, as among psychotherapists in general, that the patient has very little chance of improvement unless he wants to get better, but the vast majority of people who have reached the point of openly considering divorce do not want to be reconciled. In Wayne County, Michigan, which includes Detroit and its environs, an agency called "The Friend of the Court" offers marriage counselling to every divorcing couple that wants it, but although 11,000 couples filed for divorce in 1965, only 401 of them accepted the offer of counselling; about one quarter of these couples were reconciled. A somewhat better success record has been compiled by the Conciliation Court of Los Angeles County, which manages to work out reconciliations, through counselling, for a little over half of those couples where both partners voluntarily enter into the process. But in recent years, even though these services have become more popular, only between four and six per cent of the couples filing for divorce in Los Angeles County have been using the Court; the net result is that the salvage rate of all dissolving marriages is still very small. A compulsory reconciliation service, like that just enacted into New York's new divorce law, may force a great many people to confer with the counsellors, but it is very doubtful that this will save any large percentage of marriages. Even working with motivated voluntary clients, marriage counsellors throughout the country report significant improvement in less than half the cases; with unmotivated and unwilling clients, the rate of success is bound to be much smaller. Marriage counselling, though it can often heal a sick marriage, has little chance of saving a dying one and almost no chance of bringing a dead one back to life.

It would seem, then, that in the great majority of cases where marriage has become thoroughly unsatisfying, or is racked by deep emotional conflict, non-divorce is unlikely to result in happy marriage. Yet this is not the same as saying that divorce is necessarily a more successful alternative. To find out whether it is or not, let us turn again to the evidence.

The success or failure of divorce, first of all, does not depend solely on whether or not it leads to a new and happier marriage. We have seen that marital dissolution can of itself have results ranging anywhere from the profoundly beneficial to the profoundly harmful. At one extreme, an unremarried divorcee says that she is "surrounded by the wreckage of all that meant anything to her" and is unable ever to care for, or to trust in, anyone again; at the other extreme, an unremarried man says that divorce has brought him "terrible years but wonderful years, a second chance at life, a wholly new outlook on myself and the people around me. I shudder to think that I might have lived out my life without all this happening to me."

Thus, even among unremarried FMs, we can distinguish between the successfully and the unsuccessfully divorced. What we have seen indicates that the unsuccessful ones constitute a small minority of FMs, and the very successful a somewhat larger minority; in between, the great majority are reasonably successful. Most of the latter will not consider themselves wholly successful until they remarry, yet most of them feel they are better off than they were and have no regrets about the divorce. Four-fifths of Dr. Goode's sample, for instance, apparently had no reservations about the wisdom of their choice, since they felt that if they had stayed married, their marriages would only have deteriorated further, or at best shown no improvement.

Beyond this, however, people do very commonly weigh the outcome of divorce in terms of remarriage. The success of divorce, so judged, is not overwhelming, but it is at least respectable; as we have just seen, except for the severely neurotic and other special types, most of the Formerly Married have an even chance, or better, of achieving a satisfactory second marriage, and a very good chance of achieving one that is an improvement over the first. For the great majority of them, that is success enough.

The divorcing persons themselves are not, of course, the only ones whose lives are affected by their choice. Children are involved in sixty per cent of today's divorces, and it has long been standard for those who write about divorce to deplore the damage done to the children by the shattering of family life. Quite a few years ago, some of those who were scandalized by the climbing divorce rate pointed with horror to the very high proportion—sometimes said to be as high as eighty per cent—of delinquent children who came from broken homes; even today the bald assertion that divorce causes delinquency is still repeated, usually by opponents of divorce-law liberalization. But more searching analyses have suggested a larger cause associated with both divorce and delinquency—namely, social and economic deprivation: divorce and delinquency are both more common among poorer people, and occur side-by-side, perhaps not so much as cause-and-effect as two effects of the same general cause.

One way to prove this would be to compare the delinquency rates from intact and broken homes at the same economic level. Sheldon and Eleanor Glueck, in their careful study, *Unraveling Juvenile Delinquency,* attempted to do just this —they studied children from intact and broken homes in the same neighborhoods. They did find some degree of connection between the broken homes and delinquency, but it was very much smaller than had been supposed: within this one stratum of society, not eighty but only twenty-one per cent of delinquents came from homes where the parents were separated or divorced. A somewhat larger proportion of delinquent children came from broken homes than from unbroken ones, but this difference could not be ascribed solely to the fact that the family had split up: although the Gluecks had drawn upon homes in the same or similar neighborhoods, they found that economic and physical conditions in the broken homes were quite a bit worse than those in the intact homes; those conditions may have been partly responsible for the difference in the delinquency rate. A number of other investigations of the subject have shown that the delinquency rates for children from broken and unbroken homes are not very far apart; and even where there are definite differences in the rates, those differences are not greater than one might expect on the basis of pre-existing economic or psychological inferiority of the broken homes. One may reasonably conclude that divorce is responsible only to a limited extent for delinquency.

But even if divorce is far less likely to result in delinquency than has been alleged, perhaps it does produce other forms of damage to the personality. Nearly all FMs are deeply concerned over the harm they feel sure divorce must do to their children, and very often these fears are confirmed by the symptoms they see in them at the time of separation and for a while thereafter: crying spells, guilt feelings, nightmares and bed-wetting, sudden babyishness or aggressive playing, stammering, loss of interest in school, and many more. Longer-range effects are harder to identify, though they are said to include fearfulness about love and marriage, resentment toward men or toward women, and inability to relate to other people.

Putting aside for a moment the question of how frequent and how real such difficulties are, the crucial question is whether non-divorce would create fewer or more of them. The traditional view has long been that people should stay together, at least until the children grow up, on the assumption that this is far more healthful for them than divorce; conversely, people who do divorce are thought to be robbing their children of the benefits of a secure and happy childhood. But the testimony of nearly all the experts sharply contradicts these notions. Dr. J. Louise Despert, the author of *Children of Divorce* and a child psychiatrist who has had wide clinical experience with children both from divorced and from unhappy unbroken homes, says that "divorce is not automatically destructive to children; the marriage which divorce brings to an end may have been more so." Divorce, she says, may be "a cleansing and healing experience for the child." Other psychiatrists have found that the ending of a bad marriage seems to bring great relief to children; that it creates security and consistency in the family pattern, ending an intolerable vacillation in the children between hope and fear; and that it brings the child's fears of desertion out of the unconscious into the open, where he can finally learn to handle them.

To test such clinical impressions on a broad scale, F. Ivan Nye, a sociologist now at Florida State University, compared a large group of adolescents from broken homes with another large group from unhappy unbroken homes; the former turned out to be less often delinquent, better adjusted to their parents, and to have distinctly fewer psychosomatic ailments. Dr. Nye feels that this important phenomenon has been generally over-looked because family counsellors and child guidance workers focus their attention on the difficulties and tensions children experience at the time of the break-up; after a while, however, in a life free from the previous conflicts, the children adapt and reach a new equilibrium—but by that time no one is looking.

Divorce therefore seems preferable, from the viewpoint of the children's well-being, to the continuation of a seriously unhappy marriage. Nonetheless, many FMs continue to believe that in breaking up their marriages they have permanently harmed their children. Even if divorce is the less damaging alternative, the thought that they have done any damage at all makes them suffer from a continuing guilt. But how much actual damage have they done? Social scientists who have studied the children of divorce, seeing them without the dis-torting influence of guilt feelings, have found relatively little evidence of lasting emotional trauma due to the divorce itself. Children of divorce, and children living in intact and, for the most part, normal homes, have emotional problems in about the same numbers and degree of severity. In one of the most recent studies of the subject, published in 1964, Lee G.

Burchinal, a professor of sociology at Iowa State University, gathered information about two large groups of seventh-grade and eleventh-grade students and compared those from intact homes with those from broken homes and homes where there had been a remarriage; he could find almost no difference among them.

What, then, of the effects of divorce outside the family itself? Does it or does it not do any harm to the society in which the divorcing people live? Most Western societies seem to think of it as potentially harmful; they regulate marriage and divorce, but maintain far more stringent controls over the latter than over the former. In the United States, whether people use a religious or civil marriage ceremony, the resulting union has the legal value of a private contract between two consenting parties, such as is made by people going into a business partnership; but while every one of the fifty states permits all other private contracts to be dissolved at the mutual wish of both parties involved, it does not do so in the case of marriage. This is the only form of private contract from which partners can be released only by permission of the state, which retains the right to decide whether dissolution is or is not justified.

The only valid ground for the state's interference in this private contract is its interest in the preservation of social order, which would presumably be threatened if any large number of children became dependent on the state, or delinquent, as a result of divorce. Those who oppose easier divorce laws often point out that even the Soviet Union, though it made marriage and divorce a personal matter after the Revolution, had to pull in the reins again by means of the family edict of July 8th, 1944, which put an end to the legal recognition of unregistered marriages and to easy divorce. The inference is that easy divorce had proven hurtful to social order in the U.S.S.R., and had to be eliminated. In actual fact, there is no evidence whatever that it did so; it was ended primarily because it conflicted with the Stalinist goal of population growth, for which family stability, rather than freedom to pursue happiness, seemed a necessary condition.

It is fairly well known that freedom to divorce has existed in certain deteriorating societies; this was the case in the later years of the Roman Empire. What is less well known, freedom to divorce has existed in certain stable and healthy societies—especially those which have mechanisms other than the father-mother family for insuring the well-being and socialization of the children. The Hopi Indians, and various other preliterate peoples, had very high divorce rates but without creating serious problems concerning child-rearing and socialization. Among the Hopi the married couple lived with the wife's family; if there was a divorce, the husband moved back to his mother's house, while the wife remained in a household with her relatives, where her children were cared for and educated without difficulty. Although this is a pattern more often seen in primitive societies, something analogous to it exists in the pioneer communities of Israel—the *kibbutzim*—where the effects of divorce on the children have been minimal because they live apart from the parents in children's quarters and are cared for by trained specialists.

"There is no reason to believe," writes Dr. Kingsley Davis, of the University of California, Berkeley, an eminent researcher of family and social problems, "that a highly tolerant attitude toward divorce in the United States will mean the decline and fall of our civilization. . . . The only necessity is that some sort of social machinery be worked out for rearing the child properly—a necessity hard to supply in our culture."

For the time being, we can only piece together makeshift machinery—the use of schools after hours, day care and play-group facilities (both privately and publicly supported), co-operative nurseries, and the like. Yet even in advance of the fuller development of such devices and the creation of new ones, all those divorcing people who either can afford private facilities to aid them in the care and training of their children, or who have familial and other help with these tasks, may feel reasonably certain that they are not impairing the health of society. Indeed, if, as we have seen, their children would be somewhat more likely to grow up emotionally disturbed in an unbroken unhappy home, the decision to divorce is, even from society's standpoint, the better one.

Critics of divorce have raised the question of whether it is in conflict with the fundamental American way of life. They often see it as a repudiation of the American belief in family life, and a threat to moral values. They offer a number of alternatives: the conservatives among them urge acceptance of one's marriage, for the good of all concerned, the liberals stress the use of professional help to keep marriage intact, and a handful of radicals argue that freely condoned adultery will relieve the intolerable demands and tedium of monogamy. On one thing all three groups agree: the idealized romantic concept of marital love is a major reason for discontent and divorce; a more practical and down-to-earth view would be better for us all. But all these approaches to the divorce problem are, curiously, more impractical than the romantic notion of marriage, and more in conflict with the American philosophy of life than divorce itself.

Marriage, after all, is the only way Americans can find a great many of the emotional rewards they urgently need in life; to accept an unhappy marriage, to adjust to a loveless one, or to separate sex from marital love, is to ignore the most important benefits modern marriage has to offer, which are almost unobtainable elsewhere. In a world that has grown huge and impersonal, marriage is our principal source of emotional satisfaction, security, and individual happiness. Until society invents and perfects some new forms of grouping, some new kinds of attachment among people, we will need to have our marital partners be romantic as well as companionable, sexual as well as parental, exciting as well as domestic. This being so, we are right to be idealistic about marriage and to hope for much from it. We naturally rejoice greatly when it yields most of what we want, and cast it aside grievingly when it fails us.

And even if one agreed that it was foolish to hope for so much from marriage, is it not every man's right, in the United States, to commit follies in his pursuit of happiness? The meaning of the right to this pursuit has changed greatly since Jefferson first wrote it into the Declaration of Independence, but in recent decades the courts have more and more often equated it with both the freedom of contract and the freedom to labor, provided no harm is done to the rights of others. Divorce, as long as it does no harm, or at least less harm than continuation of a poor marriage, is clearly justified by this doctrine. The freedom to divorce is therefore a truly American right, which it is unjust to abridge by social or psychological pressure or by passing or maintaining restrictive laws.

It is for these reasons that divorce has become so common despite the existence of legal impediments. Between 1867 and 1960 the United States divorce rate increased more than sevenfold, even though the divorce laws of a number of states were made more stringent and conservative during that same period of time. If divorce were banned by law in all the states tomorrow, family life would be no better preserved; the deep needs and the basic philosophy of the people would lead them to disobey the law and live according to their consciences in illegal but satisfying unions, as is the case in Italy—a country without legal divorce—where some two and a half million people now live in such liaisons.

The wide use of divorce today is not a sign of a diminished desire to be married, but of an increased desire to be happily married. Never before in our history has marriage been more popular than it is today; in 1900 when, according to fond literary legend, everyone lived in warm familial contentment, only a little more than half of all men and women fourteen years old and over were married; today almost two-thirds are. More than ever, Americans want to marry well; more than ever they are willing to seek a good marriage, even if it means undergoing the long and often wretched experiences of divorce; more than ever they are coming to believe that divorce is morally justifiable in terms of the well-being of all concerned. For in the light of its consequences, divorce clearly appears to be a highly moral act, not only in many specific situations but in a broader sense. It is the necessary corollary of our elevated ideal of marriage, our valuation of emotional health, and our respect for the individual's right to seek happiness.

The sources on which I drew, in writing this portrait of the separated and divorced in America, are three-fold.

First, I combed through the pertinent published literature, especially the studies made by psychologists, psychiatrists, and sociologists. The major items I used are listed in the Bibliography, and referred to in the following notes by the author's name or, where needed, the author's name and publication date or short title. Three of these sources were so valuable and formative in my thinking that I should mention them here: Willard Waller's *The Old Love and the New,* though rather out of date, has a number of stunning insights; Jessie Bernard's *Remarriage* is both packed with useful information and humanly wise; and William J. Goode's *After Divorce* is an indispensable storehouse of quantitative sociological findings on almost every aspect of the lives of divorcing women.

Second, over a two-and-a-half-year period I interviewed some two hundred separated or divorced persons from various parts of the United States, attended their social functions, and visited their homes and haunts; I also talked or corresponded with scores of those who serve them, ranging from marriage counsellors to travel agents, from psychoanalysts to dance-hall operators.

Third, with the help of two psychologists and a market researcher, I devised a lengthy questionnaire containing nearly a hundred and fifty items; my more diligent respondents needed anywhere from three to ten hours to complete it. Some questions required only a check-mark by way of answer, while others called for essay-type answers; all, however, were designed to permit precise scoring and tabulating. I was therefore able, wth professional help, to extract a number of quantitative findings; most of them corroborated, but a few of them contradicted, my subjective impressions. The questionnaire was answered and returned by 169 middle-class and upper-middle-class adults of all ages, religions, and educational attainments, scattered all around the country. The sample is therefore a reasonably good one; nevertheless, since the proportions do not match those of an ideally representative sample, and since the respondents were all volunteers, I have used my statistical findings sparingly and with caution.

CHAPTER ONE

p. 3: *the man in Room 27.* . . . As stated in the Prefatory Note, all case histories or quotations from anonymous informants come from interviews or questionnaire replies unless otherwise identified in these notes. *Three thousand Americans.* . . . There is no official figure on the number of married couples that separate daily. My figure is a conservative estimate, taking the annual total number of divorces (over 400,000—i.e., over 800,000 persons), and correcting to allow for the fact that at least a third more persons separate with intent to divorce but are reconciled. Burgess (1953), p. 585, cites studies showing that about one out of every four divorce suits filed is withdrawn before it comes up in court. See also note to p. 211.

p. 4: *subculture.* . . . Among the social scientists who think of it this way are Kirkpatrick, who calls it a "subinstitution" (p. 512), and Monahan (1958), who speaks of a "dual pattern" of American marriage, in which monogamy is the standard institution, sequential polygamy (divorce and remarriage) the alternate.

p. 5, footnote: *annulments accounted for three per cent.* . . . U.S. Public Health Service (1962), p. 5.

p. 8: *ambiguity.* . . . Goode (1956) discusses this in detail on p. 11 f.

pp. 15–22: The most useful and recent compilation of data on divorce is *Divorce Statistics Analysis, United States, 1962,* referred to in the Bibliography as U.S. Public Health Service (1965); many of the figures in this section come from that report. The other sources on which I drew most often for current statistics include U.S. Public Health Service (1963) and (1964), the U.S. Bureau of the Census (1962) and (1966), and Jacobson, who uses marriage and divorce data for several past decades to calculate the risk of divorce for each year of marriage, the chance of remarriage, etc.

p. 16: On the risk of divorce in general, see Jacobson, p. 148. The divorce rates for various occupations come from U.S. Bureau of the Census: *U.S. Census of Population, 1960, Final Report, PC(2)-7A: Occupational Characteristics*, Table 12: "Marital Status of the Experienced Civilian Labor Force"; U.S. Public Health Service (1964), p. 3–3; and Goode (1962). The divorce rates in other countries can be found in Goode (1956), p. 11, and Goode (1961), p. 405.

p. 17: Divorce rate by socio-economic status is discussed in Goode (1956), pp. 46–53. On whites versus non-whites, see U.S. Bureau of the Census (1962).

pp. 18–19: The changing divorce risk, according to length of time married, is discussed in Jacobson, pp. 93–95 and 134, Monahan (1962), and U.S. Public Health Service (1964).

pp. 19–20: The Kansas City Study is listed in the Bibliography as Burgess (1960).

p. 20: Per cent of divorces involving children: Bernard, p. 80, Jacobson, p. 129, and U.S. Public Health Service (1964), p. 3–3.

pp. 20–21: For the relation between religion, urbanization, and the chance of divorce, see Locke, pp. 240–241, Goode (1956), p. 105, and Jacobson, p. 103.

p. 22: *ninety per cent. . . .* Ernst, p. 7, says ninety-five per cent; Pilpel, pp. 265 and 283–287, says "at least eighty-five per cent." On the changing grounds for divorce, Baber has a thorough but somewhat dated discussion on pp. 451–461; for more recent comment, see Bell, p. 402.

p. 23: On the number of divorces granted on grounds of cruelty, incompatibility, etc., see U.S. Public Health Service (1965), pp. 28–29.

p. 24: *What, then, do FMs name. . . .* Harmsworth, *passim,* and Goode (1956), p. 123.

p. 28: *sexual problems are not a major cause. . . .* Goode (1956), pp. 118–119; for the contrary view, Calderone, p. 177, Bergler (1948) *passim,* and Louis Nizer, quoted by Decter.

p. 31: The *Harper's* article is by Decter.

pp. 35–36: *Americans take months or years. . . .* Goode (1956), pp. 137–138, and Cuber, p. 90.

p. 36: *And there were the talks. . . .* Waller (1951), p. 517, discusses truth-sessions eloquently.

p. 37: *a symbolic graph. . . .* LeMasters (1957), p. 582. See also, on the process of marital conflict, Beck (1966). *Anger is the knife. . . .* The use of anger is examined by Waller (1951), pp. 515–520.

p. 38, footnote: Goode's suggestion about deliberate provocation appears in Goode (1956), pp. 135–136.

CHAPTER TWO

pp. 42–43: The symptoms of distress are compiled from interviews and questionnaires, but see also Goode (1956), p. 186. On the suicide rates of the divorced, see Jacobson, p. 138, and U.S. Public Health Service (1956), pp. 370–371 and 426–427.

p. 46: *damages the ego.* . . . Waller (1930), p. 8, Waller (1951), p. 157, and Kirkpatrick, p. 524, are among the many who make this point. *One sixth of all the family heads.* . . . Beck (1962), p. 8.

pp. 46–47: On the number of FMs who seek help with their emotional problems, see Gurin, pp. 280–281.

p. 47: *A few leading psychologists have begun to think.* . . . See Aronson (1964) and Aronson (1964a) for fuller treatment of this intriguing trend in psychiatric thought.

pp. 49–50: *"role disturbance".* . . . Bernard, p. 126. *Co-parent.* . . . *ib.*

p. 50: *nine-tenths of the time.* . . . The percentage of women getting custody varies slightly in different surveys: Jacobson, p. 131, says about eighty per cent, but he was including lower-class homes, where foster-parent arrangements are common; Goode (1956), p. 311, finds custody going to the women ninety-five per cent of the time; others report figures in between these two.

p. 51: *marriage may have proven uncomfortable and overly demanding.* . . . Cuber speaks of such people often; in order to remain married, they use special methods of preserving distance. See Cuber, chap. 3.

p. 53: *"chain lovers".* . . . The term is used by an anonymous correspondent quoted in Jessie Bernard *et al, Dating, Mating and Marriage* (Cleveland, Howard Allen, Inc., 1958), p. 290.

p. 54: *The large majority do offer some explanations.* . . . An impression based on my own survey; Burgess (1953), Locke, and others, however, say much the same thing.

p. 56: *rather paranoid.* . . . Baber, p. 498.

pp. 57–58: On divorce in ancient Rome, see Hunt (1959), pp. 25, 65, 67–68. On Christian ecclesiastical control of marriage, *ibid.*, pp. 113–114, 146; also, Bryce, vol. II, pp. 116 and 805. On the absorption of romantic love into marriage, see Hunt (1959), chaps. VI and VII.

p. 58: *'alarming and terrible' divorce rate.* . . . President Dwight's comment, and the divorce rate, are cited in Blake, p. 57. *Plays and novels.* . . . The history of plays dealing with divorce is reviewed by Koster; that of novels by Barnett. *"A sly way,"* etc. . . . The quote

is from Davis (1957), in which article he analyzes the view of divorce
as a pathological or neurotic act, and finds it a disguised moral judgment. See also Goode (1956), pp. 4–5 and 182.

p. 59: *tolerant . . . but resentful*. . . . Cuber, chaps. 2 and 5.

p. 62: *recent Broadway comedy . . . Fair Game* by Sam Locke,
produced in November, 1957. On the matter of the attitude of men
toward the divorced woman, see Roulston, p. 62, Bernard, p. 154,
Gordon, p. 132, and Bell, pp. 427–428.

p. 65: *In only two to three per cent of the cases*. . . . Kephart
(1961), p. 584.

p. 69: *a sign of returning health*. . . . Goode (1956), pp. 214–215
and 258, considers the actual beginning of dating the sign of returning
health, but I think that even the appearance of thoughts of doing so is
significant. *There is a very marked difference*. . . . The generalizations that follow in this paragraph are from my own survey, plus Goode
(1956), p. 262.

p. 74: *self-love . . . the basis of emotional health*. . . . This crucial point is discussed by Fromm, pp. 57–63, Maslow, chap. 12, and
Suinn. For a popularized summary of the evidence, see Hunt (1966).
Optimism may expand beyond sensible bounds. . . . Waller (1951),
p. 516 f., discusses the "great increase in egocentricity" that is a normal
accompaniment of the divorce process.

CHAPTER THREE

p. 76: *after the colonial period, most young men and women began
to have a good deal to say*. . . . Nearly all histories of the family stress
the degree of parental control existing until the beginning of the present
century, but a recent paper points out that in America a considerable
degree of self-selection of the mate existed even early in the nineteenth
century; see Frank Furstenberg, "Industrialization and the American
Family," *Amer. Sociol. Rev.*, June, 1966.

p. 78: On friends as the principal source of new contacts, see Goode
(1956), p. 255, and Hollingshead.

p. 83: *job or professional employment milieu*. . . . Goode, p. 250,
and Hollingshead.

p. 86: The P.W.P. quotation and historical details are from Egleson,
pp. 10 and 165–173.

p. 89: *hundreds and perhaps thousands of little groups*. . . . My
estimate is based on impressions gleaned from P.W.P. officers, entre-
preneurs of ski clubs and dances, etc.

p. 96: Marian Champagne's suggestions are found on pp. 247 and
288 of her book.

p. 97: *seeping upward to the middle class.* . . . So says Bernard, p. 59. Goode (1956), p. 67, takes a somewhat equivocal stand on the matter.

p. 98: The class differences with regard to the use of the "pick-up" are spelled out in Lerner, p. 586. The Grafton article, "The Twisted Age," appeared in *Look* for December 15, 1964.

p. 99: *the bar . . . is used by only about one out of ten.* . . . This, like other ratios given in this book and not ascribed to another source, is based on my own survey.

p. 101: *roughly 150.* . . . The figure is from an article by Martin Tolchin entitled "The Lonely Turn to Public Dances," in *The New York Times,* Nov. 19, 1963, p. 43.

p. 102: The ads are excerpted from the *New York Post* for October 6 and 9, 1964, and Dec. 1, 1965. Origins of the friendship club are from Block, and Bernard, p. 139.

p. 103: *"In essence"* etc. . . . The statement is by Block.

p. 104: On the history of matchmakers, see Fielding, pp. 19–21. The estimate of the total number of marriage brokers is from Vedder's study of lonely-hearts clubs.

pp. 104–105: The material on the Scientific Marriage Foundation is based on its own literature and personal communications from Dr. Crane.

pp. 105–107: The material on Friends Finders Institute is based on its literature and personal communications from Mrs. Richmond, Miss Thornton, and a number of their clients.

p. 107: The description of the typical marriage broker is based on my own visits to a number of them plus literature from others. *Perhaps three per cent.* . . . I derive this as follows: 800 marriage brokers (Vedder's figure) each averaging anywhere from 200 to 1,000 active clients (my own figure), for a national total of somewhere on the order of 500,000 clients. About a quarter to a third—say, 140,000—are FMs; about ten per cent of these, or 14,000, get remarried through the efforts of the brokers in a given year, out of a total of nearly 500,000 FMs remarrying annually. Hence, three per cent.

CHAPTER FOUR

p. 111: *Those who do not.* . . . This point is supported by Goode (1956), pp. 261–262; he finds that women with a "high trauma index" date less often than those with a "low trauma index."

p. 114: For the anecdote of the four-year-old in pajamas, I am indebted to the October, 1964, newsletter of the Washington, D.C. chapter of Parents Without Partners.

pp. 124–125: On the antagonisms between FMs and the widowed, see Langer, *passim*. Hanna Kapit, Ph.D., reports on the differences and conflicts in a two-part article, "The Widowed and the Divorced," in the *Journal* of Parents Without Partners for May–June, 1965, and July, 1965; and Waller (1951) mentions it on p. 476.

pp. 127–128: On the mores of the young, see Ehrmann, *passim*, and Andrew Hacker, "The Pill and Morality," in *The New York Times Magazine*, Nov. 21, 1965, p. 32.

CHAPTER FIVE

p. 142: *the first and second Kinsey Reports say.* . . . Kinsey (1948), pp. 278–280 and 295; Kinsey (1953), pp. 519, 533, and 549.

p. 143: *the widowed are sexually much less permissive.* . . . Kinsey's explanation for lumping them together is in Kinsey (1948), pp. 266 and 294–295, while the evidence for greater permissiveness of the FMs comes from a survey conducted by Professor Ira L. Reiss of the University of Iowa, about which I have a direct communication from him; the survey will be published in 1967 by Holt, Rinehart and Winston under the title, *Liberals and Conservatives: A Study in the Sociology of Sex.*

p. 146: *The causes of sexual incapacity are many.* . . . The literature on this subject is huge; one useful survey of it is Bergler (1961), although some of Dr. Bergler's psychoanalytic formulations are rather special. Brief eclectic explanations of both impotence and frigidity can be found in Arieti.

p. 148: On the Judeo-Christian tradition, see Hunt (1959), chap. IV.

p. 150: *Kinsey found masturbation.* . . . Kinsey (1948), p. 272, and Kinsey (1953), pp. 536 and 562. See also Waller (1930), pp. 207–208. Dr. Calderone's statements appear on p. 188 of her book.

p. 153: *Some observers.* . . . The first two interpretations (moral decay, solace) are widespread; the third (neurotic acting-out) is primarily psychoanalytic, and is asserted in its most unequivocal form in Bergler (1948), *passim. Redefining the self, repairing the ego*, etc. . . . . The functions of sexual experimentation were stated by Waller back in 1930; see Waller (1930), p. 56 f. and pp. 144–147. But writing when he did, he gives the subject a somewhat depressing and desperate sound. Today the general attitude of FMs toward sexual experimentation is more positive, less despairing.

p. 157: *"the erotomania of the newly divorced".* . . . the phrase is that of Lehrman, q.v. Waller (1951) speaks of the feelings of omnipotence of the separated or divorced person at this juncture.

p. 167: Miss Knakal's description of the romance addicts is embodied in an unpublished paper entitled "The Impact of Our Changing Sex Mores on the American Family," delivered at the 1963 Biennial of the Family Service Association of America in San Francisco.

p. 168: *We are all forbidden to desire our parents sexually.* . . . The disjunction between love and sex, and their later reunion, has been explained countless times in psychological literature ever since Freud's first formulation in *Contributions to the Psychology of Love*. One of the best resumes of theory and clinical findings on the matter is that of the sociologist Robert F. Winch, in chapter 13 of *The Modern Family* (N.Y., Henry Holt and Company, 1952). *"Good" women* . . . *"bad" women*. . . . Not all of the blame for sexual incapacity, however, rests on faulty psychodynamics in the family. A split between the good woman and the bad, the Mother and the whore, the Madonna and Eve, is embedded in Christian cultural tradition and has plagued western men since the early centuries of Christianity. I have dwelt on this throughout much of my own earlier book (1959).

CHAPTER SIX

p. 174: The quote is from Waller (1930), p. xv.

pp. 180–181: The various statements about the difficulties of obtaining divorce from an unwilling partner are drawn from Ploscowe, and Pilpel, in both of which this subject is dealt with extensively.

p. 182: *a third to a half of a man's net income.* . . . Jacobson, p. 127, emphasizes the smallness of alimony and child support, but he is basing his figures on the population at large. Pilpel, p. 240, gives a picture more typical of the middle class. See also Ploscowe, chap. 7, esp. p. 195.

p. 183: *grounds for cutting off the alimony.* . . . Ploscowe, p. 207, says that in most states there is no requirement that the unremarried ex-wife be chaste, but that in some states the law does provide hat the court may modify an alimony decree upon proof that the ex-wife is living with another man and holding herself out as his wife.

p. 198: *A majority of the divorced remarry within five years.* . . . Jacobson, pp. 69–70, reports that slightly less than half of the divorced remarry within five years, but the latest cohort on which he is reporting is that of people divorced in 1934; Glick, drawing on later years, states that about three quarters of the divorced remarry within five years of the actual divorce. See also note to p. 232.

CHAPTER SEVEN

p. 209: *FMs of certain categories.* . . . The three generalizations which follow are based on my own observations. In addition, Goode (1956) reports that "high-trauma" (unwillingly divorced) wives are more likely to continue yearning for the old marriage than low-trauma wives (p. 303), that the longer-married wives are slower to remarry than those married a short time (p. 297), and that the women who almost never date include a higher proportion of those still emotionally bound to their former husbands than is true of the women who date often (p. 265).

p. 211: *one out of four couples change their minds.* . . . I base this ratio on the results of surveys in Indiana and in Ohio, as cited in Burgess (1953), p. 585. *About one out of ten . . . would at least consider remarriage.* . . . My survey showed one out of ten unremarried FMs were willing to consider it. Goode (1956) says anywhere from one out of five to one out of twenty, depending on the intensity of the trauma associated with the divorce, the more severely traumatized being more willing to reconcile (p. 303). Paget reports that in the marriage counselling experiment in San Bernardino, one out of eight couples contacted by a reconciliation agency came in for at least an initial interview (p. 33), which indicates at least a residuum of willingness. *One out of every fifteen pairs . . . actually do remarry each other.* . . . Jacobson, p. 67; the three-year average duration of the hiatus is, however, from Popenoe, p. 695. *Less than half of the people were happy.* . . . Popenoe, p. 695.

pp. 212–213: *Only two states . . . make alimony temporary.* . . . Pilpel, pp. 293–294 and 298, says that in Pennsylvania there is no permanent alimony except in the case of support of an insane spouse; in New Hampshire, the law prohibits the court from granting a wife more than three years alimony where there are no children; at the end of the period, the alimony may be renewed for another three-year period, but only if there is good reason. On the continuance of alimony after the wife's remarriage, see Ploscowe, pp. 203–204.

p. 214: *he or she is still bound to the other by other bonds.* . . . The point is made by Bernard, p. 205.

pp. 214–215: The Kirkpatrick quotation appears on pp. 552–553 of his book.

p. 216: The effects of repressed anger are discussed briefly by Cobb, pp. 136–137, Spotnitz, chap. 4, and Menninger, pp. 375–377.

p. 219: *the negotiations are a crude therapeutic experience.* . . . A number of lawyers and psychologists to whom I have spoken agree with this formulation, but I have found no published clinical studies of the matter.

p. 220: *In nearly every state.* . . . I make this qualification because in a few states, mostly in the West, a specified period of voluntary living apart is sufficient grounds for a divorce action; under such conditions, even a reluctant spouse can exert relatively little pressure for a heavy penalty. See Pilpel, pp. 277, 283, and Appendix.

p. 221: *for all of which he will have to pay.* . . . Pilpel, p. 442, points out that a newspaper notice by a man claiming to be no longer responsible for his estranged wife's debts does not relieve him of responsibility unless she deserted him or is otherwise at fault. But a separation agreement or court decree does relieve him, while obligating him to make specific payments to her.

p. 222: *more than half the children of divorce.* . . . J. T. Landis (1960), p. 9, reports that 55.6 per cent of the group he surveyed specified one or more ways in which one or both parents had tried to use them in the struggle. The harm done by such uses of the children is attested by Blaine, p. 101, and Despert, p. 63.

p. 224: *Such continuing anger is probably more frequent.* . . . The sources for the following generalizations are the same as for the note to p. 209 above; also, Goode (1956), pp. 301–302. The figure for wives as plaintiffs is from U.S. Public Health Service (1965), p. 29.

p. 226, footnote: *three to five per cent.* . . . Jacobson, p. 109. The more recent U.S. Public Health Service (1965) is of no help on this issue.

pp. 226–227: The statements about the rarity of real court fights are based on Ernst, p. 7, and Pilpel, pp. 283–287.

p. 227: *ninety per cent.* . . . same as preceding note. *Anywhere from over a year to more than three years.* . . . Monahan (1962).

p. 228: On the process of recovery from a bereavement, see Lindemann. *Over sixty per cent.* . . . U.S. Public Health Service (1965), p. 25. *Possibly half.* . . . There are no published figures concerning the number of childless middle-class ex-wives getting alimony; this is only an informed guess, based on conversations with a number of divorce lawyers. *Most divorced persons do achieve near-finality.* . . . This contradicts the finding of Goode (1956), p. 289, that there was little decrease, as time passed, in the negative feeling of ex-wives toward their husbands. But three-quarters of his subjects had been divorced less than fourteen months; I think that a significant decrease would have shown up in his sample, as it did in mine, if he had had a larger proportion of people who had been divorced longer.

p. 230: The quote by the woman executive appears in Cuber, pp. 95–96.

CHAPTER EIGHT

p. 232: *Over a third of all FMs remarry within two years of their divorce.* . . . Jacobson, p. 70, shows that 30.6 per cent of the men and 33.8 per cent of the women who were divorced in 1934—his latest year in this table—remarried within two years; Goode (1956), however, found that within twenty-six months of the divorce, 53 per cent had remarried (p. 331). See also note to p. 198 above. *At least a quarter of all FMs are still unremarried.* . . . Jacobson, p. 70, shows only 45.5 per cent of men and 47.5 per cent of women divorced in 1934 were remarried within five years. Glick, on the basis of census studies made in 1948, says that as of that time three-fourths of all ever-divorced persons were remarrying within five years after the divorce, and six-sevenths were remarrying within fourteen years. This latter figure is also higher than Jacobson's; he expected only 78 per cent of the men and 71 per cent of the women to eventually remarry.

p. 233: Earlier remarriage of the very young: Goode (1956), p. 279; earlier remarriage of those who wanted the divorce: Goode (1956), pp. 276 and 283; earlier remarriage of those with higher income: Glick, p. 733. Jacobson, p. 70, shows women remarrying a little faster than men, but Bernard, p. 57, reporting on a middle-class sample, shows them remarrying considerably more slowly.

p. 239: *Frigidity is much more common than impotence.* . . . Kinsey (1948), pp. 236–237 and 323; Kinsey (1953), pp. 514, 526, and 532. For the quotation by the woman writer, I am indebted to Beryl Fox of the Canadian Broadcasting System, Toronto, who lent me the raw transcripts of interviews she conducted for a documentary on single women.

p. 251: *divorce itself is a cause of divorce.* . . . Kirkpatrick, pp. 522–523.

p. 256: *FMs seem to seek . . . new and mostly divorced friends.* . . . Waller (1930) and (1951) portrays this clearly; so do a great many popular writings. Goode's disagreement with this (see footnote to p. 256) is in Goode (1956), pp. 242–245.

p. 257: The C. S. Lewis quote is from *The Four Loves* (New York, Harcourt, Brace and Company, 1960), p. 96.

p. 258: *roughly four hundred thousand of them are Long-Termers.*
. . . Census data contained in "The American Family," a report by
the Population Reference Bureau of Washington, D.C., dated Dec.
30, 1963, show one and a half million unremarried FMs as family
heads with dependent children; of these FMs, about one quarter are
Long-Termers (see page 232 above); thus, roughly 400,000. On the
proportion which are headed by women: custody goes to the mother
about nine-tenths of the time, as per note to p. 50 above. The Population Reference Bureau report says that 93 per cent of the one-parent
families broken by separation or divorce are headed by women.

p. 259: *her position in the community remains unclear.* . . . The
ambiguous social status of the divorced woman is discussed by Winch,
pp. 729–730 of the 1963 edition of *The Modern Family*.

p. 262: *their effective attitudes are distinctly more permissive.* . . .
This is a finding of the survey made by Ira Reiss; see note to p. 143.

p. 263: *the many shortcomings in the parental performance.* . . .
See, for instance, Freudenthal, and Goodman.

CHAPTER NINE

p. 266: *only one out of three.* . . . Waller (1930), p. 335, Cahen,
pp. 98–109, and Popenoe. *Six out of seven.* . . . See note to p. 232.

p. 267: Comparative chances of remarriage of FMs and single people
are drawn from Jacobson, p. 82, and P. Landis (1950).

p. 268: *Divorced people marry other divorced people about sixty
per cent of the time.* . . . Glick, p. 278. *But their preference . . . is
even stronger than these figures indicate.* . . . The material in the balance of the paragraph is drawn from Bowerman (1953). Bowerman
also refers to a similar study done by other researchers, in Madison,
Wisc., which showed that FMs chose each other four times as often
as chance would account for.

p. 270: *half of those who finally remarry.* . . . Hollingshead reports that 89.4 per cent of the never-married people he surveyed got
engaged before marriage, while only 53.8 per cent of FMs did so (in
unions where both partners were FMs); the never-marrieds averaged
10.3 months of engagement, the FMs only 4.9 months.

p. 273: *FMs spend less than half the time.* . . . Hollingshead.

p. 274: *Only about half of the remarriages are held in churches.*
. . . Hollingshead.

p. 275: Bergler's statements are on his pp. viii, and 117–119; the
view exists throughout his book.

p. 276: *human nature remains much more plastic.* . . . See, for instance, Allport, Bossard, and Coutu; for a popularized summary of the evidence, see Hunt (1964), pp. 143–145. The quote by Abraham Stone appears in Scheinfeld; the quotes by Bernard are from her book, pp. 86 and 272. Others with this same general view of divorce and remarriage include Goode (1956), Cuber, Blood, Waller (1951), and Simpson.

p. 278: *higher than those for first marriages.* . . . P. Landis (1950) reported them to be one third to one half greater; Bernard, p. 66, finds second marriages fifty per cent riskier. The Iowa study is that of Monahan (1958). Others are quoted in Monahan (1952). *At least sixty per cent . . . do endure.* . . . There are no official figures available on this point—not even in U.S. Public Health Service (1965), in which see pp. 14–16. But one out of five first marriages breaks up (see Jacobson, p. 148), and if Monahan's figures are generally applicable, we can assume that two out of five second marriages break up; hence three out of five, or sixty per cent, endure.

pp. 278–279: *Some . . . are acting upon what they have learned.* . . . Bernard, pp. 30, 100, and 272.

p. 279: Locke's data are on pp. 301–302 of his book. Bernard's data and discussion are on pp. 108–113 of her book. Goode's data are from Goode (1956), pp. 331 and 335.

p. 283: *Landis once studied 409 long-term marriages.* . . . J. T. Landis (1946). LeMasters' study of conflict-ridden marriages is LeMasters (1959a).

p. 284: *Marriage counsellors throughout the country.* . . . Beck (1966), requoting Beck (1962), points out that nearly half the marital cases in counselling terminate prematurely at client initiative, and that others continue in deadlock, or deteriorate despite treatment. Similarly, Hollis found 52 out of 96 cases unimproved; see Hollis, p. 189 f.

p. 285: *Four fifths of Dr. Goode's sample.* . . . Goode (1956), p. 342.

p. 286: *eighty per cent.* . . . Allegations to this effect are referred to by Baber, p. 504. *Two effects of the same general cause.* . . . Goode (1956), p 308, summarizes evidence gathered by others on this point. The Glueck material is from pp. 90–92 of their book.

p. 287: *A number of other investigations have shown that delinquency rates.* . . . These are summarized in Wootton, pp. 118–123. *The testimony of nearly all the experts.* . . . Some of the published testimony to this effect is summarized in Goode (1962). Others who agree that divorce is better for the children than continued marital discord include Bernard, Bowerman (1962), Burchinal, Despert, Illsley, Nye, and Perry.

pp. 287–288: Dr. Despert's statements are on pp. 10 and 18 of her book. *Other psychiatrists.* . . . See, for instance, Plant, Blaine.

p. 288: *To test such clinical impressions.* . . . Nye, q.v. *Relatively little evidence of lasting emotional trauma.* . . . J. T. Landis (1960); Burchinal.

p. 289: *This is the only form of private contract.* . . . Jacobson, p. 88.

pp. 289–290: The statements about the Soviet family edict and its purposes are from Juviler, q.v., who is an associate professor of government at Barnard College, and spent three semesters at the Faculty of Law, Moscow University.

p. 290: *The Hopi Indians.* . . . Queen, pp. 32–33. *The kibbutzim.* . . . Kargman. Kingsley Davis' statement is in Davis (1944), p. 710.

p. 291: *the idealized romantic concept of marital love is a major reason for discontent and divorce.* . . . This view has been expressed in numerous writings by persons as diverse as the Catholic theologian Denis de Rougemont, the psychoanalyst Ernest van den Haag, the sociologists Robert Winch and Ray Baber, the anthropologist Ralph Linton, a number of professors of marriage and family life, and moral philosophers as unlike as Bertrand Russell and Hugh Hefner.

p. 292: *equated it with both the freedom of contract and the freedom to labor.* . . . Jones (1953), *passim,* but especially p. 49. The divorce rate for 1867 is in U.S. Bureau of the Census, Dept. of Commerce, *Historical Statistics of the United States, 1789–1945* (Washington, D.C.: 1949), p. 49. The rate for 1960 is from U.S. Public Health Service (1964), pp. 3–4.

p. 292: *two and a half million people.* . . . *Time,* Feb. 19, 1965, p. 56. *Never before in our history.* . . . U.S. Bureau of the Census, *Statistical Abstract of the United States: 1965* (Washington, D.C.: 1965), Table 29, p. 31.

This is neither an exhaustive nor even a representative list of published materials relating to the subject of the present book. I have included only those works referred to in the Notes on Sources and in the text itself, plus a very few additional items which were of particular value to me and, presumably, would be to those readers who wish to pursue the matter further.

Allport, Gordon W. *Pattern and Growth in Personality*. New York: Holt, Rinehart and Winston, 1961.

Altus, William D. "The Broken Home and Factors of Adjustment," *Psychol. Reports*, 1958 (vol. 4).

Anon. "Is Alimony Legal Robbery?" *McCall's*, Aug. 1955.

Anon. "Nobody Tells You; by a Divorcee," *Woman's Home Companion*, Jan. 1951.

Arieti, Silvano, ed. *American Handbook of Psychiatry*. New York: Basic Books, Inc., 1959.

Aronson (1964), Jason. "The Positive Role of Mental Crisis," *Saturday Review*, Dec. 5, 1964.

Aronson (1964a), Jason, ed. *Positive Disintegration*. Boston: Little, Brown and Company, 1964.

Baber, Ray E. *Marriage and the Family*. New York: McGraw-Hill Book Company, 1953.

Bacal, Jacques, and Louise Sloane, "Are Second Marriages Better?" *Look*, Nov. 25, 1947.

Barnett, James H. *Divorce and the American Divorce Novel, 1858–1937*. Philadelphia, 1939.

Beard, Charles A., and Mary R. Beard. *The Rise of American Civilization*. New York: The Macmillan Company, 1934.

Beck (1962), Dorothea Fahs. *Patterns in the Use of Family Agency Service*. New York: Family Service Assoc. of America, 1962.

Beck (1966), Dorothea Fahs. "Marital Conflict: Its Course and Treatment as Seen by Caseworkers," *Social Casework*, Apr. 1966.

Bell, Robert R. *Marriage and the Family*. Homewood, Ill.: The Dorsey Press, Inc., 1963.

Bergler (1948), Edmund. *Divorce Won't Help*. New York: Harper & Brothers, 1948.

Bergler (1961), Edmund. *Counterfeit-Sex: Homosexuality, Impotence, Frigidity*. New York: Grove Press, Inc., 1961.

Bernard, Jessie. *Remarriage: A Study of Marriage*. New York: The Dryden Press, 1956.

Blaine, Graham B., Jr. "The Children of Divorce," *Atlantic*, Mar. 1963.

Blake, Nelson Manfred. *The Road to Reno*. New York: The Macmillan Company, 1962.

Block, Jean Libman. "Where to Meet a Man for $1.50," *Cosmopolitan*, Apr. 1951.

Blood, Robert O., Jr. *Marriage*. New York: The Free Press of Glencoe, 1962.

Bossard, James H. S. *Parent and Child*. Phila.: Univ. of Pennsylvania Press, 1953.

Bowerman (1953), Charles E. "Assortative Mating by Previous Marital Status: Seattle, 1939–1946," *Amer. Sociol. Rev.*, Apr. 1953 (vol. 18).

Bowerman (1962), Charles E., and Donald P. Irish. "Some Relationships of Stepchildren to Their Parents," *Marr. and Family Living*, May 1962.

Bryce, James. *Studies in History and Jurisprudence*. New York: Oxford Univ. Press, 1901.

Burchinal, Lee G. "Characteristics of Adolescents from Unbroken, Broken, and Reconstituted Families," *Marr. and Family Living*, Feb. 1964.

Burgess (1953), Ernest W., and Harvey J. Locke. *The Family*. New York: The American Book Co., 1953.

Burgess (1960), Ernest W., ed. *Aging in Western Societies*. Chicago: Univ. of Chicago Press, 1960.

Cahen, Alfred. *Statistical Analysis of American Divorce*. New York: Columbia Univ. Press, 1932.

Calderone, Mary S. *Release from Sexual Tensions*. New York: Random House, 1960.

Carter (1963), Hugh, and Alexander Plateris. *See* U.S. Public Health Service (1963).

Carter (1964), Hugh. "Eight Myths about Divorce and the Facts," *The New York Times Magazine*, May 3, 1964.

Champagne, Marian. *Facing Life Alone*. Indianapolis: The Bobbs-Merrill Company, Inc., 1964.

Cobb, Stanley. *Emotions and Clinical Medicine*. New York: W. W. Norton & Company, Inc., 1950.

Coutu, Walter. *Emergent Human Nature*. New York: Alfred A. Knopf, 1949.

Davis (1944), Kingsley. "Children of Divorced Parents: Sociological and Statistical Analysis," *Law and Contemporary Problems*, Summer 1944 (vol. 10).

Davis (1950), Kingsley. "Statistical Perspective on Marriage and Divorce," *Annals of the Amer. Acad. of Polit. and Social Sci.*, 1950 (vol. 272).

Davis (1957), Kingsley. "Divorce and Its Effects," in Fishbein, q.v.

Decter, Midge. "Young Divorcee," *Harper's*, Oct. 1962.

Despert, J. Louise. *Children of Divorce*. Garden City, New York: Doubleday & Co., Inc., 1953.

Dublin, Louis. *The Facts of Life from Birth to Death*. New York: The Macmillan Company, 1951.

Egleson, Jim, and Janet Frank Egleson. *Parents Without Partners*. New York: Ace Books, Inc., 1961.

Ehrmann, Winston. *Premarital Dating Behavior*. New York: Bantam Books, 1960.

Eisenstein, Victor W., ed. *Neurotic Interaction in Marriage*. New York: Basic Books, Inc., 1956.

Ernst, Morris L., and David Loth. *For Better or Worse: A New Approach to Marriage and Divorce*. New York: Harper & Brothers, 1952.

Fielding, William J. *Strange Customs of Courtship and Marriage*. Garden City, New York: Garden City Books, 1960.

Fishbein, Morris, and R. J. Kennedy, eds. *Modern Marriage and Family Living*. New York: Oxford Univ. Press, 1957.

Freudenthal, Kurt. "Problems of the One-Parent Family," *Jour. of Social Work*, Jan. 1959 (vol. 4).

Fromm, Erich. *The Art of Loving*. New York: Harper & Brothers, 1956.

Glick, Paul C. "First Marriages and Remarriages," *Amer. Sociol. Rev.*, Dec. 1949 (vol. 14).

Gold, Herbert. "Divorce as a Moral Act," *Atlantic*, Nov. 1957.

Goode (1947), William J. "Education for Divorce," *Marr and Family Living*, May 1947.

Goode (1956), William J. *After Divorce*. Glencoe, Ill.: The Free Press, 1956.

Goode (1961), William J. "Family Disorganization," in Merton, q.v.

Goode (1962), William J. "Marital Satisfaction and Instability: A Cross-Cultural Class Analysis of Divorce Rates," *Internat. Social Sci. Jour.*, 1962 (vol. 14).

Goodman, David. "The Torment of the Divorced Man," *Coronet*, May 1961.

Gordon, Richard E., et al. *The Split-Level Trap*. New York: Bernard Geis Associates, 1960, 1961.

Gurin, Gerald, et al. *Americans View Their Mental Health*. New York: Basic Books, Inc., 1960.

Harmsworth, H., and M. Ninnis. "Nonstatutory Causes of Divorce: The Lawyer's Point of View," *Marr. and Family Living*, Nov. 1955

Haussaman, Florence, and Mary Ann Guitar. *The Divorce Handbook*. New York: Putnam, 1960.

Hollingshead, A. R. "Marital Status and Wedding Behavior," *Marr. and Family Living*, Nov. 1952.

Hollis, Florence. *Women in Marital Conflict*. New York: Family Service Assoc. of America, 1949.

Hunt (1959), Morton M. *The Natural History of Love*. New York: Alfred A. Knopf, 1959.

Hunt (1964), Morton M. "The Self-Healing Powers of the Mind," in his *The Thinking Animal*. Boston: Little, Brown and Company, 1964.

Hunt (1966), Morton M. "Do You Underrate Yourself?" *Family Circle*, May 1966.

Hurvitz, Nathan. "The Measurement of Marital Strain," *Amer. Jour. of Sociol.*, 1960 (vol. 65).

Ilgenfritz, Marjorie P. "Mothers on Their Own—Widows and Divorcees," *Marr. and Family Living*, Feb. 1961.

Illsley, Raymond, and Barbara Thompson. "Women from Broken Homes," *Sociol. Rev.*, 1961 (vol. 9).

Jacobson, Paul H. *American Marriage and Divorce*. New York: Rinehart & Company, Inc., 1959.

Jones (1953), Howard Mumford. *The Pursuit of Happiness*. Cambridge: Harvard Univ. Press, 1953.

Jones (1963), Eve. *Raising Your Child in a Fatherless Home*. New York: The Macmillan Company, 1963.

Juviler, Peter. "The Soviet Family" (a book review of a Soviet sociological work on the family), *Counterpart: A New Review of Contemporary Life in the United States and the Soviet Union*, Jan.–Feb. 1966.

Kargman, Marie. "Divorce—From Husband–Wife to Ex-Husband–Ex-Wife: New Role Expectations in the Divorced Family," paper read before the Eastern Sociol. Society, Phila., Pa., April 1962.

Kephart (1954), William M. "The Duration of Marriage," *Amer. Sociol. Rev.,* June 1954 (vol. 19).

Kephart (1961), William M. *The Family, Society, and the Individual.* Boston: Houghton-Mifflin Co., 1961.

Kinsey (1948), Alfred C. et al. *Sexual Behavior in the Human Male.* Phila.: W. B. Saunders Company, 1948.

Kinsey (1953), Alfred C., and Paul H. Gebhard. *Sexual Behavior in the Human Female.* Phila.: W. B. Saunders Company, 1953.

Kirkpatrick, Clifford. *The Family as Process and Interaction.* New York: The Ronald Press Company, 1955.

Kling, Samuel. *The Complete Guide to Divorce.* New York: Bernard Geis Associates, 1963.

Koster, Donald N. *The Theme of Divorce in American Drama, 1871–1939.* Phila.: 1942.

Kunz, Phillip R. "Mormon and Non-Mormon Divorce Patterns," *Jour. of Marr. and the Family,* 1964 (vol. 26).

Landis (1946), Judson T. "Length of Time Required to Achieve Adjustment in Marriage," *Amer. Sociol. Rev.,* Dec. 1946 (vol. 11).

Landis (1956), Judson T. "The Pattern of Divorce in Three Generations," *Social Forces,* Mar. 1956 (vol. 34).

Landis (1960), Judson T. "The Trauma of Children When Parents Divorce," *Marr. and Family Living,* Feb. 1960.

Landis (1962), Judson T. "A Comparison of Children from Divorced and Nondivorced Unhappy Marriages," *Family Life Coordinator,* 1962 (vol. 11).

Landis (1963), Judson T. "Social Correlates of Divorce or Non-Divorce among the Unhappily Married," *Marr. and Family Living,* May 1963.

Landis (1950), Paul H. "Sequential Marriage," *Jour. of Home Econ.,* Oct. 1950 (vol. 42).

Langer, Marion. *Learning to Live as a Widow.* New York: Gilbert Press, Inc., and Julian Messner, Inc., 1957.

Lehrman, Philip R. "Psychopathological Aspects of Emotional Divorce," *The Psychoanalytic Rev.,* Jan. 1939 (vol. 26).

LeMasters (1957), E. E. *Modern Courtship and Marriage.* New York: The Macmillan Company, 1957.

LeMasters (1959), E. E. "Courtship of Older Persons," *Midwest Sociologist,* 1959 (vol. 21).

LeMasters (1959a), E. E. "Holy Deadlock: A Study of Unsuccessful Marriages," *Midwest Sociologist,* 1959 (vol. 21).

Lerner, Max. *America as a Civilization.* New York: Simon and Schuster, 1957.

Lindemann, Erich. "Symptomatology and Management of Acute Grief," *Amer. Jour. of Psychiatry,* 1944 (vol. 101).

Lobsenz, Norman. "Are Divorce and Alimony Unfair to Men?" *Reader's Digest,* Oct. 1959.

Locke, Harvey J. *Predicting Adjustment in Marriage.* New York: Henry Holt and Company, 1951.

Martin, John Bartlow. "Divorce," *The Saturday Evening Post,* Nov. 1, 8, 15, and 22, 1958.

Maslow, A. H. *Motivation and Personality.* New York: Harper & Brothers, 1954.

Menninger, Karl. *Man against Himself.* New York: Harcourt, Brace and Company, 1938.

Merton, Robert K., and Robert A. Nisbet, eds. *Contemporary Social Problems.* New York: Harcourt, Brace & World, Inc., 1961.

Monahan (1952), Thomas P. "How Stable Are Remarriages?" *Amer. Jour. of Sociol.,* Nov. 1952 (vol. 58).

Monahan (1958), Thomas P. "The Changing Nature and Instability of Remarriages," *Eugenics Quarterly,* 1958 (vol. 5).

Monahan (1962), Thomas P. "When Married Couples Part: Statistical Trends and Relationships in Divorce," *Amer. Sociol. Rev.,* Oct. 1962 (vol. 27).

Mowrer, Ernest R. *Family Disorganization.* Chicago: Univ. of Chicago Press, 1939.

New Jersey. Committee on Reconciliation. *Report of New Jersey Supreme Court's Committee on Reconciliation.* Trenton, 1956.

Nye, F. Ivan. "Child Adjustment in Broken and in Unhappy Unbroken Homes," *Marr. and Family Living,* Nov. 1957

Paget, Norman W., and Marcella R. Kern. *Counseling Services to Parents and Children Involved in Divorce Proceedings.* San Bernardino, Calif.: State Dept. of Social Welfare, et al., 1960.

Perry, Joseph B., and Erdwin H. Pfuhl. "Adjustment of Children in 'Solo' and 'Remarriage' Homes," *Marr. and Family Living,* May 1963.

Pilpel, Harriet F., and Theodora Zavin. *Your Marriage and the Law.* New York: Collier Books, 1964.

Plant, James S. "The Psychiatrist Views Children of Divorced Parents," *Law and Contemporary Problems,* Summer 1944 (vol. 10).

Ploscowe, Morris. *The Truth about Divorce.* New York: Hawthorn Books, Inc., 1955.

Popenoe, Paul. "Remarriage of Divorcees to Each Other," *Amer. Sociol. Rev.,* Oct. 1938 (vol. 3).

Queen, Stuart A., and John B. Adams. *The Family in Various Cultures.* Phila.: J. B. Lippincott, 1952.

Rochford, Elbrun. *Mothers on Their Own.* New York: Harper & Brothers, 1953.

Roulston, Marjorie Hillis. *You Can Start All Over.* New York: Harper & Brothers, 1951.

Russell, Bertrand. *Divorce.* New York: John Day, 1930.

Scheinfeld, Amram. "Why Men Pick the Wrong Women," *Cosmopolitan,* May 1953.

Simpson, George. *People in Families.* New York: Thos. Y. Crowell Co., 1960.

Spotnitz, Hyman, and Lucy Freeman. *The Wandering Husband.* Englewood Cliffs, N.J.: Prentice-Hall, Inc., 1964.

Suinn, R. M. "The Relationship between Self-Acceptance and Acceptance of Others," *Jour. of Abnormal and Soc. Psychol.,* 1961 (vol. 63).

U.S. Bureau of the Census (1962), Dept. of Commerce. *1960 Census of Population, Supplementary Reports:* "Marital Status of the Population, 1960," PC (S1)–39. Wash., D.C.: 1962.

U.S. Bureau of the Census (1963), Dept. of Commerce. *Current Population Reports: Population Characteristics,* Series P–20, No. 122. Wash., D.C.: March 22, 1963.

U.S. Bureau of the Census (1966), Dept. of Commerce. *United States Census of Population, 1960: Marital Status,* PC (2)–4E. Wash., D.C.: 1966.

U.S. Public Health Service (1956), Dept. of Health, Education, and Welfare. *Vital Statistics—Special Reports,* vol. 39, no. 7: "Mortality from Selected Causes by Marital Status." Wash., D.C.: May 8, 1956.

U.S. Public Health Service (1963), Dept. of Health, Education, and Welfare. Hugh Carter and Alexander Plateris, "Trends in Divorce and Family Disruption," *Health, Education, and Welfare Indicators,* Sept. 1963.

U.S. Public Health Service (1964), Dept. of Health, Education, and Welfare. *Vital Statistics of the United States, 1960: Vol. III: Divorces.* Wash., D.C.: 1964.

U.S. Public Health Service (1965), Dept. of Health, Education, and Welfare. *Divorce Statistics Analysis, United States, 1962.* Na-

tional Center for Health Statistics Series 21, No. 7. Wash.,
    D.C.: Dec. 1965.

Vedder, Clyde B. "Lonely Hearts Clubs Viewed Sociologically," *Social
    Forces,* Dec. 1951 (vol. 30).

Waller (1930), Willard. *The Old Love and the New.* New York: H.
    Liveright, 1930.

Waller (1951), Willard. *The Family: A Dynamic Interpretation,* re-
    vised by Reuben Hill. New York: The Dryden Press, 1951.

Winch, Robert. *The Modern Family.* New York: Holt, Rinehart and
    Winston, 1963.

Wootton, Barbara. *Social Science and Social Pathology.* New York:
    The Macmillan Company, 1959.

INDEX

Adjustments to new life, 47, 246
patterns of, 4, 25
Adultery, 22–23, 24, 181, 291
Alcoholism, 52, 199, 205, 283
grounds for divorce, 23–24
Alimony, 65, 203, 205, 211–213,
220–221, 237
child-support payments and, 181–
182
(*See also* Child support)
for childless women, 212
effect on chances for remarriage,
182–183, 211–213, 243
emotional dependency continued
by, 211–213, 224
number of women receiving, 182*n*,
228
as per cent of husband income,
182, 212
permanent and temporary, 212–
213
request for additional, 224
state laws, variations in, 212
withholding of, by husband, to
express hostility, 224
Anger
healing power of, 37–38, 247
necessary to break old ties, 37–38,
215–225, 247
provoking marital partner to, 38*n*
role of, in marital dissolution, 37–
38, 215–225
Annulments, 5*n*

Bergler, Dr. Edmund, 275, 277, 280
Bernard, Dr. Jessie, 276, 279
Boredom, effect on marriage, 15, 108
Burchinal, Lee G., 288–289

Calderone, Dr. Mary S., 150–151
Catholics, formerly married, 20–21,
243
Celibacy among the Formerly Married, 144, 169
Champagne, Marian, 96
Child support, 181–182, 220–221
effect on chances for remarriage,
243
number of women receiving, 228
Childlessness, 14–15, 37
as cause of divorce, 24
Children of the Formerly Married,
20, 258–259
attitudes toward FM parents, 260
behavior of FM parents in front
of, 7
changing role of FM parents, 64–
68, 257–265
initial changes in, 221–223, 229,
258–260
long-term changes in, 260–265
custody of, 50, 241, 256, 258
given to father, 259, 267
discussing problems with ex-mate
concerning, 66–67, 209, 218–
219, 221–222
education of, 9, 209
effect of divorce on, 225, 261–
263, 286–291
damage to personality, 261–
263, 287
guilt-feelings of parents, 287–
288
psychological impact, 19–20,
286–291
psychosomatic ailments, 287–
288

317